Teaching Basic Skills in College

* * * * * * * * * * * * * * * * *

*A Guide to Objectives,
Skills Assessment, Course Content,
Teaching Methods, Support Services,
and Administration*

Alice Stewart Trillin
and Associates

❋ ❋ ❋ ❋ ❋ ❋ ❋ ❋ ❋ ❋ ❋ ❋ ❋ ❋ ❋ ❋ ❋

Teaching Basic Skills in College

Jossey-Bass Publishers
San Francisco • Washington • London • 1981

TEACHING BASIC SKILLS IN COLLEGE
*A Guide to Objectives, Skills Assessment, Course Content,
Teaching Methods, Support Services, and Administration*
by Alice Stewart Trillin and Associates

Copyright © 1980 by: Jossey-Bass Inc., Publishers
433 California Street
San Francisco, California 94104
&
Jossey-Bass Limited
28 Banner Street
London EC1Y 8QE

Library of Congress Cataloging in Publication Data

Main entry under title:

Teaching basic skills in college.
  Includes bibliographical references and index.
  CONTENTS: Trillin, A. S. Introduction.—Gray, B. Q.,
Slaughter, V. B. Writing.—Waters, M. M. Reading.—
[etc.]
  Basic education—United States—Addresses, essays,
lectures. 2. Universities and colleges—United States—
Curricula—Addresses, essays, lectures. I. Trillin,
Alice Stewart.
LC1035.6.T4   378'.199'0973   79-92469
ISBN 0-87589-456-9

Manufactured in the United States of America

JACKET DESIGN BY WILLI BAUM

FIRST EDITION
First printing: August 1980
Second printing: May 1981

Code 8016

*The Jossey-Bass
Series in Higher Education*

Preface

✳ ✳ ✳ ✳ ✳ ✳ ✳ ✳ ✳ ✳ ✳ ✳ ✳ ✳ ✳ ✳ ✳ ✳

I once saw in the *New York Times* a map of New York City decorated by large black dots scattered among the boroughs. The dots, I discovered, represented the seventeen branches of the City University of New York (CUNY), and I realized as I studied them that this dotted map was very much like the picture of the City University that existed in my mind almost five years ago when I began to work with Mina Shaughnessy at CUNY's newly formed Instructional Resource Center. I had taught on one of those campuses—City College—for eight years, and I knew it intimately. Although its Gothic towers rose majestically above Convent Avenue, it looked nothing like the Ivy League campuses where I had studied; temporary quonset huts had become our permanent offices and classrooms, and the Gothic hallways seemed to grow darker and dirtier and more crowded each year. But the landscape of City College had been the backdrop for classes that were so much more exciting for me as a teacher than those I had attended as a student that I had long before stopped seeing the dirt and the darkness and the crowding as obstacles to learning.

It was strange, then, that when, as writing program specialist at the Resource Center, I began the series of long subway and bus and car rides that would take me to campuses in Queens, the Bronx, on Staten Island, I was often shocked, and then angry, at what those campuses looked like. I remember saying once to a colleague, as we stood outside the main building of a college in the Bronx, a building that had formerly been a rehabilitation center, "How can anyone learn anything here? This place doesn't even *look* like a college." I know better than to say that now. One of the things I discovered while I worked on the reports that became the basis for the chapters in this book, as I visited almost every campus of the City University, was that students were learning and teachers were teaching, in spite of the fact that this was to be one of the most difficult times in the history of the City University. After a while the black dots on the map in my mind became real places, each with its particular character and landscape, its colors and its sounds and its smells, and, as I had at City College, I soon stopped looking at the dirt in the hallways and began to look instead at the faces of teachers and students in classrooms.

We began the studies on which this book is based in the spring of 1975, as the first project of the Instructional Resource Center. When Mina Shaugnessy agreed to take on the job of directing the center, after having created City College's pioneering basic writing program, she thought for a long time about just what the proper function of a resource center should be. There were some of us who thought that the center's greatest resource was Mina, but she, characteristically, was skeptical about her own ability to perform miracles. She felt instead that the greatest resource of the university was its teachers and its students, and that anything the center might accomplish would have to grow out of their talents and their energies. Thus she decided that our first job would be to identify what was best in the skills programs as they existed on the different campuses of the university rather than to embark on ambitious research or curriculum development projects. Although descriptions of these programs' administrative structures were available, no one had ever reported on what really went on between students and teachers in their classrooms. Mina felt that only when we had found this out, when we knew what our resources truly were, could we begin to mobilize them and help make them more effective.

Five years later, this book is the result. The task turned out far less modest than we had expected it to be. First of all, our work was done during a period of extraordinary turmoil in the university. It was a time of cutbacks and retrenchments, a time when the entire concept of the open admissions program that had been initiated in 1970 was being questioned. Skills programs that had been set up to meet the needs of the large numbers of underprepared students who entered CUNY under Open Admissions were constantly being threatened, and we frequently had the experience of finding out about a promising new program or approach just as it was about to be eliminated. At the same time, we began to be overwhelmed by the quantity of material that we were gathering. As the stacks of syllabi and lesson plans and CUNY-authored textbooks grew higher, as reports on skills programs at the various campuses began to spill out of filing cabinets, we realized we had to find a way to organize the information, to make it accessible to more people than those who could visit the center and sort through all the documents. Perhaps most important, we needed to make a permanent record of some of the accomplishments of the skills teachers who were being threatened daily by retrenchment. And so we assigned specialists to write about what we have learned in four related but, at least for analytic and administrative purposes, four separate skills areas—reading, writing, English as a second language, and mathematics.

We began the project with the help of a grant from the Field Foundation, and we are particularly indebted to Leslie Dunbar of that foundation for encouraging us in the early critical stages of our work. We also thank Marilyn Maiz, the administrative coordinator of the Resource Center, for her help on this project. Not only was she the only person who ever knew where all the pieces of our complicated puzzle might be found at any one time, but she also has the rare ability to combine absolute dedication to teachers with intelligent skepticism about answers that seem to her not carefully enough thought out. For this reason, she has been one of our most valuable critics. Other extremely helpful critics have been Sarah D'Eloia of the English department of City College, Robert Lyons of the English department of Queens College, and Barry Kwalick of the English Department of William Patterson College, who read the manuscript of Chapter One; Wendy Maloney of the School of Education, Brooklyn College, who read Chapter Two; Ann Raimes of the Developmental English Program at Hunter College, who read Chapters One and Three; and Martha Maxwell, author of *Improving Student Learning Skills* (1979), who offered useful comments on all the chapters.

Of course, the person most responsible for this book, for so many reasons that I will not attempt to list them here, is Mina Shaughnessy. Because of our love and admiration for her, the book is dedicated to her memory. And because her work so strongly influenced our professional development, we have included in the list of references at the end of the book citations of all her published writings, so that her insights can teach others as we have been taught.

We also dedicate this book to the CUNY skills teachers and their students who have continued to confront the problems of teaching and learning daily in their classrooms, no matter what shifts and strains have threatened to disrupt the university and the city of New York during the past years. When, several years ago, it became the fashion in New York to rail against the shocking illiteracy of college students and the lowering of standards in City University, while columnists and headline writers railed against the "race of barbarians" who were ruining our institutions of higher learning, skills teachers and their students kept going to class. During the worst of that time—a time that is by no means over—it must have been difficult, after being threatened with retrenchment or hearing the latest attack on City University on the evening news, for teachers to stay up late grading essays, inventing new assignments, devising exercises, even writing textbooks, and for students to keep responding to their teachers' challenges and to ask for even greater ones. What astonishes me most is that so much was accomplished during such a difficult and insecure time. This book documents some of this accomplishment and only exists because those teachers and their students never thought of the university as it was depicted on that map in the *New York Times,* the one that showed the CUNY campuses as dots, abstractions that could be blotted out in a moment by a politician's felt-tipped pen. For these students and their teachers, those dots had become real places, as they became for all of us who worked on this book, and they can never be blotted out. For us, the reality of CUNY will always be inside its classrooms. No wonder Mina was so anxious to find out what went on there.

New York City   ALICE STEWART TRILLIN
March 1980

Contents

✻ ✻ ✻ ✻ ✻ ✻ ✻ ✻ ✻ ✻ ✻ ✻ ✻ ✻ ✻ ✻ ✻ ✻ ✻

The Authors

❋ ❋ ❋ ❋ ❋ ❋ ❋ ❋ ❋ ❋ ❋ ❋ ❋ ❋ ❋ ❋ ❋ ❋

ALICE STEWART TRILLIN is currently curriculum consultant to the Office of Higher and Continuing Education of New York's public television station, WNET/Thirteen. She first became involved with the teaching of basic writing in 1965 at Hofstra University when she helped start Project NOAH, one of the first college programs for underprepared students. In 1967 she joined the English department at City College and specialized in the teaching of basic writing. When Mina Shaughnessy set up the City University of New York's (CUNY) Instructional Resource Center in 1975, Trillin became the Resource Center's writing program specialist. While at the Resource Center, she, with colleagues, produced *The English Modules*, a series of videotapes and a textbook dealing with sentence structure.

Geoffrey Akst is currently professor of mathematics at Borough of Manhattan Community College, where he is coordinator of all of the basic skills programs; he has been teaching at CUNY since 1966. Akst holds a doctorate from Columbia University in the teaching of college mathematics. He has done extensive research in the field of mathematics remediation and serves as co-chairman of the CUNY Mathematics Discussion Group, an organization of mathematics faculty concerned with the problems of undergraduate instruction. His professional interests include individualized instruction, logic, problem solving, and program evaluation.

Barbara Quint Gray is assistant professor of humanities at the Polytechnic Institute of New York, where she administers the freshman writing program. She has been teaching basic writing since 1970 when she joined the English department of the City College of New York. She has also taught at Newark State College, Rutgers University (Newark), and Hostos Community College of CUNY. Gray is a founder of the *Journal of Basic Writing* and remains a member of its editorial board. In addition to basic writing, she has a special interest in applications of linguistics to the teaching of writing.

Miriam Hecht has taught mathematics at Hunter College since 1967. She coordinated the college's remedial arithmetic program from its inception in 1972 until 1978. Currently she chairs the CUNY Faculty Task Force on Mathematics Assessment and is a member of the Educational Media Committee of the Mathematical Association of America. Hecht was director of the CUNY-SUNY Mathematics Remediation Project, which produced audiovisual resources, and coauthor of the accompanying text, *ModuMath Arithmetic.* Her chief professional interest is nontraditional and alternative education, particularly at the college level.

Linda Ann Kunz is an assistant professor of English at Hunter College, as well as a consultant-in-training of the Aesthetic Realism of Eli Siegel. Her grammar and basic writing textbooks include *26 Steps: Controlled Composition for Intermediate and Advanced ESL Students, X-Word Grammar: An Editing Book,* and, with Robert R. Viscount, *Write Me a Ream: Exercises in Controlled Composition.*

Virginia B. Slaughter is co-director and a consultant in basic skills teaching at the Instructional Resource Center of the City University of New York. Her interest in literacy and the needs of underprepared high school and college students began in the early seventies when she taught English in an inner-city high school and was instrumental in developing a citywide school volunteer program in Connecticut. She has taught writing at City College and Hunter College. In 1975, Slaughter joined the Resource Center to coordinate, among other projects, a survey of remedial programs in the seventeen branches of CUNY that was the genesis of the present work. She also edits, with a colleague, the Center's newsletter, *Resource*.

Margaret M. Waters is an associate professor and a coordinator of elementary education at Brooklyn College's School of Education. During the period of open admissions at Brooklyn College she developed the Comprehensive Reading Program for entering college students. Waters is a member of the Reading Task Force appointed by the chancellor of CUNY to determine minimum competency assessments in reading for students throughout the university. She currently teaches courses in reading methodology at the master's degree level. One of her professional interests is the education of gifted and talented children.

Teaching Basic Skills in College

* * * * * * * * * * * * * * * * *

A Guide to Objectives,
Skills Assessment, Course Content,
Teaching Methods, Support Services,
and Administration

Alice Stewart Trillin

Introduction

❋ ❋ ❋ ❋ ❋ ❋ ❋ ❋ ❋ ❋ ❋ ❋ ❋ ❋ ❋ ❋ ❋ ❋

This volume stems from the most monumental attempt to educate underprepared students in the history of higher education: basic skills instruction at the City University of New York (CUNY) since the inception of its SEEK program in 1965. The SEEK program (Search for Education, Elevation, and Knowledge) was one of the first in America to recognize that large numbers of students were barred from success in higher education because of their inadequate preparation in high school. In the mid 1960s, it was becoming more and more difficult to take for granted that young people would have the kind of access to college that for so long had seemed an integral part of the American dream. The City University had traditionally been the place where New York City's poor were educated. When City College was founded in 1847, it had a policy of open admissions: its original mandate was to provide "free education for the sons and daughters of the immigrant poor who

1

could not afford to attend college." Only two decades later did the college begin to restrict admissions, although it continued in this century to educate "the sons and daughters of the immigrant poor."

By the 1960s, however, it was clear that something had gone wrong. In a city where minority students constituted 38 percent of the high school population, by 1969 only 5 percent of the student body of CUNY's senior colleges were minority students. The SEEK program was only a small step toward making CUNY's enrollment more adequately reflect the ethnic balance of the city's high schools, but by the end of the decade the open admissions policy was reborn. On July 9, 1969, the New York City Board of Higher Education passed the following three resolutions to launch the new open admissions program (pp. 188–189):

1. It shall offer admission to some University program to all high school graduates of the City.
2. It shall provide for remedial and other supportive services for all students requiring them.
3. It shall maintain and enhance the standards of academic excellence of the colleges of the University.

Reading these resolutions now, ten years later, one is struck by both their optimism and their naiveté. Even then it was clear that it would be extremely difficult to carry out these three somewhat contradictory policies. It was also clear that the success of the first and third would depend upon how well the second resolution was carried out. There could be no open admissions and no maintenance and enhancement of standards without an effective system of support for the new students. I suspect that no one at the time understood exactly what this meant or understood the enormous commitment that would be necessary to build this support system.

The seventeen colleges of the City University were asked to respond to the challenge offered by the Board of Higher Education by instantly creating, some from scratch and some from the early experiments with remediation that had evolved under SEEK, a complete system of support services for the thousands of students who would enter in the fall of 1970 under the open admissions plan. Although "Open Admissions" as it was originally conceived officially ended in 1976 with the reimposition of entrance requirements at the senior colleges, it left the University irrevocably changed. It is not the intention of this book to provide a history of open admissions or of how these changes came about. (For a more general discussion of open admissions, the 1979 study by Lavin, Alba, and Silberstein is useful.) Instead, we intend to describe some of what we have learned from our experience as teachers of the students who came to us through open admissions. We will not deal in statistics, nor will we attempt to document the success or failure of programs, but instead will describe some of the things that have gone on in classrooms at the City University during the past decade. We have tried to capture some of what we saw on our visits to campuses, to identify promising teaching methods, to suggest some of the more interesting approaches that teachers at the City University are pursuing.

Exchanging Ideas

When we began the series of reports for the Instructional Resource Center on which this book is based, we were all enormously curious about the innovative teaching methods that we would discover on our visits to campuses. City University was a vast laboratory, offering an unparalleled opportunity to discover new teaching techniques. Surely out there, in one of those many classrooms, someone must have found an "answer," a secret key that would unlock the potential we all knew our students had. Some readers of this book may be looking for that same key. We found no single key, no modern alchemy, in our search; but we did find a great deal that we think will be useful to anyone teaching skills or setting up a skills program anywhere in this country.

As teachers, we have tried to concentrate on methods of teaching rather than on the structure of programs. But, unfortunately, it is often difficult to describe the moments when learning takes place, the kinds of moments we often witnessed on our visits to classrooms, or to say anything very definitive about what makes teaching effective. As programs evolve, a great deal is done by instinct, and it is only after a few years that the best results of a series of trials and errors get written down, codified, passed on as advice and guidelines. Though we do in fact occasionally pass on advice and guidelines, parts of this book should be read as the kind of rich, friendly interchange of ideas among teachers that goes on while a program is evolving. During the early days of the writing program that Mina Shaughnessy developed at City College, we used to have frequent meetings of the staff, and in these meetings lay the beginnings of many of the principles that shaped the program. There was an intensity and a closeness in our relationships then, strengthened by our sense that we were all allies in a difficult battle. Although we often disagreed about how to help our students write better, we all agreed that we had a great deal to learn, that there were very few successful models that could give us guidance, and that our most important lessons were to be learned by listening to one another and our students. And so we listened, in staff meetings, in one another's classrooms, over lunch or in hallways. This book, contains some of what we heard. It by no means offers the kinds of guaranteed-for-success methods promised by the titles so often found on the best-seller list these days. Perhaps what we are offering is best described as a modest "bag of tricks," a phrase Mina used to describe the various teaching methodologies and ideas that every teacher carries into the classroom. Mina had a healthy respect for this bag of tricks—and she had a good-sized one of her own— but the phrase also conveyed her sense that we should not rely too much on any one method or point of view but instead see each as a prop for a performance that relies for its success not on tricks but on knowing when and how to use them.

Knowing when and how to use the things that go on in other people's classrooms is a difficult business, as all teachers know. We have all had the experience of trying to reproduce a moment we observed over a colleague's shoulder, or to imitate an approach we read about in a journal, only to find it fall flat. Some of the ideas in this book might work beautifully on a particular day and fail dismally on another. Sometimes I suspect that the success or failure of a particular class has something to do with the tides or the phases of the moon. But most of the time, I think our ineffectiveness has more immediate—and more remediable—causes. And so, before turning to these ideas, it may be worth considering for a moment

what besides a bulging bag of tricks the skills teacher must bring
into the classroom.

Most obviously, we would probably agree, teachers need to
be convinced that it is possible for our students to learn. Mina
(Shaughnessy, 1977c) wrote that the teacher must "hypothesize the
educability of his students and . . . look at their behavior as writers
from such a perspective, assuming . . . that while what they write
may be wrong or inappropriate in relation to the models they must
learn, their behavior is neither random nor illogical but ingeniously
adaptive at one moment, linguistically conservative at another, or
relentlessly—albeit wrong—logical at still another." The necessity
of this point of view is not discussed in this book; rather, it is taken
for granted.

We would probably also agree that effecting significant
changes in an underprepared student's mathematical and verbal
skills depends on a great deal more than a dedicated and optimistic
teacher. Mina knew, better than anyone, that dedication and optimism are only what prepare teachers to take the next step, to
begin to ask questions about how learning takes place. Effective
teaching involves not only what goes on in the classroom but a long
series of interwoven steps that lead up to a particular learning
experience and eventually take the student beyond that experience. Before using any specific method or approach described in
this book, it is essential to think first about what is causing the
problem the method is designed to remedy. What is the rationale
on which this method is based? Why are students making the mistakes that this method is meant to correct? Does this method get at
the reason for the error, or does it merely help the student correct
the error? And what might the student need to learn before this
approach will be most effective? In addition, it is essential that we
think about where the approach is taking the student. Is there a
carryover from what the student has learned in this exercise to
other assignments? What is the next step?

We have tried, therefore, in the following chapters to raise
such questions of purpose and direction, the kinds of questions that
we think should be asked before adopting any particular "bag of
tricks" or designing any basic skills course or program. We have
sought to make each chapter comprehensive and have risked the

danger of seeming overlap among chapters on some questions, since some readers will turn to the chapter of particular interest to them. Thus, in each we address six major questions.

What are the objectives of the skills program? The most obvious answer to this question is that the objective of a skills program is to bring students to the point where they can deal effectively with college level material. But defining just what this means can be difficult. "College level material" obviously varies not only from institution to institution, but even within an institution and its departments. For example, in a mathematics skills program it is essential to determine exactly just what students are being prepared for. Which mathematics skills are prerequisite to success in other college courses? Should there be different objectives in courses designed for students who intend to major in the sciences and those who plan to study the liberal arts? In language skills courses there is, in one sense, no limit to what a student needs to learn. Obviously, everyone should learn to read and write as well as possible. And yet, exactly how much can a beginning student realistically be expected to learn? And should the objectives in reading and writing courses for students whose first language is not English differ from those for native speakers?

If there has been any trend in defining the objectives of skills courses, it has been toward making the objectives of individual courses more modest and more precisely articulated. This does not mean that standards have been lowered, but simply that skills programs need to provide the student with more time and more support to reach their goals than we may have originally assumed.

What are the different skills levels of entering students, and how can these skills levels be determined? This question involves first of all defining discrete levels of skills, and then devising methods for determining the level at which to place each student. In the past, it was possible to determine a student's level of skills according to his high school records. Since open admissions is based partly on the premise that large numbers of students have been inadequately prepared by the city's high schools, the high school record can hardly be relied on as an indicator of competence. Often a student who has completed four years of high school English will not have written a single composition, and so grades in these courses may have little relationship to whether a student can write. As a result, diagnostic and placement tests are increasingly essential.

Any instrument designed to determine placement of entering students has to be designed with the objectives of the skills course in mind. This is relatively easy to do in a math program, where objectives can be precisely defined, but more difficult in a language skills program. If the objective of a writing skills course, for instance, is to teach students to write papers which are relatively free of error and which are logically organized, then a placement instrument must test a student's ability to write such papers. However, if such testing is to be done successfully, faculty must be trained to agree upon just what the terms *relatively free of error* and *logically organized* mean. An objective test is easier to use than a writing sample but often does not measure relevant skills. An objective test that measures a student's knowledge of grammar, for instance, may only be useful if the objective of the course is to teach knowledge of grammatical principles in isolation rather than the application of these principles in written composition. At CUNY, placement procedures have improved as there has been more faculty involvement in deciding on objectives and interpreting the results of placement tests.

What should be taught at each skills level? The answer to this question is complicated because the learning of skills seldom progresses in a completely orderly, predictable manner. It is, however, easier to determine course content and the order in which material should be taught in a mathematics skills program than in a language skills program because the way that mathematics skills build on one another is well known. One of the greatest needs in the field of language competence is research that will tell us more about the way that adult learners acquire language skills. Our experience has taught us a great deal about this, and the skills programs we describe reflect the effort that has been made to teach skills developmentally. However, specific suggestions about the content of courses, such as the syllabi that appear in Chapter Two, should be seen as possible course models, rather than as prescriptions for course content. And any advice about what to teach and the order in which it should be taught should be taken with the caveat that learning—especially language learning—often takes place in spurts and in defiance of neat hierarchical arrangements.

What teaching methods should be used at each level of skills? The emphasis of this book is on this question. The authors have tried, whenever possible, to examine the rationale on which a particular method is based, as well as the ways that a teacher can integrate the approach into the rest of the curriculum, asking always, "What has gone on *before* the experience in the classroom, and what will go on *after* it?" Besides discussing teaching approaches—linguistic approaches to grammar, prewriting exercises, and controlled composition, for example—the authors have also discussed structures that seem to enhance the learning experience, structures such as learning labs, peer tutoring arrangements, and modularized instruction.

Methods that are recommended for one skills area are not necessarily endorsed in another. Thus Miriam Hecht and Geoffrey Akst, in Chapter Four, strongly favor mastery learning and self-paced, individualized instruction in mathematics courses. In other chapters, my associates express more reservations. Although mastery learning and self-paced instruction undoubtedly have their value in language learning, and particularly in the language laboratory, and although many programs based on mastery learning of language skills have been shown to be successful in achieving certain specific goals, administrators and teachers of reading and writing should not be drawn to these programs, as some have been drawn to objective tests, simply because of their ease of administration and evaluation. English teachers must be especially careful to ask themselves what, exactly, it is that their students are mastering. And they have to be sure that the information being mastered, which is often something like a lexicon of grammatical rules, will help students achieve the objectives of their course.

How do you find out what has been taught and how effectively it has been taught? This issue has been dealt with in more detail in some chapters than in others, simply because evaluating some basic skills, such as writing, is necessarily more complicated than evaluating others, such as mathematics. The question of evaluation has been considered in recent years to be a university-wide problem, and

CUNY is now in its second year of centrally administered proficiency testing. These tests are an attempt to make more uniform the standards of competency that have evolved on individual campuses over the past decade. In Chapter Five Geoffrey Akst and Miriam Hecht consider some of the more technical aspects of the question of evaluation, since this is a question that will be demanding more and more attention in the future of skills programs.

How should a skills program be administered? We have devoted relatively little space to this question, although occasionally some administrative issues, such as the awarding of credit and departmental responsibility for skills programs, are considered. The colleges of the City University are semiautonomous units, separately administered, and the evolution of a program's administrative structure often has more to do with the history of a particular institution than with deliberate choices. Moreover, as teachers, we felt that it would be difficult for us to evaluate the effectiveness of administrative structures, although we know these structures are often responsible for the success or failure of a particular program.

However, a word needs to be said here about departmental responsibility for skills programs. Compelling arguments can be made for setting up a separate department of developmental skills (Roueche and Kirk, 1973). Equally compelling ones can be made for keeping skills programs within existing departments (Hecht and Akst, Chapter Four). There is no one right answer to this question, but a guide to the best solution seems to lie in the answer to another question: What kind of administrative structure will provide the most support for the skills program? Ideally, the academic departments of a college or university should assume responsibility for skills programs. The finest teachers, the greatest resources of the academic community, should be involved in the teaching of skills. But effecting this kind of involvement is often difficult. Faculty who have taught nothing but advanced courses to traditional students for years are often as unprepared as they are unwilling to teach the new students. But, if an academic department is committed to its skills programs, and if faculty members are willing to "dive in," as Mina Shaughnessy called that act of faith necessary if teachers are to change and learn in response to the new students, both the department and the students will be enriched.

There have been many instances, at CUNY and elsewhere, of the willingness of teachers to "dive in," for example: E. D. Hirsch of the University of Virginia, when he was chairman of the English department, decided to devote himself to the teaching of composition after years as a scholar and teacher of literature. But there have also been instances when skills programs have simply not been a high enough priority within traditional academic departments. Then, to ensure that the needs of underprepared students were taken seriously, separate skills programs had to be set up, forming what Roueche and Kirk call "a community of learning specialists who can collectively know and relate to each individual student as a person" (1973, p. 84). One hopes that this description might accurately describe the entire academic community and not only these members of it who teach skills.

Future Directions

The authors have, for the most part, avoided talking about trends in teaching methods. We have all attended too many academic conferences not to be wary of discussing a trend that seems in particular favor one year, only to disappear from the calendar of events the next year. We have also tried to avoid making predictions. But if there has been any significant trend—perhaps pattern is the more accurate word—in skills teaching at CUNY over the past decade, it has been toward the recognition that the job we have to do is even more difficult than we knew it was in 1969 when we were given the mandate by the Board of Higher Education to "provide for remedial and other supportive services for all students requiring them." The pattern of the past decade at CUNY has been one of discovering more about what our students need and learning more about how to teach them. As we have discovered and learned, programs have become more clearly articulated, more carefully defined. A program that might have begun with only one level of mathematics remediation might now have three. An English department that began with one developmental skills course might now include a separate department for English as a Second Language (ESL) students, with five levels of courses for these students alone.

Although we have come a long way in articulating programs, in defining objectives, and in refining teaching strategies, we have just begun to do the kind of solid research essential to the development of skills programs, the kind of research begun by Mina Shaughnessy in *Errors and Expectations* (1977b). In the last piece that Mina published during her lifetime, "Some Needed Research on Writing," she called for more research on two questions—how young adult learners develop skills and "what skills we have failed to take note of in our analysis of academic tasks" (1977c, p. 319). Recently much promising work has been going on at CUNY and elsewhere, particularly on the first of these questions.

During the first decade of skills teaching at CUNY, programs were often designed before there was time to engage in the kind of carefully documented research that Mina called for. As we devise ways of serving our students better during the second decade of this educational experiment, we have the advantage of now knowing how difficult the job we took on ten years ago really is. We also have the advantage of starting this second decade with the kind of rich experience that this book documents, the kind of information that research on skills teaching is beginning to provide, and, most importantly, with the sure and certain knowledge that our students, whatever the trends and shifts in the priorities of the University and of the city, will continue to come to class, asking to be taught, and demanding by their presence and their constancy that we become better teachers.

1

Barbara Quint Gray
Virginia B. Slaughter

Writing

✳ ✳ ✳ ✳ ✳ ✳ ✳ ✳ ✳ ✳ ✳ ✳ ✳ ✳ ✳ ✳ ✳

The arrival of great numbers of underprepared students at universities and colleges across the country, some as a result of open admissions policies as at the City University of New York (CUNY), others as a consequence of the decline in literacy skill development at the elementary and secondary school levels, has posed a substantial challenge to both the teaching style and the content of traditional freshman composition courses. Those old, familiar courses have generally assumed competence at the level of writing sentences and focused, therefore, on control of expository prose techniques, often in academic essays analyzing literary works.

Teachers of those traditional courses have sought, generally to introduce literary analysis by providing examples of it in lectures or by leading discussions in which the class participated in analysis. They have graded each paper not only according to its discussion of the topic but also to the presence, or absence, of a handbookful of possible grammatical or stylistic lapses; but they have rarely discussed these lapses systematically in class. Instead, they have assumed that such problems are mistakes, or perhaps inelegancies of style, that more reading and writing and the nudge of the red pencil will lead the writer to outgrow.

If these teachers have addressed grammar at all, traditional school grammar has been the usual source of rules governing the niceties of the written word, niceties that often do not, and do not need to, contradict students' individual senses of the language. Students have been expected to assimilate the more arcane subject-verb agreement rules governing such situations as a compound subject consisting of singular and plural nouns coordinated by *neither . . . nor,* or they could ponder the current dicta on beginning, or not beginning, sentences with *but.* They could then append the entire body of newly memorized knowledge to their existing instincts about the workings of English when applying themselves to that special and specialized form of the language called upon when writing.

To meet the needs of students unprepared to write at the level required for college work, the traditional freshman composition course has been supplemented by a "basic writing" sequence especially tailored to bring underprepared students up to the level of skill required for competent college work. This process has brought change in several areas.

First, teachers committed to teaching new kinds of students often have to adopt new modes of communicating with their classes, for these students are often intimidated by the erudition of their professors and shrink from criticism of their writing that calls into question not only their knowledge of their native tongue but sometimes the cultural assumptions that their work expresses. In addition, teachers can no longer assume the body of literate knowledge and experience that had been the shared capital of earlier students. Many students now have come through high school English courses in which they have done virtually no writing. Others have written only short factual answers to quizzes on their reading, formulized book reports, or highly subjective "creative" papers in which anything has been approved in the name of self-expression. Many students report that their high school teachers have rarely suggested that grammar and spelling might "count" or demanded organized and grammatical work. When their teachers have criticized, they have tended to do so in an unfocused barrage of unexplained rewritings, circled errors, and cryptic symbols that have left students convinced that they cannot write but uncertain where their problems lie and uninspired and unequipped to address them.

This new breed of entering student, furthermore, is often uncertain of the forms peculiar to standard English, in either its spoken or its written varieties. While students may be painfully aware of different registers in the language, of variations in their own speech from one social situation to another, they lack the experience in the formal registers of academic and professional life that would familiarize them with the speech or writing of literate persons. When asked to create dialogue illustrating their informal language, they can do so with comfort and gusto, but when asked to act out a job interview or a conference with an English professor, the major changes in presentation that they often rely upon are omission of overtly slang terminology, such as *ain't,* combined with dressing neatly and sitting up straight. The effect is that for students whose admission to college would not have been possible by traditional standards, learning about writing is often not a matter of memorizing a few linguistic and stylistic amenities. It is, instead, learning all the syntactic, morphemic, and stylistic features of an unfamiliar register.

Many students who now populate basic writing courses, however, are demographically the same as students who formerly took traditional freshman composition courses. For, even in the most prestigious colleges and universities, more students than ever before read and write at a level that was formerly regarded as inadequate for college. Many independent signs point to a general decline in the writing abilities of entering freshmen. One is that scores on the communications skills sections of college admissions tests, like those administered by the Educational Testing Service or the American College Testing Program, are not as high as in past decades.

A similar trend emerged from the findings of the National Assessment of Educational Progress, a federally funded study that has monitored the educational attainments of students at three grade levels. A comparison of high school seniors studied in the first assessment, in 1969, with those monitored in the subsequent, 1974 assessment, showed "an overall decline in the quality of essays written for the second assessment," and, more specifically, "increases in awkwardness, run-on sentences and incoherent paragraphs" (National Assessment of Educational Progress, 1975, p. 1). Although for both assessments some writers' work was judged to be excellent, more writers in the 1974 survey were judged to write poorly, and they were substantially worse than the poor writers of the 1969 survey. In response to this trend, many institutions have inaugurated a written proficiency examination as a requirement for graduation; this kind of policy change acknowledges that entering students may need to improve their writing skills substantially before the admitting institution can graduate them.

There is, however, a critical difference between traditional college freshmen, even in their less well prepared incarnation, and the new kinds of students that broader admissions policies have included in many freshman classes. Students in the more traditional college population have always assumed, along with their teachers, parents, and friends, that they would eventually go to college somewhere; that assumption has underlain their formal, and informal, education. In contrast, many of the new students never thought of college as even a remote possibility.

From her knowledge of CUNY students and samples of their writing, Mina Shaughnessy, the CUNY dean who coined the term "basic writing," discerned common characteristics in the divergent backgrounds of nontraditional students (1976a, p. 139): "We can infer that they have never written much, in school or out, that they have come from families and neighborhoods where people speak other languages or variant, nonprestigious forms of English, and that, while they have doubtless been sensitive to the differences between their ways of speaking and their teachers', they have never been able to sort out or develop attitudes towards the differences that did not put them in conflict, one way or another, with the key academic tasks of learning to read and write and talk in standard English."

A few semesters of basic writing courses can provide such nontraditional entering college students with the writing skills they need for success in college and beyond. This is a difficult job, but it is not an impossible one. It requires a carefully designed program of several levels, nourished and sustained by a belief in the students' ability to learn and a willingness to pursue increasingly effective ways to teach them.

Levels of Basic Writing Skills

If "basic writing" consists of all the work required of underprepared students before they reach a level of writing performance that allows them to work without direct instruction in writing, the phrase "basic writing skills" designates a spectrum of ability that can be divided into three broad categories. At the least skilled end of the spectrum are the semicoherent, misspelled, syntactically fractured first attempts of marginally literate high school educated adults. Students entering a basic writing course on this most fundamental level might produce an initial sample like one written in response to the following question:

> Question (from the CUNY Writing Skills Assessment Test, 1978):
> It always strikes me as a terrible shame to see young people spending so much of their time staring at television. If we could unplug all the TV sets in America, our children would grow up to be healthier, better educated, and more independent human beings. Do you agree or disagree? Explain and illustrate your answer from your own experience, your observations of others, or your reading.

> I agree, "is harmful effect on young people." Most children is more effect than adult because young children watch on T.V. like one Sample *violent* is bad for children eyes, someday—they mind think is fun; I know one neighbor she had a son and once he watch T.V. on the program he saw Batman and Robin climbing the building so he try it, he climb the rope and the rope broke lose and fell on the floor bleeding top on his head—they rush him to the hospital he had about 10 or 15 stitches. He never doing again he know only just fantasy on T.V.
> T.V. cause more trouble like putting some sample on children mind; They should take out more violent, too many police series on t.v. and they should put good thing on Television program for the children, the world is too many violent already. like cop and Robber—someday they children grow up—they do same thing on T.V. I wish parent do something about this; parent should

watch they children to be sure children don't allow watch violent or other thing on T.V. parent should spend more time with the children such as: give something keep away from T.V. I read in the magazine they said, "Rate to high on violent on T.V. should put down less violent on T.V. many people is complain all the time; I believe they should put no violent and other things on T.V. for young people, T.V. is harmful on people mind, And children.

Beginning writing samples at the most unskilled end of the basic writing spectrum may vary a good deal depending on the writer and the topic, but they generally share the same difficulties: (1) sentences whose boundaries are not accurately marked or which set up syntactic requirements that are not met, (2) verb forms that deviate from the standard English conventions for indicating tense and number, (3) words whose forms are inaccurate for the function they are fulfilling (*violent* for *violence*) and words that are not part of the standard vocabulary at all, (4) inaccurate internal punctuation, and (5) spelling problems that range from the correct spelling of a word other than the one meant (*they* for *their*) to incorrect or omitted letters that distort the intended word.

These errors are sprinkled with distracting consistency through writing that is unfocused and full of vaguely suggestive, but undeveloped, ideas. A passage typically makes little concession to the needs of a reader who is not already intimately familiar with what the writer is trying to say; the meaning may be clear only to its author.

A second level of student writing style, showing greater control of the grammar of standard English but still exhibiting the writer's difficulty in producing coherent, sustained prose might look like this:

Recently I have watched some of television's top rate shows. The shows have no educational value at all. The violence and sex that the networks put out is outrageous. Not only that, but it has an overall bad afect on grades in school. The time these shows are air, interfers with time for study, term projects book reports, and homework.

I do however; disagree that everyone should pull the plug on television. Television does have its' positive side. With the PBS (CHANNEL 13) education shows (NOVA, etc.). Television is an excellent means of communacation. Television news has more information plus films so you have a feeling of what's happening and so you would be a bore.

A solution is to allow maybe one hours of air time [one hour of prime time] for network show an evening on Weekdays and unlimited air time for weekends and holidays.

The television could if used properly new tool of education if it is used wisely and by programming more educational series.

Television is also a great advance. It's a good feeling to come home and watch a show to relax you after a long days work.

Writing at this level may retain some grammatical errors, but they should not be as pervasive or as disorienting as those at the first level. Sentence structure problems are likely to consist of fragments and run-on sentences rather than the nonsyntactic structures that appear in the work of less skilled writers. Or, students may confine themselves to the relatively simple structures that they know, avoiding those they are afraid to try. Some Level 2 students who have entered college at the first level may continue to exhibit types of error more characteristic of Level 1 writing, but their work should show evidence of partial control over those elements—getting them right more often than not—that will usually grow more complete with further experience in writing and editing.

Development of thought in Level 2 writing may be quite disjointed at the outset. Writers may start off with a sentence that looks as if it intends to establish a topic but is too vaguely expressed to establish the topic with much certainty. And they may abandon that topic altogether, or at least appear to, in their subsequent sentences. Such writers also evince little understanding of the convention of paragraphing and remain unfamiliar with the traditional rhetorical modes, continuing to present highly egocentric writing which evolves by a private logic of associations that is only dimly accessible to readers and sometimes even, after a short span of time, to themselves. However, their impromptu passages may continue, albeit repetitively, for several hundred words, suggesting the Level 2 writers' conviction that they have something to say and that they can say it in writing.

The third level of writing is produced by students who are comparable to traditional freshman composition students. Their writing is grammatical most of the time although it may retain some lapses in spelling and an occasional sentence fragment or comma splice. It also exhibits the writer's ability to establish a topic and stick to it, to create sensible paragraph divisions, and to produce an orderly essay. Writing at this stage generally meets traditional college entrance standards but may still demonstrate the writer's difficulty with semantics, logic, or appropriateness of expression and tone. Writing produced in an initial impromptu essay at Level 3 might look like this:

> I disagree with this passage. The writer of the passage believes that the children of America are in many ways harmed by watching television and would be better off without it. I agree that excessive television watching is not good for anyone. Children who watch too much TV tend to become lazy and show a lack of imagination, and therefore they are harmed by it. Television can also benefit children in many ways. They seem to learn things much quicker and at a younger age by watching educational TV shows such as "Sesame Street" and "Electric Company," than children who don't watch these shows. Shows like "Sesame Street" teach them things through repetition and they catch a child's attention easily through their use of bright colors, cartoons, music and puppets. Children enjoy these shows and also learn from them.
>
> I believe that children should be guided by their parents as to what shows they can and cannot watch. Children should watch shows that are suitable for them, that is, simple enough for them to understand but not so simple that they are bored by it. They should not be allowed to watch shows that are excessively violent because these shows leave a bad impression on them. I don't think that this pertains just to children, though, because adults are affected by these shows too.
>
> From my own observation, I have concluded that children between the ages of three and ten watch the most television. These are very important years because the child's whole character is formed during these years. If the child watches too much TV it can be harmful to him, especially if he is watching "junk" TV shows, that is shows with no educational value whatsoever. Later on, it seems that young adults seem to drift away from TV and don't start watching it to an excess again until they hit about thirty. By this time many of them have children of their own and are sitting down to enjoy it with them.
>
> In conclusion, I think that television watching has both advantages and disadvantages but in my opinion, the advantages far

outweigh the disadvantages. Children can really benefit from watching TV and I think the children of the generations will be smarter than we could have ever dreamed possible.

In general, students whose writing places them initially at the most skilled end of the spectrum of basic writers are likely to differ somewhat from those who have traveled across the spectrum from the other end by laboriously completing several basic writing courses, for writers who have developed their skills in a year of basic courses may continue to have occasional lapses. At the third level, however, all students should be expected to have enough control over standard English, or enough information about how to exercise such control, that grammar need no longer be a focus of attention.

Diagnosis and Placement

A carefully designed writing program needs to identify the strengths and weaknesses of each student's writing performance at the outset in order to place students into broadly homogeneous instructional groupings appropriate to the levels of skill that its courses address. Wherever possible at CUNY, departments have opted to use a writing sample to measure writing ability and so determine placement. There are several reasons for this, the most important being the conviction of most English faculty that standardized tests measure not writing skills but editorial skills such as identifying correctly formed sentences and recognizing appropriate usage, punctuation, and capitalization.

Nevertheless, experience in the use of standardized objective tests as placement instruments suggests that, although they do not give as accurate an indication of writing ability as a writing sample does, they can provide a practical, easily scored, and fairly reliable method for assessing verbal skills, and they can save time and money. There is, furthermore, a strong correlation between placement designations based on some standardized test scores and independent placement by essay evaluation.

Objective Tests

Colleges that developed their own objective placement instruments have largely abandoned them as they have proved no more reliable or valid than published tests and are both costly and time consuming to administer and score. Among the objective tests that various CUNY campuses have found most useful are the Sequential Tests of Educational Progress (STEP) English Expression Test, the California Achievement Test (CAT), the Stanford Test of Academic Skills, and the Stanford Achievement Test in Reading. Many also endorse the Effectiveness and Mechanics subtests of the Cooperative English Test (CET). Of these, the CET, STEP, and Stanford Test in Reading are representative.

The CET subtests both follow a multiple choice format that offers one best answer and three content distractors for each question. The Effectiveness subtest asks students to select a written expression that most suitably completes each of thirty sentences, and the Mechanics subtest asks them to identify the line in each of sixty three-line sentences which contains a mechanical error or to recognize that no error in usage, spelling, punctuation, or capitalization exists.

The STEP English Expression Test also evaluates students' ability to assess correctness and effectiveness in sentences. The first part, "Correctness of Expression," tests students' English proficiency, rather than their familiarity with formal terminology, asking them to consider contexts that require subject-verb agreement, pronoun-antecedent concordance, and correct selection of adjective or adverb forms. In the second part, "Effectiveness of Expression," students demonstrate sensitivity to language by selecting an alternative that is grammatically correct, outstanding in sentence structure or word order, and most precise and appropriate in idiom and diction. The Stanford Achievement Test in Reading measures reading comprehension by means of sixty-five multiple-choice questions on several short passages.

Scores on these objective tests, either alone or in conjunction with a writing sample, have been used successfully on a number of CUNY campuses for placing students into the three levels of basic writing course. Although each campus or institution would need to discover how a test score can be converted into a placement designation for its particular purposes, here are scores on three different tests used at CUNY and their placement equivalencies:

Standardized Test	Score	Placement
Cooperative English	below 132	Level 1
Test (CET):	132–140	Level 2
Effectiveness and	141 or better	Level 3
Mechanics subtests		
STEP English	below 40	Level 1 or 2 (gross
Expression Test		discrimination)
	41–57	Level 3
	58 or better	Exempt from entry level writing course
Stanford	below 22	Level 1
Achievement Test in	22–43	Level 2
Reading	44 or better	Level 3

These equivalencies have been established by comparing students' scores on the standardized tests with independent assessment of the same students' writing abilities on an essay test. Many campuses, even relatively small ones, that do not want to rely solely on a standardized placement instrument nevertheless find that reading an essay for each incoming freshman places an enormous burden on faculty. Thus, they use a combination of both kinds of tests. The objective instrument determines general levels of verbal skills and establishes placement for students who most clearly fall into one or another level. The only essays that are read are those of students whose objective scores cluster at the dividing point between two different levels. How broad a cluster of scores will receive an essay reading may vary from one campus to another, but the procedure of replacing some essay readings by objective scores can reduce the number of necessary readings by one half and still result in accurate placement.

Although high school records may contribute to an assessment of writing ability, they are generally not as reliable a measure as the placement testing procedure due to wide discrepancies in grading standards of different high schools and to the small amount of writing required for successful completion of many high school English courses.

Writing Samples

Although a standardized test may provide a practical instrument for assessing verbal skills, writing instructors generally consider the most valid measure of writing performance to be writing, since unlike multiple-choice tests, it is the one measure that involves students in the entire complex activity of generating and sustaining writing. A resolution of the Conference on College Composition and Communication (1978) endorses that position, stating that "no student shall be given credit for a writing course, placed in a remedial course, exempted from a required writing course, or certified for competency without submitting a piece of written discourse." A writing sample is the fullest means of discovering how well students can combine rhetorical, grammatical, and stylistic skills to produce material that will serve them adequately as college students and graduates.

Who should set the standards for placement at a given level, and who should evaluate the placement essays? To say that English faculty are best qualified to make these judgments is only to say that they have worked most closely with students' writing and they are most interested in improving the writing performance of their students. Faculty from any department could, of course, read essays.

More important than who should evaluate the essays is the question of how they should be evaluated. Whether the writing sample is used alone or in combination with a standardized test, following certain procedures will improve the reliability of the assessment. Essays should be anonymous, and they should be read by faculty trained to apply departmental standards quickly and accurately. Each essay should be read by two readers, each of whom assigns a grade without knowing the other's assessment. When there is a discrepancy between the two judgments, a third reader resolves the dispute. Essays read for placement are scored effectively using the holistic, or impressionistic, method detailed in the discussion of the CUNY evaluation scale later in this chapter.

During the first week of classes, students in basic writing sections write a second essay which enables the teacher to verify placement and to plan a course of instruction. Individual reassignments may need to be made at this time.

At midterm, many teachers again assign in-class essays to all basic writing students; these are, ideally, exchanged among faculty for grading. This procedure allows instructors to monitor individual students' progress and allows students to see whether they are progressing apace. It is essential if regularizing standards for passing is a goal because it allows students and faculty alike to ascertain how they are faring in relation to the general standard rather than just in terms of the single class.

The same procedure that is used for placement may also be followed at the end of a course. This will help to align initial placement standards with exit criteria. Exit examination readings are often done in committee so that discrepancies can be resolved immediately by a third reader.

CUNY Evaluation Scale. There are two major difficulties to be considered when assessing students' writing performance. As outlined by Cooper and Odell (1977, p. 2) they are "making judgments that are reliable, that we can reasonably assume are not idiosyncratic; and making judgments that are valid, that provide significant information about the writing we are dealing with." Cooper and Odell endorse holistic reading methods, which consider a sample of discourse as a whole entity, for these offer reasonable solutions to both problems especially for the purpose of grading essays for placement and exit. Atomistic scoring methods, which assess particular features associated with skills in discourse, are more useful for diagnostic purposes once the student's placement level has been established.

The most commonly used holistic method of evaluation, developed by the Educational Testing Service and adapted both by CUNY and by the California State University and Colleges (White, 1973–1979), is a procedure for sorting or ranking writing. The rater matches a writing sample with another piece in a ranked series of pieces or with a description of characteristics on a graded scale of descriptions that correspond to the ranked examples. On the basis of this matching, the rater then assigns the writing sample a number or grade. The placing, scoring, or grading occurs quickly and impressionistically, taking no more than two minutes.

The CUNY Task Force on Proficiency in Writing, convened to articulate university-wide criteria for minimum competence in writing, developed the following scale for use as a guide to readers of the Writing Assessment Test developed as a CUNY-wide placement instrument. The scale is accompanied, for each session, by a set of student papers gleaned from earlier test responses to exemplify performance at the six levels that the guide outlines.

City University of New York
Freshman Skills Assessment Program
Evaluation Scale for Writing Assessment Test

6: The essay is competently organized and the ideas are expressed in appropriate language. A sense of pattern or development is present from beginning to end. The writer supports assertions with explanation or illustrations.

Sentences reflect a command of syntax within the ordinary range of standard written English. Grammar, punctuation, and spelling are generally correct.

4–5: The writer introduces some point or idea and demonstrates an awareness that development or illustration is called for.

The essay presents a discernible pattern or organization, even if there are occasional digressions.

The essay demonstrates sufficient command of vocabulary to convey, without serious distortion or excessive simplification, the range of the writer's ideas.

Sentences reflect a sufficient command of syntax to ensure reasonable clarity of expression. The writer generally avoids both the monotony of rudimentary syntax and the incoherence created by tangled syntax.

The writer demonstrates through punctuation an understanding of the boundaries of the sentence.

The writer spells the common words of the language with a reasonable degree of accuracy. Exceptions can be made for the so-called spelling demons which frequently trouble even an advanced writer.

The writer shows the ability to use regularly, but not necessarily faultlessly, the common forms of agreement and of grammatical inflection in standard written English.

2–3: An idea or point is suggested, but is undeveloped or presented in a purely repetitive way.

The pattern of the essay is somewhat random and relationships between sentences and paragraphs are rarely signaled.

The essay is restricted to a very narrow range of language, so that the vocabulary chosen frequently does not serve the needs of the writer.

The syntax of the essay is not sufficiently stable to ensure reasonable clarity of expression. The syntax often is rudimentary or tangled.

The writer frequently commits errors of punctuation which obscure sentence boundaries.

The writer spells the common words of the language with only intermittent accuracy.

The essay reveals recurrent grammatical problems; if there are only occasional problems, this may be due to the extremely narrow range of syntactical choices the writer has used.

1: The essay suffers from general incoherence and has no discernible pattern of organization. It displays a high frequency of error in the regular features of standard written English. Lapses in punctuation, spelling, and grammar often frustrate the reader.

Or: The essay is so brief that any reasonably accurate judgment of the writer's competence is impossible.

At CUNY, essays to be evaluated holistically are read by two readers and scored on the scale from 1 to 6, with a score of 4 representing the CUNY standard of minimal competence and the required score for placement in Level 3 courses. In any instance where one reader rates the essay 4 or above and the other at 3 or below, a third reader is required and the third score places the essay above or below the line of competence.

Reading for Diagnosis. Once classes have begun, teachers can use a different testing procedure to quantify the specific needs of each individual and tailor the instruction in the course accordingly. The Hunter College Writing Profile and Score Key (see Exhibit 1) is an atomistic evaluation guide that pinpoints troublesome aspects of an individual's writing performance. It focuses on subskills that correlate with features of CUNY's holistic scale. The reader assigns a number, on a six-point scale, to the writer's performance of each of the subskills under examination, making checks in the appropriate numbered column. The overall score is the average of the numbers checked for each subskill.

The score key may serve to define course entrance and exit criteria. It may be used by instructors as a device for referring particular students to tutors for assistance with specific skills. Or, it may help the students themselves to identify problem areas and writing goals to keep in sight during a course.

The top half to the profile and score key deals with definable sentence errors, the bottom half with the student's ability to carry an idea to a suitable conclusion. The top half is the primary concern of instructors of basic writing, Levels 1 and 2, whereas the bottom half is of greater concern in the Level 3 course. If scoring in the top half results in a majority of checks in columns one and two, the student should be working in the Level 1 course. Level 2 papers should score mostly in columns two and three of the top half of the key. Checks in columns four and five of the top half indicate that the writer is working in the range of Level 3, in which case the sample paper would also be scored for the skills outlined in the lower half of the profile.

Basic Writing Courses

Although some colleges may offer only one homogeneous remedial writing course prior to freshman composition, writing programs that serve the broadest spectrum of basic writing students will benefit from a structure based on the three broad stages of writing development outlined earlier. The courses can aim toward competency which, in a particular program, will mark students' readiness to move from one level to another and finally to manage college-level writing tasks. These stages may often correspond to three semester-long courses, but the disparate needs of changing student populations and the growing interest in ensuring that students achieve an established minimal level of competency in writing may result in some students' taking more than two semesters of work to move through the first two levels and arrive at the level of freshman composition.

The following discussion of the three basic writing levels suggests course content that can serve student needs at each level. The discussion considers, as well, some ongoing faculty debates over the content or organization of these courses. Such debates, although perhaps suggestive of dissension and distress among basic writing faculty, are rather symptomatic of their continuous struggle to find and promote the best methods of solving the complex problems that their students face. Disagreement over pedagogical approaches is widespread at CUNY and is often considered a sign of a

Exhibit 1. Hunter College Analytic Score Key.

Student: _____

Reader: _____

Technical Aspects	6	5	4	3	2	1
	error-free	almost error-free	competent but some errors	several errors	frequent errors	severe problems
Sentence Structure fragments, run-ons, subordination, parallelism, incorrect word order, missing or repeated subject						
Verbs form, endings (-s, -ed, -ing), tense sequence and consistency, voice, subject-verb agreement, verb ties						
Grammar plurals, possessives, quantifiers, articles, pronoun form and reference, negation, comparison, adjective/adverb mix						
Idiomatic Diction choice of word and structure, prepositions, repeated words, no slang or second language interference						
Mechanics manuscript form, punctuation, capitalization, spelling, editing errors (for example, omitted word)						

Content, Style, Organization	skillful	good	adequate	some flaws	many flaws	severe problems
Sentence Variety varied sentence length and type, effective constructions						
Style and Usage appropriate level of diction, usage and sentence structure, clear, interesting "voice"						
Paragraph Development controlling idea, adequate detail, unity and clarity of development, transitions						
Essay Structure thesis and support, quality and quantity of information, clear and logical organization and development						
Placement	Exempt	Fresh. Comp.	Fresh. Comp.	Level II	Level I	Pre-Level I (ESL)

Length: adequate: _____ under 250 words: _____

Comments: _____

_____

_____

Pass _____ Fail _____

Source: Office of Freshman and Developmental English, Hunter College, CUNY.

program's health and vigor. Shaughnessy (1977b) is an excellent source of additional assignments and rationales for basic writing courses.

Level 1 Courses

In writing programs that begin at Level 1, faculty often disagree about how best to help their students develop the necessary skills to advance to the next level, but they rarely disagree, at least in theory, about what skills their students need to gain during the semester. The work of students coming into Level 1 shows that they need both to build confidence in their ability to express their thoughts in writing and to learn to produce written English according to the standard conventions.

Some faculty feel that the primary task for Level 1 students is to develop confidence as writers and a new commitment to the written word as a vehicle for thought and self-expression. These faculty often feel that formal considerations—grammar, capitalization, paragraph indentation, internal punctuation—are best left alone for much of the semester. They feel that concentration on formal matters inhibits students' flow of writing, focuses their attention too narrowly on the written product and their need to make it correct as opposed to meaningful, and generally diminishes the likelihood that students will learn to enjoy the process of writing and to find it important to themselves.

Other faculty take a substantially different position, that from the beginning Level 1 writers are painfully aware of what they have been taught to call "proper" English and are self-conscious about their inability to produce it. These faculty feel that students, understandably reticent to appear foolish or inept especially in such a concrete medium as the written word, are anxious to learn to control the formal aspects of their work and, therefore, gain confidence and self-assurance as they increase their control over standard forms. Although these two pedagogical positions stimulate ongoing discussion among faculty (see Farrell, 1977, and Laurence, 1977), the actual success of any individual teacher does not seem to result from subscription to one or the other.

The instructor of a Level 1 course must help students get

their thoughts down on paper and respond to these thoughts through conferences, class discussions, and written comments. Students at this level need to practice writing constantly. Emphasis should be on the process rather than the end product of writing as content moves from the personal to the more analytical. The writing process can be explored from several vantage points as students compose themes, write regularly in a journal outside of class, and produce frequent extemporaneous writing in class, including ten-minute free writing exercises, practice hour exams, and notes of criticism and suggestion in reaction to reading one another's work. The course also addresses standard English form, offering practical instruction in controlling sentence structure, verb forms, subject-verb agreement, noun plurals, form-class correspondences, spelling, and basic punctuation. Training in proofreading for error is an appropriate accompaniment to this emphasis on form.

Students moving out of Level 1 should have made sufficient progress to rank a step or two higher in a holistic evaluation, but they may well retain some of their old problems in grammar. They should evince growing ability to produce the standard written idiom; their ability will not be faultless, for complete mastery often develops over a person's full career as a writer. Although control of error in student writing must be viewed in relation to the length and content of the writing sample, students' grammar and spelling should no longer constitute a substantial distraction to their readers if they are to move to Level 2.

The following syllabus for a Level 1 course represents one teacher's idiosyncratic approach. It is offered not as a recommendation but rather as an example of how such a course might be structured to combine substantial writing experience and growing control of standard English form.

Syllabus for Level 1. In this course, students read and write autobiographical material to allow them to concentrate on the business of writing without having to worry about the added complications of dealing with academic subject matter. If they write on the subject about which they have an unlimited, accurate, and unquestionable fund of information—themselves—then they can turn all of their attention to effective self-expression and not have to worry whether their content is "correct." The writing assignments are structured, however, to introduce students to a variety of expository techniques.

Grammar discussions in class concentrate on areas of confusion about standard written English grammar that characterize the writing of Level 1 students. Individual difficulties are discussed in conference and, where necessary, in sessions with private tutors. The primary goal of discussing grammar is to provide students with criteria of correctness that do not depend on judgments of whether given structures "sound right." Because some Level 1 students speak nonstandard English, what sounds proper to their ears will not always be correct written form.

One text used for this course is Petrie (1970), an anthology of largely autobiographical writings by students from previous semesters of basic writing courses. It provides samples of how one might approach some of the writing assignments made in class and is useful, therefore, for examination of the particular writing techniques being taught. It also allows students to see that others who were in their exact situation, who were as frightened and self-conscious as they are at the outset, actually produced good, readable, grammatical and publishable prose.

Another text, Muscatine and Griffith's *First Person Singular* (1973), is an anthology of autobiographical writings by established authors and by persons in public life who aren't professional writers. Similar texts include Coursen's *As Up They Grew* (1970) and Lyons' *Autobiography: A Reader for Writers* (1977).

A growing number of texts are addressing themselves to the grammatical confusions of Level 1 students. Useful ones include Gould's *Groundwork* (1977) and Loewe's *The Writing Clinic* (1973). Daiker, Kerek, and Morenberg's *The Writer's Option* (1979) and Strong's *Sentence Combining* (1973) provide excellent exercise in generating sentences and practicing structures, and Skurnick (forthcoming) makes strong and productive links between grammar study and proofreading for grammatical correctness.

In a typical syllabus, writing assignments might elicit two kinds of work. The first, a weekly journal, continues throughout the semester. Students write a minimum of 350 words a week on their responses to the events, major or trivial, of their lives during the semester. Any subject matter can be included, with the understanding that the semipublic nature of a journal that is read by the instructor places some restriction on the depth and range of the personal material included. Writing a journal encourages students to examine their experience as college students, family members, inhabitants of a particular city or region, and writers. It provides students an opportunity to experience writing as a meaningful and pleasurable activity.

In-class writing assignments constitute a second kind of experience in composition. They are discussed and explained in class and begun in class, but may be taken home for completion. Beginning the papers in class offers students an opportunity to consult with the instructor for advice, direction, and reassurance on the initial stages of the composing process; it allows the instructor to discover any general difficulties with the assignment and to guide individual students having particular problems. These assignments fall into three major units: description, narrative, and analysis.

The purpose of the description unit (three to four weeks) is to focus the students' attention on providing precise, vivid descriptive detail and selecting and arranging that detail so that it produces a unified impression. Students begin by describing a place—a street scene, a familiar room, a location in their neighborhoods. They work to choose the most accurate, most concrete possible terms to replace old standbys like *great, nice,* and *beautiful.* In a second assignment, they describe a person, extending their concerns from simply providing details to selecting and arranging their information to create an overall sense of their subject.

Writing narrative draws on an old skill, storytelling, and places new demands on it. The purpose of this unit (three or four weeks) is to lead students to view their experiences selectively so that they can relate an episode that makes a point using only relevant details and excluding details that might well be true but that are not related to the chosen point. The first assignment requires students to choose a specific day or journey that had overriding significance in their lives and to tell about it in such a way that its significance is clear. The second assignment asks students to write a dialogue between two people that reveals the nature of each or the nature of their interaction. Students continue to exercise the skills developed in the first unit, those of providing clear and precise descriptive detail focused around a central theme. In writing the second paper, they begin to learn the meaning of quotation and the conventions for its use, information that they will draw upon in all of their academic writing.

The analysis unit (six to eight weeks) introduces several methods of analysis by asking students to apply them to their own experience. The first assignment requires students to analyze the parts of a whole. Students are asked, for example, to analyze the elements that make up their neighborhood as a social unit. The second assignment involves writing a comprehensive definition of oneself as a member of one's ethnic group. The third assignment is to write an autobiography, and this requires the student to consider virtually all the expository devices discussed in the course. The students must discover a consistent theme that has run through their life and view the events of that life in terms of it. The fourth and final assignment is an exercise in comparison. It asks students to compare themselves with another person of their choice, perhaps a parent or sibling. It requires that students make the bases of comparison clear and specifically related to a central point to be made by the comparison.

All writing assignments are presented on detailed, written assignment sheets that set forth discrete steps for students to follow in considering separately the many tasks involved in completing the assignment. Students are instructed to: (1) Choose a topic. (2) Jot down details, in phrases or single words, that come to mind in thinking about the topic. (3) Find a word or words that summarize the overall sense or tendency of the list and use that designation in a simple statement that establishes the point to be made about the general topic. (4) Organize the details into categories, recognizing that there are any number of possible organizations and that the process of finding one will require working from the items (step 2) to the statement (step 3) and back, adding or deleting items, and perhaps altering the statement until the result is a short set of categories that all relate to the statement and that contain solid supportive material. (5) Write a first draft, paying little attention to grammatical correctness but concentrating on getting the ideas down on paper. (6) Reread the draft, revising it first for content, then for specific elements of grammar. (7) Write a final draft. And (8) proofread the final draft before submitting it. The process outlined in these steps is useful beyond its application to the assignments at hand as it introduces students to an effective method of controlling the writing of all academic papers and examinations.

The second focus of the typical Level 1 course is on development of standard English conventions. Prior to each writing assignment the class also tackles one problem in standard written English grammar. In completing their compositions, students must pay special attention to the elements of grammar discussed. Thus, since the first topic in grammar to come under discussion is the concept of complete sentences, the first paper requires a final draft that contains only complete, well-formed sentences. Before the second written assignment, the class will have discussed subject-verb agreement, so that in their second paper students must not only write well-formed sentences but they must also produce subjects and verbs in concord. Papers that contain errors in the areas of grammar already discussed are returned for revision. Other errors that may occur are ignored until considered in class. This allows students to concentrate on learning to write grammatical standard written English one step at a time rather than overwhelming them at the outset with all the areas which they must master.

Topics in grammar, in the order in which they are discussed, are (1) components of a sentence (two weeks), (2) writing sentences: an introduction to sentence combining (two weeks), (3) agreement of subject and verb (one week), (4) formation of verb tenses (three weeks), (5) the use and punctuation of quotations (one week), (6) agreement of pronouns with antecedents (one week), (7) standard use of particular, troublesome prepositions as distinct from specific regional usage (one week), (8) punctuation, particularly the use of commas in series, after initial adverbials, between coordinated sentences, and surrounding sequence signals like *however* and *nevertheless* (one week), and (9) specific kinds of spelling difficulties (one week), although spelling mistakes are marked for revision all semester long. In addition to these topics, exercise in sentence combining throughout the semester can produce continued growth in sentence control and variety.

Level 2 Courses

The instructor of a Level 2 basic writing course can assign writing tasks that are closer to traditional academic forms using a number of rhetorical modes. Students require further work in grammar control, but they can concentrate on writing analytical essays. The conventions and rules that govern analytical writing inform the course content. Students can write short expository papers, often in response to readings or other stimuli, such as cartoons, posters, or art works, from which they draw information and to which they formulate a reaction. At this level, there can be more careful attention to the formal constraints of essay structure. Attention to grammar continues in conferences and critical responses to student writing, but formal presentations in class are limited to elements of grammar that continue to trouble large segments of the group and so will vary from semester to semester.

Practice in sentence combining is useful at this level to help students develop precision and style in their writing by expanding their options for presenting meaning in sentences. Students can also be encouraged to imagine an audience for their writing and to anticipate the responses of various types of readers. Like Level 1 students, those at Level 2 need to write as much as possible—expository papers, in-class essays, free writing, and journals—generating about 10,000 words during the semester.

Students leaving Level 2 should ideally be able to place into freshman composition, Level 3, on a holistically scored placement or exit examination. Their writing should demonstrate some solid control of structure and organization, some awareness of audience and tone, and substantial control over standard grammar and spelling.

Like the earlier syllabus for Level 1, the syllabus that follows represents only one teacher's approach to the course.* It omits

*The authors are grateful to Sarah G. D'Eloia for contributing her syllabus for a Level 2 course.

specific consideration of grammar since needs for grammatical instruction may vary dramatically from student to student and term to term. It demonstrates, however, one way to build sophisticated rhetorical capacities starting at a very basic level.

Syllabus for Level 2. This course introduces students to the *form* of complex argumentation with rebuttal: one interpretation, solution, or course of action is preferable to others because it better takes into account the range of facts or because it produces results deemed more desirable as measured against common values. Complex arguments require the integration of a number of high-level cognitive skills. It requires students to reach a generalization of sufficient breadth and depth to account for a wide range of facts, to uncover causal connections in complex processes, to consider opposing points of view and to make extended comparisons between alternative points of view, and, in the case of proposing or defending a course of action, to assess results in terms of stated intentions and values. The course is organized so that each new skill builds on preceding ones and increases in complexity. For the greater part of the course, students write short, three-to-five paragraph, thesis-support essays with an introduction, body, and conclusion.

The first few assignments address the problem of reaching generalizations which draw conclusions from raw data. For example, students may look at rates of death and serious injury in automobile accidents over the last decade and at rates of death and serious injury in automobiles traveling at different speeds, on different surfaces, and on divided or single roads. Or they may look at charts and maps showing total rates of cancer, rates of cancer by kind, estimated levels of nonorganic air, water, and soil pollution, the distribution of heavy and light industry, and the rate of death from cancer by occupation. Or they may survey a table of salaries paid New Yorkers of both sexes and various occupations and ethnic groups in attempts to find the explanation which best accounts for the wide range and the clustering of incomes.

In each case, students must organize or reorganize the data in order to find a pattern which supports an explanation or generalization that accounts for the data. The best generalization is the one which takes in the widest range of information while not contradicting any of the facts. For example, the generalization that men earn more than women is true, but weak, because some of the male and female New Yorkers earn exactly the same salary. In class discussions of completed assignments, students rank each other's generalizations for their relative "power." The best generalization not only gives the most reaching explanation but also most explicitly anticipates or most clearly implies all that the writer subsequently asserts by way of support. All these assignments require students to seek out causal connections which are relatively clear-cut; for example, excessive speed is the greatest single cause of deaths and serious injury in automobile accidents; a sharp reduction in the legal speed limit resulted in a sharp decline in rates of death and injury.

In the next few assignments, students favor or oppose various social policies—capital punishment, stricter penalties for juvenile offenders, living together before marriage, or tracking in schools, for example—giving at least two reasons for their conclusions. They discuss the effects of a particular policy on the wider population and in their own lives, affecting their own needs and values. This kind of subject matter adds to the assignment the complexity of uncertainty, for the causal connections between these policies and their projected personal or societal effects are often tenuous, even in the most proficient analyses. Here, too, differences in students' values will clearly appear. Occasionally, sharp conflicts of personal and social interests may occur. The purpose of these assignments is to make the students examine their assumptions and qualify their assertions, to see that their values shape their judgments, to see the circular nature of some processes, and to see that results can be mixed.

The next set of assignments directs students toward making their first complex argument. Again the topic should be one which affects students directly or one about which sentiment runs very high. In the first assignment, students write an essay in which they advance their three best reasons for supporting or opposing the policy. As before, they argue in terms of the results and in terms of the values that are supported. In the second essay, they must take the opposite position and advance the three best reasons for supporting that position. The third assignment has two parts. In the first part, students write a paragraph attacking the arguments they used in their previous essay on social policy: holding that the policy does not really produce the results stated, or not to the extent asserted, or produces other negative results which weaken, equal, or more than offset the positive results, or holding that the policy does not necessarily support and may conceivably undermine the stated values. In the second part, students write a paragraph attacking the arguments of the opposition in similar fashion.

The fourth assignment is to write a long complex argument which synthesizes the three previous assignments. Students can often compose this essay by cutting and pasting the previous assignments. The finished paper should have (1) an introduction, (2) a few expository paragraphs stating the student's proposal and the three reasons he has for supporting it, (3) a brief, perhaps one paragraph, statement of the alternative and the reasons advanced for it, with an explanation of what is wrong with the alternative, (4) a consideration, probably in one paragraph, of what points may appear to be weaknesses in the present proposal but are actually strengths or instances of lesser evils, and (5) a one-paragraph conclusion. Some students will need to have help condensing the arguments of the opposition into a single paragraph and making the seams disappear as they put the pieces together. Unsatisfactory essays should be revised, preferably under the instructor's direct supervision, so that the student has, at last, a satisfactory model for the complex argument. The beauty of this set of assignments is that students simultaneously learn how to expand and revise, how to think a topic through from several angles, and how to accommodate complexity. They have the satisfaction, in addition, of producing a paper whose length astonishes them.

During the remainder of the term, the students write one or two other complex arguments, using the first argument as a model of the process and the product.

Any anthology of topical essays may be used as a text for this course. The instructor may supplement the text with photocopied magazine or newspaper articles. One rhetoric text that is useful for this course is Kytle's *Clear Thinking for Composition* (1973), which treats some of the major pitfalls in constructing a good argument—cultural conditioning, unconscious needs and fears, vague abstractions, false analogies—in a down-to-earth way that students like. Also appropriate is Gehle and Rollo's *The Writing Process* (1977), which establishes a good connection between description, narration, analysis, and argumentation. It emphasizes prewriting and rewriting as parts of the total process, treats logical fallacies, and contains a segment on sentence improvement and mechanics. It is, unfortunately, written in a style more appropriate to Level 3 students.

Level 3 Courses: Freshman Composition

Practice in academic essay writing can continue at Level 3 and can draw increasingly for its content on academic material: literary works, critical essays, and informative reports. By the end of this last semester of basic writing, students will need to be able to sustain a paper of five to ten pages and to perform the kinds of writing tasks likely to be assigned to college students.

The major point of contention among faculty over the content of this course concerns whether it should culminate in a research paper. Many writing programs do not concentrate on research techniques. Many faculty, no longer as confident about the value of term papers as they once were, are abandoning the term paper in favor of examinations. Their confidence in student papers may have eroded because of the proliferation of commercial businesses that sell term papers, or, more alarming, because when students produce their own papers, they seem to have trouble understanding just what research entails. The students' confusion may be the result of the traditional approaches to teaching research, which have concentrated on the forms of doing research rather than on the reasons for doing it. Countless textbooks tell students how to find a book in the library, how to put notes on index cards, how to write a proper bibliography, and how to footnote. Although these forms are puzzling to students and must eventually be taught, if students are to be equipped to do solid academic work, it is more essential that they learn the spirit of research, the rationale for it.

Students need to discover that research is not simply a form, a series of blanks to be filled in with pieces of information extracted from sources. They need to find that it is a way of giving weight to their own process of reasoning, a way of exploring, integrating, and evaluating their internalization of what they have read.

Thus, more important than teaching the formal conventions of the research paper is teaching the basic processes of research: how to assess source material and how to integrate it sensibly into one's own work. Instructors must address the major questions among students learning to do research: how a paper that is largely based on the ideas of others can be considered the student's own work and how the lines can honestly be drawn between the proficient use of sources and the feared but often dimly understood spectre of plagiarism.

Students need to learn how their own interpretation can emerge from their reading of other people's presentations of a subject. Once they develop confidence that they can use sources with an integrity that meets their own as well as their professors' demands, they can easily learn to deal with the formal procedures of research: using card catalogues, writing footnotes, and the like.

Although the traditional research paper may remain unpopular on many campuses, a writing program must provide training in elementary research techniques if it is to produce writers capable of conventional college-level work. The syllabus that follows illustrates one CUNY teacher's design for introducing students to using source materials in a Level 3 class.

Syllabus for Level 3. In this course, students discover how to manipulate published source material responsibly and productively; the course draws on library resources as well as textbooks. However, although the instructor may wish to take students on a tour of the library and demonstrate how to use a card catalogue and other library facilities, that kind of activity is not at all essential. A premise of this course is that, if students learn the responsible use of library resources in their writing, they will discover on their own how to find what they need in a library. Once students understand how to gather, sort, and reformulate information, they will know that what they seek in a library is not a particular, illusive, "right" answer to a problem but an aggregation of items from which they can create one possible answer to a problem.

Students also discover how to find and make use of those reference materials that are related to their particular projects.

Having learned that, they can explore other parts of a library, indexes other than those they have already consulted, or resources that they did not know existed, perhaps asking a librarian for a specific direction or two, but knowing that what they find in a library must be determined by their own needs and cannot be determined by a librarian, whose purposes and interests are different from their own. Thus, students must learn to reshape the subject under study in ways that their own intellects can mold into logical and sound form.

A course with this grand an ultimate goal begins, nevertheless, very simply, with several essays from any contemporary anthology. Students spend the first two weeks of class reading and summarizing essays. They also take notes on an essay or two, coming to class prepared to explain what they noted down and why. In class discussion, students consider the thoroughness and conciseness of their summaries as well as the soundness of their several approaches to notetaking.

In the next two weeks, students continue to summarize, adding some evaluation of each essay, perhaps a consideration of the writer's bias as apparent either through direct statements or through word choices. Or, they comment on the usefulness of an essay's contents for inclusion in a hypothetical paper of their own.

Having had opportunities as a group to summarize, take notes, and evaluate those procedures as represented in one another's work, the students spend the next two weeks doing a note project on a subject of current interest using material from *The New York Times,* which nicely confines the project and gives students experience working with an index. For this small research project, students take notes on three-by-five-inch slips or cards. They learn, in the process, how to identify notes from multiple sources of information and how to make use of slugs on note cards. Next, they learn how to reorder their material to create a new work as opposed to merely paraphrasing one and then another source. This project, an exercise in taking and using notes, allows the class to grapple with the issue of how a paper becomes the writer's when all of its information comes from sources written by others. In the course of arranging and rearranging note cards, and having to justify an organization to themselves, to one another, and ultimately to the instructor, students come to realize that they have created a new whole, one that is totally different from any of the sources and, thus, one that is legitimately theirs. The product of this exercise is simply a packet of arranged notes, preceded by an outline and divided by heading cards that allow a reader to understand the logic of the order. Since these notes are never converted into a paper, students need not yet learn how to include quotation in a text, to footnote, or to write a bibliography. Thus, the exercise remains tightly focused, allowing students to develop confidence about one critical aspect of research without overwhelming them with a number of new conventions at once.

The last six weeks of the term focus on a novel as a primary source, and essays about that novel constitute a group of secondary sources. An edition of a popular classic that includes critical essays about the novel is useful for this purpose. After reading the text, students begin writing an assignment on a topic that is considered in the critical essays. But, before reading those essays, they first deal with the topic on their own. For example, students reading *Huckleberry Finn* might be asked to describe Huck's relationship to the society in which he lives. They would scan the text, taking notes on passages that reflect, for them, evidence of this relationship; they would formulate a thesis and write a paper. For their next assignment, they would read an essay that considers the entire text, such as Lionel Trilling's "The Greatness of *Huckleberry Finn*," and write a paper that first outlines Trilling's perception of Huck's relationship to his society and then accepts or rejects it. A third assignment would ask students to read two additional and complementary essays, perhaps T. S. Eliot's "An Introduction to *Huckleberry Finn*" and Leo Marx's "Mr. Eliot, Mr. Trilling, and *Huckleberry Finn*," and then to write a paper that details the scholarly argument among the three men and takes a position regarding it.

This series of three papers presents controlled opportunities for students to learn conventions for writing a research paper, including forms for footnotes, bibliography, and citations. Students use the *MLA Handbook* (1977), Turabian's *A Manual for Writers* (1967), or whatever other style manual a department considers most appropriate.

Students are finally ready to write a long paper on their own, now that they have worked through the separate components of such a project. The final assignment of the course asks them to write a paper of eight-to-ten pages on a choice of several topics related to *Huckleberry Finn*. It requires the use of some of the essays they have already read and other secondary sources that students find independently in the library. The paper may be a literary analysis or a consideration of historical or sociological subjects tangentially related to the novel, such as slavery, life on the Mississippi River, or confidence men.

Methodology

The grammatical and rhetorical skills that basic writers must develop need to be addressed simultaneously at every level of writing course, and it is in this requirement that the teaching of basic writing differs from the teaching of other basic skills. For example, one must know the basic arithmetical operations before moving on to algebraic questions. But, in basic writing, there is not a discernible hierarchy of skills to be mastered; it is not sensible to require a student to achieve total control of one element of writing, let us say verb forms, before he can go on to consider another, like internal punctuation. Every act of writing requires the integration of many related skills. At each level, instructors must address both syntactic and rhetorical considerations, but in increasing complexity as the students' capacity for comprehending and controlling that complexity grows.

To meet the needs of new kinds of composition students at whatever point they may enter a writing program, their teachers will have to explore a variety of pedagogical techniques, evaluating their effects and refining them to meet the specific needs of the students. Through their experience with this ongoing pedagogical experimentation, CUNY faculty have developed a number of new approaches, have made some new applications of traditional pedagogy, and have endorsed and adopted methods and materials developed at other institutions.

Their experience suggests that faculty entering into this exploration need to consider three broad areas: (1) the development of methods to help students cultivate (in the short space of a semester or two) the intellectual skills necessary for expository or analytical writing, (2) the development of methods to facilitate quick acquisition of syntactic and grammatical skills, and (3) the creation of alternative instructional modes that facilitate, and perhaps accelerate, students' progress.

Although no one practice is endorsed by a majority of CUNY faculty, and although many techniques reported here will have already changed considerably through the continual effort to improve them, it is instructive to consider some methods that have been found successful at CUNY.

In the first area of exploration, faculty seeking new methods for developing analytical skills have not deviated from the long-established principles of ordering expository prose, but present those principles differently. They have developed exercises that allow students to observe and to practice different formulas for organizing subject matter depending on the type of essay a student needs to write, and they have drawn on accessible subject matter that encourages student thought in ways that literary analysis has largely ceased to do. In the second area, instructors have sought to foster acquisition of new language skills by applying contemporary developments in linguistic theory to the teaching of the standard language. And in the third area, teachers have developed instructional methods that encourage students to draw on their own internal resources as well as those of their peers, so that students depend on their teachers for guidance and structure but do not view them as the sole source of rules, explanations, or perceptions.

Developing Expository Skills

The ultimate goals of basic writing programs remain identical to those of traditional composition courses. Both seek to introduce the conventional modes of expository writing—description, narration, analysis, argumentation—with the intention of preparing students to write the kinds of academic papers that they are likely to encounter during their college careers. In addition to that central focus, both traditional composition and basic writing courses at all levels may also include some creative writing, but in both cases these assignments are more for the purpose of encouraging students to write and to enjoy writing than they are for the purpose of teaching techniques of creative writing. In basic courses, creative writing often takes the form of prewriting or free writing that will act as the first stage in producing what will ultimately become an expository work. Or it may be the start of a course which begins with narrative or descriptive writing that will lead to more complex, analytical writing assignments.

In basic writing courses, instructors only sometimes rely on the traditional technique of using literary or other academic essays as models, as sources of information to be drawn upon for an assignment's content, or as positions against which a student is to respond in an essay. They have found other methods that help students get started on writing projects, maintain their interest in the process of writing, and lead them through productive steps for polishing their writing into respectable academic papers.

Prewriting. Many teachers introduce the process of prewriting, which emphasizes the stages of thought that prepare a student to write. Inexperienced writers tend to jump into an assignment without stopping to think through what they want to say, what order they want to use, or what pattern they want to impose on their discussion. Such writers often fail to establish a clear subject for a paper and spend an inordinate amount of time making and discarding false starts.

In response to these difficulties, faculty can begin to place emphasis on prewriting activities, activities that focus students' attention on constructive consideration of what they will say, that invite them or require them to consider carefully the components of what they will say and to determine a possible order of those components, all before beginning their compositions. One form of prewriting is outlined in Fawcett and Sandberg's *Grassroots: The Writer's Workbook* (1976). They instruct students starting an assignment to first limit their subject by moving from one word, like *abortion,* to a full statement, like "Abortion should be illegal," or, more elaborately, "Although there are several major problems arising from federal subsidy of abortion through Medicaid, the benefits of such support far outweigh the detriments," or some other statement that clarifies, for the writer as well as for the eventual reader, just what point the composition will make. Second, the student brainstorms, jotting down any ideas that come to mind with reference to the statement just formulated; this list should include at least fifteen items. The third step is to eliminate; by checking each item against the focal sentence, the student drops any items that do not pertain. Fourth, students group together the ideas that have something in common, that seem to be related in some way. The final step is to arrange, to decide on the order in which to present the groups in the paper. Only after completing all these prewriting steps are writers advised to begin to write their essays.

Prewriting can also take the form of students' discovering and working through a pattern of development by manipulating elements in an exercise before actually using the pattern for their own writing. Students are given groups of sentences that would form a paragraph except that they are in garbled order; for example, consider these exercises written by Rizzo and Libo of the City College of New York (other similar exercises are in Rizzo, 1978):

> 1. The horse stumbles again. 2. His bride turns to him and says, "You fool, why did you do that?" 3. The Russian shouts, "That's two!" 4. The horse stumbles. 5. A Russian and his bride were driving home from the wedding in their wagon. 6. The Russian shouts, "That's one!" 7. The Russian shouts, "That's it!" 8. The Russian responds, "That's one." 9. He pulls out a gun and shoots the horse. 10. The horse stumbles a third time. (5, 4, 6, 1, 3, 10, 7, 9, 2, 8)
> 1. The next is exercise. 2. If they aren't, you're in trouble. 3. It is a serious responsibility which involves three important areas. 4. Taking care of a dog is not easy. 5. The first is feeding. 6. All three of the foregoing areas must be considered. 7. The last is grooming. (4, 3, 5, 1, 7, 6, 2)

In the familiar process of deciding on the correct order for the sentences, and discussing their reasons for those decisions, students in basic writing classes detect the elements that hold paragraphs together and those that signal the relationships between the separate sentences in the larger unit.

This technique can be applied to the consideration of the ordering of parts in an essay. The teacher distributes the introductory, concluding, and developmental paragraphs of an essay, again in garbled sequence, and asks the students to arrange them into an essay. (Other exercises that lead students to consider various organizational possibilities are presented in Kogen and Seltzer, forthcoming.) Having determined the order of paragraphs for a sample essay, students can then add paragraphs of development, considering the justifications for their additions and the alterations that might need to be made, perhaps in the opening paragraph, to accommodate the added material. Through this kind of exercise, students learn to recognize particular kinds of structure, their demands, and the signals that unify them before they produce similar pieces of writing.

Prewriting as a problem-solving approach to composition is advocated by Flower and Hayes (1977, p. 450) who present a variety of *heuristics*—"alternative[s] to trial and error"—for achieving the goal of completing a paper. They suggest, for example, an alternative to the "tried and true" method of outlining a plan for a paper. Their method produces a similar result, but, rather than asking writers to develop an outline according to a preconceived pattern, the authors suggest that writers simply note down ideas in whatever order they occur and then "*pull* an outline *out* of the material they generate" by experimenting with drawing tree diagrams until they find one that seems to fit the content (see Exhibit 2).

Another kind of prewriting is what D'Angelo (1977) calls making "preliminary considerations." D'Angelo addresses the student who has advanced beyond the basic level, but he recognizes the difficulty these students still have in writing and so suggests a regimen for finding and developing content. Students list sources for ideas, including their own thoughts, textbook indexes, and the library card catalogue, then consider limitations on a broad topic, the audience to be addressed, the writer's purpose in doing a particular piece of work, and the attitude that the writer wishes to assume toward his subject.

Free Writing. Free writing is a variety of prewriting that has achieved wide currency at CUNY as a useful approach to overcoming the beginning writers' sense that they have nothing to say or that they cannot write. Popularized by Macrorie (1968, 1970a, and 1970b) and Elbow (1973), free writing is a way of leading students to produce prodigious quantities of writing, writing that is meaningful to themselves, in a short period of time. The instructor simply asks students to write continuously for a set period, perhaps ten minutes. When finished, students are often quite surprised to discover the length and interest of what they have produced under circumstances in which the pressure to keep a pencil moving has counteracted self-consciousness. The following example, a piece of free writing composed during the first meeting of a Level 2 class, illustrates a student's creating a topic out of what he seems to think is nothing. His calls for help in the middle are but one indication of his groping for subject matter in what he suspects is a void.

> My name is Wayne Humphrey. My moms gave me the name, it's Wayne, not Hubert. Some people call me Free Hump, which is Humphrey backwards. I have a brother in this school name Rodney Humphrey, so when people see us together they call me lil Hump and call Rodney big Hump. Oh!! Know I'm stuck stuck stuck stuck. Oh! My father calls me stinky because when I was a little tot I was was was bad. My grandmother calls me Wayne, for what reason I don't know. My big sister calls me me me me me me dummy because I don't wait on her hand & foot. Help! Help! Help! Help! I've been called many names except for my real one. I'm stuck, stuck, stuck, stuck, stuck, stuck, stuck, stuck. Oh! I have a middle name, too. St. Elmo; ha! ha!

More than simply acquainting students with their own ability to write and derive pleasure from doing so, the pieces produced through free writing exercises are useful at all levels when they become source material for a variety of other kinds of exercises and for essays. Students can revise, reorganize, and edit these pieces to yield more polished and reflective discussions of their subjects, drawing on ideas and insights in the free writing for the major content of the work. The student who wrote about his many names, for instance, might be led to expand his discussion to a consideration of the many selves within his person, a consideration that is implied in his recognition of the different names he has when he is a grandson, a son, a brother, or a friend.

Shor and Fishman (1978) present a detailed introduction to free writing in which they guide students through a procedure for recognizing interesting and sound topics within the raw material

Exhibit 2. Problem Solving with Tree Diagrams.

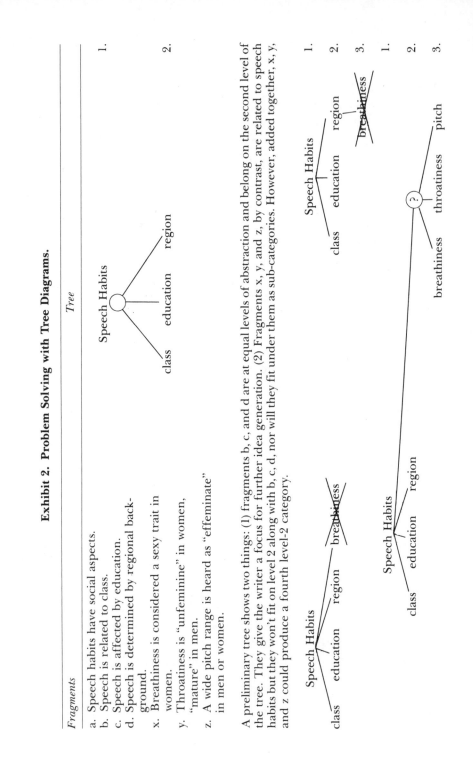

Fragments

a. Speech habits have social aspects.
b. Speech is related to class.
c. Speech is affected by education.
d. Speech is determined by regional background.
x. Breathiness is considered a sexy trait in women.
y. Throatiness is "unfeminine" in women, "mature" in men.
z. A wide pitch range is heard as "effeminate" in men or women.

A preliminary tree shows two things: (1) fragments b, c, and d are at equal levels of abstraction and belong on the second level of the tree. They give the writer a focus for further idea generation. (2) Fragments x, y, and z, by contrast, are related to speech habits but they won't fit on level 2 along with b, c, d, nor will they fit under them as sub-categories. However, added together, x, y, and z could produce a fourth level-2 category.

Trying to build an issue tree shows the writer that his/her next problem is to generate a new concept—an idea which will tie these three fragments together. The chief advantage of an issue tree is precisely this: it is a working tool which helps the writer see the structure of his/her thought as it develops and see where s/he needs to do more thinking.

In this example the issue tree goes on working. Once the writer has generated a new concept, s/he can see that while b, c, and d all "relate" to a, they do so in different ways. A more developed tree, such as the one below, might not only clarify the writer's thinking but suggest areas in which to generate ideas.

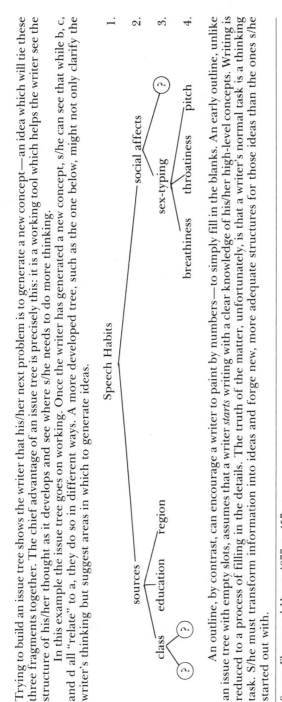

Speech Habits

1.

2.

3.

4.

An outline, by contrast, can encourage a writer to paint by numbers—to simply fill in the blanks. An early outline, unlike an issue tree with empty slots, assumes that a writer *starts* writing with a clear knowledge of his/her high-level concepts. Writing is reduced to a process of filling in the details. The truth of the matter, unfortunately, is that a writer's normal task is a thinking task. S/he must transform information into ideas and forge new, more adequate structures for those ideas than the ones s/he started out with.

Source: Flower and Hayes, 1977, p. 457.

generated in their free writing. They ask students to "record a 'first' experience . . . [and] concentrate on what happened, who did what, who said what." They then illustrate how students can look at such a piece and reform it (pp. 12–13):

> I got up out of bed at 5:00. I studied my chem notes until 8:00. Then I grabbed a piece of toast and a cup of coffee. I picked up Jeannette on the way to class and talked about the atomic number of a few elements. Later I told her about my date with Karen the night before. We got to the lecture hall at 9:28. My hands were pretty sweaty. Jeannette appeared calm.

> As a writer, you need to recognize that all of the events you experience are raw material. Even at the very beginning of the writing cycle, your freewriting encourages you to explore the events of your daily life for vivid personal details. Eventually, your writing cycle, your free writing encourages you to explore the wants to find out what the details mean to you, the writer. To find out, ask yourself questions about the events you observe:

> Why did I get out of bed at 5:00 in the morning?

> Why did I have to study my chem notes? Do I usually cram for tests? Didn't I study before? If not, why not?

> Who are the characters in this little drama? Does each one matter?

> Does Karen have anything to do with my chemistry test?
> And what about Jeannette, what do I really think of her? How does she affect me? Does she make me feel nervous? jealous? stupid? How do these events relate to the way I usually take tests? to what I *must* do in school? to what I want to do for the rest of my life?

> Now the writing cycle is turning. You have gone back to ask questions that lead to more ideas for your writing. Here is another stage of the same piece of writing incorporating some of the answers to the questions:

> I got out of bed at 5:00 because the test wouldn't let me sleep. With only the test on my mind, I studied my chem notes because I hadn't gotten to them last night. Oh, that was a great night with Jeannette's friend Karen, though badly timed, badly timed. Timing, in fact, is a big problem for me. I do reckless things at the last minute, perhaps to give myself an excuse for not doing well on my tests. Then I try to cram and my guilt feelings increase as time slips by. I managed to eat some toast and coffee and stopped for Jeannette on my way, hoping to pick her brain about the atomic number of uranium, but she wanted to talk about Karen and what I thought of her, since Jeannette, after all, had spent the evening at home, studying like crazy. Sometimes she makes me feel stupid, or at least regretful that I am such a coward and can't face up to trying my best without excuses. I wished my feet would take off in a direction away from Lecture Hall 301 but there they were, keeping step with Jeannette's, all the way into the room. I sat down like

a robot. I am a very poor test taker while Jeannette is all cool. She sat there chatting amiably with some guy she wanted to make time with later. When the tests arrived, I wondered why I subject myself to these horrifying ordeals, and I wondered if I would ever get to engineering school. I was in a panic. Jeannette, however, was calmly placing an extra Bic pen and her pocket calculator next to her paper as she began.

Students can edit their free writing exercises, concentrating on their use of one specific grammatical element. This procedure, outlined in D'Eloia (1977), calls their attention to methods for controlling that element and helps them recognize whether it is one which they must review because they tend to use it incorrectly in unselfconscious writing. In the following piece of free writing, for example, a student circling all past tense markers would discover a pattern of tense marking on verbs and see that it is extended incorrectly here to adjectives *(favorited)*, nouns *(placed)*, base verb forms *(wouldn't moved)*, and verbs whose intended meaning is present tense *(remembered)*. The pattern, furthermore, bypasses the past tense verb *happen* because it already seems to have an ending.

My Childhood Hiding Place

This seems hard to do. I remembered having a couple of placed. My favorited one was underneath my bed. It was a double-bed. Me and my sister shared the same bed. I never really through about it before this. I laid under there for hours. OH. If no one came to get me I went downstairs and pretended like nothing happen. At least I throught I convinced everyone, but there was always dust on my clothes. I could never get rid of that dust. It gave it away every time. I really don't know why I stayed under the bed. Its one of most obvious places. I remember laying on the floor. There was always a cold and hard feeling when I laid there, but I wouldn't moved until someone came to get me. I wish

With their wide range of applications, free writing exercises remain most useful in eliciting initial pieces of writing. They are of ultimate value when they are drawn upon to teach techniques that can be applied to more controlled, analytical writing.

Simulation Games and Cases. Another way of overcoming initial reticence and involving basic writing students in the writing process draws on elaborate dramatizations or simulation games. By becoming actively involved in simulated, lifelike situations, students can discover the practical importance of communication skills, both oral and written. Students draw material for their writing from a body of information that they glean from a variety of sources. The games require elaborate materials that detail imaginary situations, outline specific roles for students to play, and present information on the issues involved.

One simulation game that Troyka and Nudelman (1975) present involves a work and hunger strike at a federal prison where inmates are protesting living conditions and oppressive rules. The materials provide data on the institution, including staffing, budget, layout, and physical conditions as revealed in blueprints and photographs, daily schedules of activities, rules for dress, hygiene, store privileges, and many other aspects of inmate life. The materials establish a variety of participant roles and a number of *speaking actions, listening actions, reading actions,* and *writing actions.* These lead the players to deliver speeches appropriate to different audiences and various motivations. Students also conduct interviews, both of classmates and of informed friends and neighbors, on subjects related to the circumstances of actual correctional facilities; they read a packet of printed materials on the uprising and write responses to prisoners' complaints, plans for solving the general dilemma, narratives between players, and a variety of other possible papers related to the material provided with the game. Students in a Level 1 class write a prison position paper, a five-paragraph essay that explains the problems at the correctional facility and suggests a possible solution. Working with the materials presented in the text and a guiding outline of ways to order consideration of the problems and solutions, students at this first level of basic writing produce papers that are a far cry from the confusion and ungrammaticality that often characterize student writing at this level.

Simulation exercises encourage students both to write and to develop basic research techniques; they present realistic situations in which orderly, coherent, and accurate communication is a necessity. As with free writing, the skills learned through simulation games are ultimately applied to the rigors of more conventional writing situations in which students by themselves must establish the purpose, audience, and content for their writing.

The case approach to writing instruction draws the simulation exercise closer to mature expository writing. It sidesteps dramatic role playing and concentrates on written work to the exclusion of oral exercises. As presented in Field and Weiss (1979), the case approach draws from collected source material and establishes a hypothetical context and audience for each assignment.

Specialized Course Content. Another way to help students recognize the usefulness of improving their writing skills and the importance of applying those skills to other courses is to draw assignments for writing courses from the content of other courses. Where a number of nursing students are enrolled in composition courses, for example, a special section of a writing course can tailor its reading selections and writing assignments to the needs of future nurses. While many of their needs are identical to those of all students, a course that draws its readings from biology and medicine and that emphasizes the writing of summaries and reports will be of particular appeal to nursing students.

Or, a basic writing course may unite the traditional rhetorical modes with materials from the textbooks used in introductory science and humanities courses. Thus, Bernstein (forthcoming) shows how a cause-and-effect assignment might be drawn from economics, a definition assignment from sociology, a compare-and-contrast essay from art history, a classification essay from political science, and a process description from biology. Students can learn to interpret essay assignments according to the rhetorical mode that each calls for. They will recognize questions such as "Discuss the role of the elderly in society" as questions of definition, and questions like "What is the relationship of the desire for status to the law of demand?" as cause-and-effect questions.

Teachers can offer model answers for questions in the various modes that not only are actual responses to questions based on textual materials from the course but also can lead students to extend their understanding of a particular mode so that they can generalize that understanding to future writing contexts. Courses such as this one offered early in students' college careers may help to persuade them that the skills they learn in writing classes are useful for all the writing they have to do in college.

Both faculty and students have welcomed attempts to integrate writing with the content of specific disciplines, although there has been some faculty concern that this limitation of writing experiences may impede students should they want to alter their career plans. Basic writing courses that address both academic content and writing skills, therefore, do well to emphasize general expository techniques.

Some administrative difficulties may also arise in offering writing courses with specialized content. They are harder to schedule than regular basic writing courses when they are limited to students who are in a particular curriculum or who are enrolled in a specific, coordinated section of a particular content course. Also, they may require cumbersome collaboration between teachers in two departments.

Writing Across the Curriculum. Recently, many colleges have extended the responsibility for reinforcing writing skills to all faculty. Faculty in all departments are encouraged to maintain high standards of writing competency.

Proponents of this extension assume that students develop a richer understanding of a subject if they write about it than if they do not, and that writing helps students think by helping them to analyze and synthesize material as well as to express their ideas clearly on paper. Thus, they view the recent decline in college writing assignments with chagrin and seek to help all faculty reintegrate writing into their courses.

To initiate such a program, faculty need to arrive at a consensus on the characteristics of good writing in their fields; they need, too, to learn the vocabulary of assessing that writing. Depending on the degree of commitment of faculty and administration, and on the amount of available financing—many programs are funded by grants—a college-wide writing program can support faculty workshops, seminars, and interdepartmental faculty cooperation in strengthening and planning writing instruction. It can prepare handbooks to aid faculty in teaching writing in conjunction with their main subjects; it can introduce revised freshman composition courses in which some writing assignments are based on suggestions submitted by other departments.

Faculty workshops and seminars led by English department faculty or consultants can offer all faculty members an opportunity to learn methods of teaching writing skills and to improve curriculums for their own courses. In the workshops, teachers may consider how to phrase syllabi and assignments clearly and productively, how to teach effective textbook reading, how to improve motivation, and how to make use of both expressive personal writing and the more usual expository modes. Participants in these workshops and seminars can formulate a statement of college-wide policies for writing and requirements for freshmen courses that will help students understand from the start the place of writing in their studies. The idea that good writing skills are necessary to mastery of any academic subject matter must be placed where it belongs, as one CUNY faculty member puts it, "in students' minds, not in faculty committees."

Improving Word and Sentence Skills

While prescriptive grammar may be useful for teaching abstruse details of the formal language to people already familiar with its general conventions, and parsing sentences provides, for some students, an interesting puzzle, the evidence suggests that the study of grammar has no appreciable effect on an individual's ability to use language (see Memering, 1978). Conventional grammar study concentrates on rules for the ordering of linguistic elements but apparently does not penetrate a student's generative capabilities.

The teaching of grammar to underprepared students thus does not emphasize the study of parts of speech and prescriptive rules. It concentrates, instead, on teaching students the most fundamental rules of the standard written dialect, rules which enable them to avoid structural gaffes far more basic than sentence fragments, run-ons, and comma-splices. Teachers have drawn insights from more recent grammars, therefore, to lead students to extend their linguistic competence. Through the adaptation of nonprescriptive grammars to this kind of teaching, faculty are not simply overthrowing the old for the new; instead, they are finding practical applications for grammatical theories, applications that engender an increased language capacity in students by showing them the power and enjoyment of exploring linguistic options and the differing effects of alternative encoding styles.

Sentence Combining. One application of transformational grammar that has gained widespread and enthusiastic following among writing teachers is sentence combining. Originally developed by Mellon (1969) as an exercise to accompany the high school study of transformational grammar, sentence combining was modified significantly as a result of O'Hare's (1973) finding that dramatic gains in written syntactic maturity result from the exercise alone, without any formal grammar instruction.

The most widely used text for sentence combining is Strong (1973, p. 63), which presents long lists of kernels for students to combine into single grammatical sentences:

- A man sat on a bench.
- The man was old.
- The man held his hat.
- The man crossed his legs.
- The man uncrossed his legs.
- The man was dressed in gray.
- The gray was faded.

Combining these sentences might yield "Holding his hat, an old man dressed in faded gray sat on a bench crossing and uncrossing his legs."

The exercises lead students to explore the entire range of available structures for modification, coordination, and subordination. Strong first presents simple problems appropriate to a Level 1 class. But the text quickly and subtly moves on to exercises that make more complex demands and lead students to try more sophisticated solutions.

In the first exercise, students perform simple adjective modification (Strong, 1973, p. 10):

- French fries are loaded into a basket.
- The French fries are white.
- The basket is wire.

These sentences can be combined to form "White French fries are loaded into a wire basket." Students soon find themselves, however, using participial phrases or dependent clauses even though they may not have learned how to identify such structures or what to call them. They are given the following sentences (1973, p. 26):

- The voice is a whine.
- The whine is nasal.
- The whine is reedy.
- It echoes back to his upbringing.
- His upbringing was in the Bronx.

From these, a student might produce "His voice is a whine, nasal and reedy, echoing back to his Bronx upbringing."

When completed, Strong's exercises, only pieces of which are here reproduced, result in full paragraphs or short compositions on a wide variety of lively topics. Because there are many possible solutions to any exercise, students are encouraged to explore and this language play helps them perceive sentences as structures which the writer manipulates for his own purposes and according to his own tastes.

Since Strong's text presents materials that yield well-formed paragraphs and longer pieces of writing, it is also useful as a focus of discussion on paragraph structure. As students combine kernels into longer sentences and sometimes consider whether to join two or more expanded sentences, they experience the aggregation of sentences in what Christiansen (1967) has called the *cumulative* paragraph, a paragraph with a topic sentence as its basis and additional sentences added on at a lower level of generality to modify the initial notion.

For Level 3 students, the end of Strong's text presents opportunities to pack sentences with meaning; the lists of details to be combined are considerably longer. The text also introduces specifically literary structures, such as coordinated absolutes and elaborate appositives, that even quite capable students are unlikely to produce spontaneously. Students follow models to produce sentences like this: "Legs stiff and muscled, the tall black center went up for the ball, his long arms extended, his elbows out, his hands reaching" (1973, p. 168).

At no level is the purpose of sentence combining to lead students to write only long and complex sentences. But it does teach them to control such structures so that they have a full range of syntactic options instead of being confined to the few that they knew to be within their repertoire when they entered the course. Sentence combining provides a meaningful alternative to the advice, sometimes given to students whose sentence structures go awry, that they simply keep their sentences short. Rather than boxing them in, as that older approach did, sentence combining frees students to play with structural possibilities and choose among them on the basis of stylistic judgment rather than safety.

Another approach to sentence combining (O'Hare, 1975, pp. 2, 52) focuses specifically on the more sophisticated structures by presenting directions for coordination, subordination, and nominalization, and the punctuation required by those structures, as part of the exercise:

- Battaglia glanced at first base.
- He went into his windup. (,)
- Then he threw a hanging curve that Ryan knocked out of the stadium. (,and)

    (Battaglia glanced at first base, went into his windup, and then threw a hanging curve that Ryan knocked out of the stadium.)

or:

- Something came as a shock to the National Pickle Association.
- The government canceled the cucumber festival. ('s cancellation + of)

    (The government's cancellation of the cucumber festival came as a shock to the National Pickle Association.)

Although O'Hare's text was originally conceived for use in high schools, its designation as a text for "an elective course in writing" indicates that it goes well beyond what is generally considered the scope of high school English. It is, in fact, quite appropriate for linguistic muscle-flexing in a Level 3 course.

A third approach to sentence combining is presented by D'Eloia and others (1976). Students apply the sentence combining technique to specific sentence structures, for example, by adding to the carrier, or first sentence, a group of additional sentences that have been converted into participial phrases or relative clauses. Take the following four sentences:

- The water accumulated in the depression.
- It came from the broken main.
- It cascaded along the asphalt.
- It finally found an easy place to rest.

These sentences might be combined to yield "The water coming from the broken main and cascading along the asphalt accumulated in the depression, having finally found an easy place to rest" (1976, p. 18).

As in the other sentence combining texts, students can complete the work without necessarily having to learn grammatical terminology and without being able to identify the particular structures that the terminology designates. Instead, in leading students to generate their own kernels and elaborated sentences, to paraphrase their combinations and evaluate the contrasting structures—generally to play with language and make judgments about the results—these exercises help students to use structures rather than identify them.

Sector Analysis. Another alternative to traditional grammar, sector analysis is more often used in classes in English as a Second Language (ESL) but has found an enthusiastic following among teachers of native speakers as well. Because sector analysis is primarily used in ESL classes, it is discussed in Chapter Three.

Controlled Composition. Not based on a particular grammatical theory but compatible with the range of theories in use, controlled composition focuses students' thought on manipulation of a single element of the written language while relieving them, for the duration of the exercise, from having to cope simultaneously with any other components of the process. It allows them, for instance, to concentrate on using plural nouns and their pronoun referents without having to think, at the same time, of what topic to pursue and how to develop it.

One widely used form of controlled composition provides students with a printed passage which they must copy, making as they do so one kind of alteration. They are asked to change the tense of the verbs, or to pluralize the subject of the text, or to make some other systematic change. The following excerpt from Kunz (1972, p. 6), an excellent source of passages for controlled composition, requires control of both verb forms and pronouns if a student is to change it from the plural subject to a singular subject:

> (1) According to the stereotype, blue-collar workers are rough, half-educated men in their middle years. (2) They come home from work, open a can of beer, turn on the television set, and start complaining about their jobs. (3) Supposedly, Archie Bunker typifies them.

While this kind of exercise was designed for ESL students, it is valuable as well for native speakers who need to gain command of standard verb tense formation or concordance principles.

Another variety of controlled composition asks students to fill in blanks that have been left in partially written sentences. The exercise, for example, provides inflections and function words, carefully separated by spaces which students must fill to complete the sentence:

> In _____ of_____ _____ , _____ _____ on the _____ _____.[D'Eloia and others, 1976, Unit IV:A, p. 3.]

This technique leads students to recognize the structural force of specific elements in a sentence as well as the tendency of certain word choices to place syntactic and semantic constraints on succeeding elements.

Vocabulary and Spelling. Despite the fact that students identify vocabulary and spelling as their primary weaknesses in writing, those two areas of language study have been left surprisingly untouched by college faculty. While writing faculty agree that these are areas of conspicuous difficulty, they prefer to concentrate their teaching on grammar and rhetoric and to relegate spelling and vocabulary to the student working on his own or in reading skills courses. The rationale is that those two areas will inevitably develop from the increased practice in reading and writing that occurs in basic skills courses and from general contact with a college curriculum. While this is not an illogical position, it is unexpected from faculty whose general stance is that basic writing students do not have time, any longer, to allow their skills to develop gradually and naturally, without intervention in the process.

A second explanation for the neglect of these two areas of writing is that advances in contemporary linguistic theory have not lent themselves readily to innovative methodology. Thus, faculty who might have been eager to alter their approaches to teaching spelling, as they were to apply new grammars to teaching syntax, have been without theoretical support in that area and have been reticent to spend class time on methods that were as time-worn, time-consuming, and inefficient as dispensing lists to memorize and giving quizzes to encourage and check that memorization.

There are, however, two research reports on the teaching of vocabulary that have begun to lay the foundation for the development of curriculum. O'Rourke (1974) presents a number of broad principles for altering vocabulary instruction, although he does not provide specific details about teaching vocabulary. Most importantly, he advocates replacing the procedure of memorizing lists of unrelated words with an approach to words that groups them by concept. He suggests that there is a developmental relationship between the breadth of terminology that one can draw on in discussing a given concept and the depth of one's understanding of that concept. Thus, one's understanding of the notion *old* is broadened as one's vocabulary expands to include *ancient, elderly, archaic, antediluvian, patriarchal, senescent,* and *senile.*

In this regard, also, O'Rourke advocates working with roots and affixes, which establish one kind of basic conceptual relationship between word meanings. He suggests using the study of roots and affixes to involve students' creative abilities for example, having students make up words and definitions based on their newly acquired knowledge of the meanings of word elements. This game, O'Rourke feels, solidifies students' understanding of the principles of word formation.

O'Rourke also calls for a systematic program of vocabulary development that is integrated into the rest of students' work, at least in writing and if possible in other disciplines, in order to capitalize on the firm relationship he sees between vocabulary and concept development. This recommendation is in opposition to the more traditional format for vocabulary instruction that is sporadic and isolated, a pursuit separate from other learning.

Stotsky (1976, 1980) has applied some of O'Rourke's insights to teaching elementary school pupils and college students. Focusing specifically on the teaching of prefixes, Stotsky follows O'Rourke's proposal that the order in which elements are taught be determined by their clear visibility, high productivity, and familiarity to the learner. Thus, she recommends that a hyphenated form, as in *pre-Civil War,* be taught before a less visible form, as in *prefer,* that a prefix like *pre* be taught before one like *ab,* and that prefixes attached to words presumably known by students, like *caution* in *precaution,* be taught before those attached to roots that are not likely to be part of the students' vocabulary, like *vent* in *prevent.*

Like O'Rourke, Stotsky advocates a creative approach to vocabulary learning instead of rote memorization. She suggests formulating exercises that lead students to combine roots and prefixes to create words instead of learning them initially as bound morphemes. Thus, having learned the prefix *pre,* and presumably knowing the word *season,* a student could convert the long phrase "a coat sale that takes place before the season that requires coats" to "a preseason coat sale."

Stotsky sees a strong parallel between the condensing, word-packing power of this sort of exercise and the creation of complex structures from simple ones such as occurs in sentence combining exercises. She postulates, therefore, that just as sentence combining exercises have been shown (Mellon, 1969; O'Hare, 1973) to increase syntactic maturity by leading students to subordinate and modify rather than coordinate structures, word combining, too, may have a positive effect on syntactic maturity.

Alternative Instructional Modes

Because typical basic writing students may lack confidence, may tend to be reticent, if not silent, and may be easily intimidated, their teachers must explore ways to restructure classroom procedures to encourage student progress. They need to add new instructional techniques to their usual ones in order to engage students actively in teaching and learning.

Collaborative Learning. Students can work together in small groups to discuss, plan, and edit their writing. The teacher's role in this collaboration, as Bruffee (1972) indicates, is to set the framework for assignments and to act as a resource and guide.

Some of the reasons for using groups in a college classroom are expressed by a student in a partially peer-taught course: "Some students can relate to each other better than they can relate to a teacher. Some professors have trouble explaining ideas in the simple language that a student can understand; students can usually explain things in simpler terms" (Rizzo, 1975, p. 294). Faculty who use groups also feel that students are better able to accept criticism from a peer and that they often learn best through having to explain material to others.

A critically important factor in making collaborative learning a success, however, seems to be rigorous, if subtle, guidance on the part of the teacher through carefully structured materials that lead the groups' progress through an assignment. For, as Rizzo (1975, p. 296) points out: "The only freedom I have offered these students is significant to them—the chance to be top-dog instead of under-dog for a day. Most of them love it, but the extended opportunity would be meaningless if they didn't know, in this case, exactly what the top-dog is supposed to do. . . . Accordingly, I must be very careful to keep the lesson on one specific point, and to make sure that one point is clearly and fully illustrated by material [distributed] and fully understood by the student."

Thus, Rizzo asks her students to divide themselves, quite arbitrarily, into three groups. Once a week, she presents prepared materials on verbs, sentence structure, usage, and spelling to one or another of the groups while the others are revising a past writing assignment. The students working on these materials complete them as a group under the supervision of the teacher and then select one member to present the same materials to the rest of the class. Students who take on that task may use the handouts exclusively or may supplement them with other examples or exercises; they may also add to the materials by looking up the subject in grammar texts and gleaning additional information. While it may take a student working with group support longer to present material than it would take an experienced and qualified teacher, Rizzo finds that the students' comprehension of the subject is at least as good and their attendance is vastly improved. Ultimately, she feels, the experience of teaching others can lead students to an improved self-image and an awareness that they can also teach themselves. Rizzo (1978) presents basic writing materials in a format that can be used either by a traditional class group or by smaller, collaborative groups. Raimes (1978) also has this flexibility.

Teachers can use groups in their classrooms at all levels of writing skill to produce collaborative writings that will ultimately provide models for individually completed assignments, or to proofread, discuss, and criticize. In each case, the group's work should be carefully controlled through the use of materials that guide students' attention and energy. If students are to edit one another's work, for example, distributed materials may alert them to one or more previously discussed aspects of grammar, structure, vocabulary, or grammatical or rhetorical principles. A "reading sheet" (see Exhibit 3) designed for use early in the semester of a basic writing course might lead the editor to assess the clarity of focus in a writer's description and to point out, sentence by sentence, places either where the writing is not sufficiently specific or where it is not clearly related to the topic that seemed to be set at the beginning. It also asks the editor to make several basic assessments of the writer's grammar: to check for correct terminal punctuation of sentences, for subject-verb agreement, and for spelling errors. Such a sheet could be altered and expanded later in the semester, directing students' attention to an increasing variety of grammatical elements and to more complex rhetorical considerations like the use of transitional devices and other visible signs of one or another scheme of order.

If students are to criticize each other's work, the focus and nature of the criticism must be carefully specified so that critics will produce, and writers receive, useful and constructive criticism rather than unfocused praise or vaguely dissatisfied mumblings that one part or another "doesn't sound right." A student critic may be asked, for instance, to assess each sentence of each paragraph,

Exhibit 3. Reading Sheet—Description of a Person.

1. Number the sentences as they are marked off on the paper you are reading. This will allow you to refer to the sentences by number.
2. Can you find any statement that indicates what general impression the writer wants to give of the subject? If so, what sentence? _____
   If you can't find a particular sentence, can you still say you get a general impression of the subject? If so, what is it?_____

   If you can't get an overall impression of the subject, check here: _____
3. Have the details been clearly specified and used to contribute to the overall impression? _____ Specify which details (by sentence number) work in this way and which need to be further specified or more clearly related to the central impression.

sentence number	specific enough?	clearly related to topic?

(For more sentences, attach another sheet.)

4. Check each numbered word group to make sure that it is a full sentence but not more than a full sentence. Check also for subject-verb agreement and for spelling. Indicate errors that you find, citing sentence number and word or words involved.

sentence number	sentence?	subject-verb agreement	spelling

(For more sentences, attach another sheet.)

or each paragraph of a paper, to determine whether it is clearly and directly related to the chosen topic. He then must indicate his finding to the writer, thereby providing the writer with one reader's close assessment of what does, or does not, belong in the paper. This criticism should be written on an appended sheet, not on the actual paper, so that the student editor's advice will not be automatically incorporated into the final draft. Writers must still decide—

and this step is critical—whether or not to accept each bit of advice they receive and how to incorporate it into their work. In making these decisions, writers take final responsibility for what they include in their papers as they are consciously led through a process that skilled writers instinctively perform: the process of deciding what belongs, and what does not belong, in a piece of writing and how best to present that which is to be included.

The value of the group process often seems to be largely unrelated to the correctness of the advice that student critics give one another. It seems to lie more substantially in the requirement that students look at writing in progress critically and systematically and evaluate other readers' judgments about it, an experience students do not have when the critic is a teacher, an acknowledged expert, whose judgments few students are willing to defy.

In all of its uses, the ultimate benefit of group work lies in developing students' abilities to read their own writing critically, to correct errors in it, and to engage in the kind of critical questioning and testing of possibilities that is essential to good writing. It is important, when group work is a substantial part of the course, that students understand at the outset just what range of skills they must acquire by the end of the term. That will encourage them to complete the necessary work in one group and move on to the next. Students can be helped to recognize how much progress is required of them and which skills they need most to develop if they are given a detailed assessment of their entering performance in terms of the specific objectives of their course as well as a description of how they need to perform by the semester's end. Teachers can distribute a department's holistic rating scale, such as the CUNY evaluation scale presented earlier in this chapter, so that students can see the performance correlates of their holistic placement score and of the score they need to achieve by the end of the term. A completed writing profile, like that illustrated in Exhibit 1, is another guide by which students can survey the terrain between their entering performance and a passing assessment.

Team Teaching. A simple departure from the conventional classroom arrangement is possible if two sections of a writing course are scheduled at the same time. Then, the teachers of those sections can pool their groups and redivide the students according to the kinds of skills they need to acquire rather than having them grouped, as in a conventional class, according to the scheduling pressures exerted in registration.

If one group in a class is established on the basis of students' difficulty in controlling standard English structures, another group, whose members do not need as much work on grammar, may focus on developing the content of their writing. The grammar-oriented group may begin by considering errors that trouble the majority of its members; as some members gain control of their grammar problems, they may shift to the other group. Such a division helps to ensure that only students who actually need grammar instruction receive it.

As the semester progresses, membership in the grammar group is likely to dwindle, leaving most of the class in the content group. Then, the teachers may decide to establish more than one content group. Thus, for example, one group may work on paragraph development while another group, whose students are already aware of a need to expand their ideas by substantiating their generalities in a paragraph of discussion, may go on to apply a similar approach to development of longer pieces of writing.

Many teachers who work in teams report that collaboration strengthens their teaching. It requires joint planning, exchange of effective methodologies, constant observation of one another's teaching techniques, and conferral on final grading. Team teaching is particularly appropriate to the first and second level courses, where the emphasis on grammar and on learning basic organizational strategies may require a good deal of individualized instruction that can be aided by the attention of more than one teacher to the class.

Self-Paced Laboratory Work. While many writing laboratories function substantially as support services providing tutorial assistance to students outside of their class time, a facility may also service entire class groups. One such composition laboratory, COMP-LAB at York College, offers individualized, self-paced instruction to each student who attends (Epes, Kirkpatrick, and Southwell, 1980). The laboratory uses commercially available audio and video cassette materials as well as a number of modules written specifically for the program. Students attend the lab for two of their five weekly class hours, and any who need additional time to complete their lab assignments may go independently. In the lab, autotutorial materials allow students to focus on those discrete elements of standard grammar that they need to drill. The lab provides its own materials, self-correctable as well as self-paced, which begin with an audio cassette explanation of a particular element of grammar and then move on to a series of graduated drills that involve students in generating their own writing. Exhibit 4 presents an example from the COMP-LAB module on the verb *be* that draws on the sentence-combining technique in leading students to manipulate the verb being learned.

The use of all the COMP-LAB materials is supervised by tutorial staff whose function is primarily to see that students find and complete the exercises assigned to them. Through a self-

**Exhibit 4. Sample COMP-LAB Exercise:
Subject-Verb Agreement with Be.**

Name _____ Date _____
Instructor/Section _____ Number of Mistakes _____
Instructions: For each of the following groups of sentences, do the following: (1) Combine them into one sentence. (2) For each rewritten sentence, (a) put a slash between the subject part and the verb part, and (b) underline the verb. The first example has been done for you.

1. Tony is a birdwatcher. Seymour is a birdwatcher.

2. Clyde is a filmmaker. Gino is a filmmaker.

3. Mother is always energetic. I am always energetic.

4. She is foolish to try that. George is foolish to try that.

5. Mabel is an ugly woman. Her friend is an ugly woman.

6. The Smiths are usually late for meetings. She is usually late for meetings.

7. That desk in the corner is mine. This filing cabinet is mine.

8. The roar of the wind is frightening. The crash of the waves is frightening.

Source: Epes, Kirkpatrick, and Southwell, 1980.

paced, autotutorial model, the COMP-LAB frees the teacher whose students need considerable work on grammar from having to devote class time to drill. This allows the teacher to focus on rhetorical concerns and grammatical issues that do not need the intensive, grammar-altering drill available in the lab. In so doing, the lab offers one way of cutting the high cost of remedial writing courses by greatly reducing the number of faculty hours spent developing control of standard grammar. The method is useful, however, only for students who need considerable drill to reinforce their standard English skills. It should be combined with classwork that provides students the opportunity to incorporate those skills into their writing.

Mini-Courses. A final departure from conventional composition class structure is the mini-course, which may be conducted in a traditional style but which differs in that it lasts less than a full semester. This kind of course, which may carry modest credit, offers students with a few isolated writing problems the opportunity to rectify these problems without having to enroll in a full semester course. A mini-course, which is sometimes scheduled during a vacation break or between semesters, can provide students with intensive work on verb inflections, or sentence structure, or paragraph development, or whatever other few writing skills may be holding them back from passing to the next level of writing course. Other mini-courses may be offered to supplement course instruction that some students may want to pursue in greater depth than their course syllabi allow. Samuels (1976) describes a mini-course in writing term papers that is available on video cassettes for individual or group use.

Supportive Services

The pervasiveness of supportive services on many campuses suggests widespread agreement that traditional forms of contact between student and writing teacher—lectures, class discussions, and written comments on submitted papers—need supplementation for the basic writing student. But supplementary services clearly increase the already high costs of offering basic writing courses. As a result, the relative costs of a service sometimes become almost as important a consideration in establishing support as the apparent effectiveness of the mode of service selected.

Conference Support

Probably the most common and least expensive form of service offered to basic writing students takes the form of teacher-student conferences, which are generally required of all enrolled students. In being required, they differ from the more conventional office hours which faculty have always held but which may often have gone substantially unused. The conventional office hour was not seen by student or teacher as an integral and important component of a course; it was, instead, an extra, a time when a student might appear to discuss some issue tangential to the main work of the course or perhaps just to chat.

The conferences held by basic writing teachers are more structured and purposeful. The course descriptions of basic writing courses may include the number of conferences each student is required to attend in a semester and specify an hour, in addition to the regular class meeting hours, as a conference hour. Course guidelines may also establish a minimum number of conference hours each faculty member must keep for each basic writing course in his teaching schedule. Furthermore, many faculty may make specific appointments to fill these hours, so that while students may wander by to ask a brief question, most conference hours are broken into fifteen- or twenty-minute segments with a particular student scheduled to discuss a particular subject during each segment.

Conferences are designed to consider matters that are directly related to the course. Students may ask for clarification of a topic already considered in class that they still do not understand fully. Instructors may explain in detail the necessarily brief comments on papers, point out and explain errors, and suggest strategies for finding and correcting grammatical and rhetorical weaknesses. These conferences provide valuable contact between student and teacher that yields support for the student and allows the instructor to monitor students' confusions and difficulties. They are an inexpensive and effective form of supportive service, since they do not require independent funding—although they are

one of several reasons that basic writing courses are ideally kept fairly small—and they encourage students to confer with the person who is probably most qualified and prepared to assist them with problems they are having in their basic writing course.

Assistant Teachers

The value of having increased student-faculty contact has led some programs at CUNY to increase the ratio of teachers to students by adding a second team member to some classes. These auxiliary teachers come from a variety of sources and serve many different functions, depending on their backgrounds and qualifications.

Graduate students from nearby English departments may be assigned to a basic writing section as part of a one- or two-semester seminar in pedagogy. In addition to attending the classes, presenting material for discussion, and helping to oversee group work or individual writing projects, such auxiliary instructors can hold conferences with students who need especially intensive attention. This arrangement allows far greater individual attention to each student than one teacher could otherwise provide, and establishes a tutor for the class who has nearly as much understanding of its needs as the teacher, who can work effectively in concert with the teacher, and who constitutes, additionally, an inexpensive form of support service since the auxiliary teachers receive course credit in lieu of money for their services. The arrangement may place some additional burden on the main teacher, who needs to spend more time outside of class with the assistant discussing plans, methods, and problems, but when the arrangement works well, that time is more than repaid by the increased progress of the class, the ultimately lighter conference schedule, and the availability of a second reader with whom to share the mass of papers generated in a basic writing course.

A similar arrangement pairs a tutor from a writing laboratory with a particular section. These tutors may be receiving undergraduate course credit if their work is related to a seminar, or they may be paid at an hourly rate. In either case, they are likely to have less previous training to inform their tutoring and to have less time to devote to the work than graduate assistant teachers do. Nevertheless, these tutoring arrangements have several important strengths. They allow tutors to consult with the faculty member who is overseeing a student's course work; thus, tutors can plan a course of tutorial work that complements and supports the student's progress in class. This planning assures that tutors will pursue a program that focuses on the problems that the class will not deal with or that the class has moved beyond and avoids duplicating the lessons that the student will learn in class.

In addition, because these tutors attend the basic writing class at least occasionally, they are legitimized as adjuncts to the class in a way that a tutor operating exclusively in a laboratory is not; when students view tutors as intimately associated with the course, they attend tutoring sessions more regularly. Tutors who have attended the classes come to their sessions having experienced the course from a student's perspective, able to anticipate the confusions and distress the student may feel and to approach the student as an understanding friend rather than a superior.

Tutoring and Writing Laboratories

Beyond offering supplemental work with an assistant teacher or tutor, virtually every CUNY campus has a writing laboratory. Most are administered either by the college's English department or, less often, by a special skills department. Occasionally, they are run by the college's counseling staff as one of a number of academic services including psychological, career, and academic counseling. Some college centers have a special system that considers any student who is enrolled in two or more compensatory courses to be on "academic alert." These students are contacted by an outreach program whose special support is designed to keep emotional, economic, and academic problems from pressuring students to drop out of college.

Most tutoring in writing occurs in a laboratory established specifically for providing one-to-one or small-group tutorial support to basic writing students and, secondarily, to students in more advanced writing or elective courses who continue to have writing difficulties. Some students attend of their own accord, coming on a weekly basis for general tutoring in a range of areas in which they feel uncertain or have been told by professors that they have some weakness. Many others, though, are referred by their instructors, either for support necessary to enable them to complete a basic writing course or for assistance in learning to produce an acceptable term paper for an upper-level course. And, in some instances, use of the writing laboratory is built more formally into a basic writing course, either by making attendance in weekly tutorial sessions mandatory for all enrolled students or by designating a specific hour or two of scheduled class time for working in the laboratory. In such instances, the instructor attends the laboratory with the class, serving as a tutor or supervising the proceedings.

One last group of students who are referred to a writing laboratory's facilities are those who have failed a college-wide proficiency examination that they must pass in order to graduate. These students may choose to attend tutorial sessions in order to strengthen their writing before retaking the test; in some instances, they may be referred to the laboratory by the committee that administers the proficiency test.

Laboratories which have the requisite equipment make use of audiovisual teaching aids, largely in the form of self-paced materials that allow a number of students to work on their own with some supervision from a tutor. Notable among such materials are the *Relevance of Patterns* (Thomas, 1973) audio cassettes for drill on verbs and *The English Modules* (D'Eloia and others, 1976), a set of videotapes designed to develop control of sentence structure. Although some laboratories have experimented with the use of homemade audiovisual software, it is generally difficult to produce materials that are sophisticated enough to appeal to students who have seen a good deal of elaborately produced television. Thus, Gray and Trillin (1977) find that such materials are often unsuccessful. The commercial productions, however, have been used with some success, although tutors or instructors who prescribe them should not be lulled into thinking that they are complete cures for one difficulty or another. They may provide effective presentations of material and challenging exercises, but students regularly require discussion of the material as well as guidance in completing the exercises.

Instructors teaching career-oriented curriculums often assign laboratory exercises focusing on basic skills but drawing upon vocational subject matter or topics of concern to students in a particular field. Such materials, often written in cooperation with vocational faculty, may also provide explanation and exercise for perfecting career-related writing tasks as distinguished from the academic writing that is often the focus of both basic writing courses and the laboratories that serve their students.

Students majoring in mechanical and electrical technology, for example, can go to a writing center for help in writing lab reports and composing process essays, two tasks that they encounter often in their course work. Secretarial science majors can use the same laboratory to improve their skill at typing from a dictaphone or from stenographic notes; they learn to distinguish essay paragraphs, to use a dictionary as an aid to correct spelling, and to punctuate even the most complex structures. For nursing majors, the laboratory can also devise special materials that develop the students' abilities to use precise detail in describing symptoms, to organize reports of patients' conditions effectively, to employ specialized medical terminology accurately, and to write care plans.

The tutors who serve in writing laboratories come to their positions in a number of ways. Some are students who are enrolled in a graduate or undergraduate course in teaching writing and who receive course credit instead of monetary payment for their services. Many are graduate or undergraduate students, whether English majors or not, who see a tutoring position as providing valuable work experience that will help them in getting future teaching employment. These students are often recommended by members of a college's English faculty and are selected on the basis of such a recommendation, their knowledge of grammar, and their ability and interest in writing.

The potential tutor's knowledge of grammar is often tested by an instrument designed at the laboratory to help determine whether or not a candidate can identify errors in grammar and, in a coherent and useful manner, explain the need to correct them. Often such a test is more discerning than one that asks a candidate to parse sentences or to identify parts of speech, for, although such abilities are conventionally equated with "knowing grammar," they are less useful in a tutoring context than the ability to identify and discuss a problem pragmatically.

In order to offer top-quality tutoring, many centers train their tutors upon hiring them and then offer in-service training sessions. Training may consist of reading and analyzing student writing samples to consider what difficulties they illustrate, in what order the problems might logically be approached, and what materials would be most useful in helping the writer. It may also include role-playing games in which tutors practice working with one another prior to working with a truly confused student. Faculty with background and experience in linguistics, psychology, or the teaching of writing may address a group of trainees. In-service training sessions may do more of the same, while presenting an opportunity for tutors to discuss problems that they have encountered in their tutoring and difficulties they have had in their interpersonal interaction with students.

Once tutors have started working, they are often troubled by certain ethical problems. They are frequently confronted by the question of how much help is enough and what constitutes too much, or whether students seek services that may lead tutors into unethical practices. Such questions arise when students ask for help in writing or revising a class assignment, when they drop in to have a paper "corrected" by a tutor before submitting it, or when they require substantial help in completing a research project.

There are no clear guidelines governing dilemmas of this sort; some centers require written permission of the instructor before a tutor may help a student with course work, a practice that often reduces the faculty member's regard for the work so done and gives the student a humiliating sense of childishness. Most centers frown on tutors actually correcting work, but may allow tutors to identify with their students patterns of grammatical error or inconsistencies of organization, leaving the students, then, to do the fundamental work of altering the paper. Most centers are happy to endorse a tutor's accompanying students to the library to assist them in starting a research project, showing them how to write note cards and order them. But any actual writing is clearly beyond the scope of the tutor's role. One good rule of thumb is that tutors keep their hands, or their pens, off the students' papers; this creates a distinction between sensible and impermissible assistance and, in fact, confines tutors to a facilitator's role by requiring that students implement all changes in their work. Whatever the policy at a given laboratory, these issues should be discussed in training sessions, particularly as the tutors' ways of providing sound assistance while withholding inappropriate services will be critical to their relationships with students and to their value to the center.

Tutors who assume their roles as part of a seminar requirement have a convenient opportunity for training built into their situation. But, for paid tutors, a training hour every week or two can exhaust center funds. Some centers do not pay for time in training but make it a requirement of the job nevertheless, an alternative that does not appeal to tutors but that can be acceptable to them as long as they perceive the sessions as useful and interesting. The economies of tutor training are complicated, but the benefits to a tutoring program are substantial.

The problem of absenteeism is a common one, and even students whose course requires them to attend laboratory sessions may find other activities more pressing. Absenteeism can be quite harmful to tutor morale and to the efficient use of a center's budget. One effective method of reducing absenteeism requires that absent students pay the tutor's salary for the sessions they have missed while the laboratory continues to offer free any session which they attend. Like bills owed to the college library and other outstanding fees, the unused sessions must be paid for at the end of the term in order for students to receive their semester's credit. This financial incentive has substantially reduced student absenteeism and assured tutors of productive use of their time.

Precollege Preparation

Colleges can serve potential basic writing students in several ways that will speed their progress toward writing competency before they enter their freshman year. Two alternatives are summer intensive courses and high school articulation programs.

Summer intensive courses, offered to students who will be incoming freshmen the following fall, have met with enthusiasm on a number of campuses. Their content and methodology are not likely to differ from those for a conventional fifteen-week course, but their schedule does. Students enroll in only one course which meets for an extended class period every day. The comparatively grueling schedule of such courses may seem discouraging, yet students who enroll in them do so voluntarily and are then often swept along by the concentration of the collective effort so that attendance and success rates in intensive courses tend to exceed those in conventional courses.

In one intensive program which meets four hours a day four days a week for seven weeks, students spend an hour considering a topic in grammar, an hour discussing plans for the day's essay, and two hours writing an essay and considering a reader's response to their essay of the previous day. Essay revisions and any assigned reading are done outside of class meetings. The twenty-eight papers generated in such a course provide far more writing experience than is usually possible in a conventional semester-long course. Another intensive pattern, which Ponsot (1976) calls *total immersion,* runs as a six-week summer program meeting five hours a day, four days a week. It involves a substantial amount of in-class writing as well as a good deal of reading aloud, both from the work of recognized writers and from the students' own work.

In order to stimulate, assist, and respond to the amount of writing that students generate in intensive courses, teachers depend on substantial tutorial support. A strength of the intensive offerings, in addition to having students work on writing before they have to address their other college courses, is that the format seems to elicit an enthusiasm that is generated by students' intense involvement with writing. Not distracted by the demands of other courses, students can focus exclusively on writing. Perhaps because of this intensive experience, students seem to discover the power of writing to reveal and mold their thoughts; they begin their freshman year, therefore, with increased writing skill and enthusiasm for drawing on it.

Another way in which potential basic writing students have increased their writing skills before entering their freshman year has been through high school–college articulation programs. In these, college English faculty join English teachers at a nearby high school, one which is likely to send a substantial number of graduates to the cooperating college; from this connection come writing programs that can be specifically focused on developing the critical skills that students otherwise would lack upon their arrival at college. The idea—encouraging the development of basic skills in the high schools—is not new, but the method of putting the idea into practice departs from the more traditional posture of simply asserting that basic skills should not be taught in college.

Having abandoned that possibly correct but clearly ineffectual posture, colleges can create articulation programs in a variety of ways. They may send their faculty to the high school to conduct classes, or they may invite high school students to the college campus for a writing course, but such programs present problems with scheduling and coordination. A successful form of articulation transfers materials generated by college writing instructors working in conjunction with high school English teachers into the high school classrooms. A collaborating group can detail a syllabus that combines exercises and informative notes for the teacher on the pedagogy that underlies the exercises. The syllabus may also suggest techniques for presenting the material that it outlines. If such a syllabus can lead high school students to master the first level and possibly the second level of a college basic writing course, students may acquire in a year or two the writing skills they will need in college.

An articulation program may further bolster precollege writing programs by sending undergraduate tutors to the high school to provide tutorial services, either in classrooms or in a laboratory. In addition, proponents of collaborative learning suggest that high schools offer a course in peer tutoring so that they can begin to develop their own tutoring resources.

Perhaps the most successful model for articulated writing programs is that sponsored by the Bay Area Writing Project, a project for improvement of the teaching of writing that is centered at the University of California at Berkeley and funded by the Carnegie Corporation of New York. The Bay Area Project establishes summer courses in the teaching of composition at several college campuses across the country. The teachers who take them are selected by the faculty who teach the course rather than by the regular graduate admissions and registration processes at each institution. Preferred candidates are those who are employed as teachers during the school year, at any level from elementary to college, and who have already been recognized at their own schools as outstanding. The course meets six hours a day, five days a week, for six weeks, during which time the participants present to one another the methodologies they have found successful in their previous teaching. The participants, as one another's students, also write a lot. From the cross-fertilization that occurs, new methodologies emerge. An important by-product of this process is that participants learn to teach other teachers, for each fall they hold training sessions at their own schools. Thus, they pass new methodologies on to their colleagues. This approach has important strengths: it draws on the combined resources of college and lower school faculties, thereby avoiding the uncomfortable posture of the college, and who have already been recognized at their own schools spirit of inquiry and learning among the teachers directly involved.

Evaluation of Students' Progress

Evaluation of progress in student writing is appropriately the final issue to consider when reviewing practices for basic writing courses, for evaluation must always occur in some form at the end of a semester's work. The most common sort of evaluation, and probably the least valuable, remains the individual teacher's assessment of what each student has accomplished during the semester and, thus, what grade has been earned. The final grade, conferred in the relative vacuum of the single class, provides little information for students about how well they can expect their writing to serve them as they progress through the rest of their course work. It tells little as well to faculty, who are concerned with maintaining appropriate standards, about whether they are succeeding.

These standards, however, are seldom specified for either faculty or students within a program. Faculty often seem to feel that, as professors, they know what good writing is, and probably they are in some sense right. But that knowledge does not help them to specify what good writing of entering college students may be and how that writing may be different from the good writing of graduating seniors or of graduates writing for professional purposes. Furthermore, faculty's individual and collective senses of good writing do not begin to consider what good writing may be in a laboratory report, a term paper, a business memo, or a legal brief and whether quality in those might differ from quality in, say, narrative or extemporaneous writing.

Williams (1978, p. 12) suggests that English faculty, acting individually, may not even adhere to the standards that they think they endorse. He draws an illustration from research that he and Hake have been conducting into ways that English teachers react to what they call *nominal* and *verbal* writing styles. Here is his example:

> *Nominal:* There is a need on the part of this office for a determination in regard to the resolution of these matters.
> *Verbal:* This office needs to determine how it is going to resolve these matters.

> Given these two sentences point blank, no English teacher reading this would recommend to his students the first as a prose model. And yet when pairs of essays differing only in these two styles were at different times given to English teachers from a variety of institutional backgrounds, most tended to grade the essays written in a nominal style higher than the essays written in a verbal style. What many of us claim we reject we seem tacitly to prefer.

Faculty may experience difficulty initiating program-wide discussion of standards for entering and leaving freshman composition courses. If professors are presumed to recognize good writing when they see it, any indication that their standards of measurement may not be consistent or clear opens the possibility of their colleagues' questioning their professional abilities. And, programs that use increasing numbers of part-time faculty or draw heavily on graduate assistants to teach composition lose even the fiction of a common collegial standard.

The process of establishing a set of standards that the majority of faculty teaching in a program can endorse may be arduous, but it is also very valuable, for the more clearly teachers articulate the standards they use, and the more they learn about the rationales underlying their colleagues' differing standards, the closer they will come to recognizing the complexities of the evaluation process and realizing its benefits.

There are a number of promising models for instituting program-wide evaluation. Matthews (1968) outlines the considerations and priorities behind the evolution of a simple evaluation system for grading final essays to pass students out of Level 2 and into freshman composition. It assigns identification numbers to students and to faculty graders to ensure anonymity to both sides and asks that bluebooks be graded according to general rhetorical standards: whether writers present "a reasonably developed, logical, and coherent 300-word essay with a recognizable beginning, middle, and end" (p. 64) and whether the essay contains fewer than eight errors in grammar and syntax. A confidential list of graders' numbers allows the program to identify and confer with any faculty who depart substantially from the published standards. Matthews' assessment of the value of this procedure to her faculty is a strong endorsement of the procedure: "The process of evaluating student writing has led us, perforce, into evaluating ourselves as teachers, our assumptions, our methodologies, and our standards. The process itself has been so informative that although we constantly modify it, I doubt that we will ever abandon our exit exam" (p. 68).

Beyond the usefulness of a testing procedure for setting minimal departmental standards for writing at any stage in a sequence of courses, an evaluative instrument can provide valuable information about strengths and weaknesses, either program-wide or in individual writing samples, that can indicate what particular skills a specific student needs most to practice or what areas of teaching an entire program must accomplish more successfully. Metzger (1978) and Hake (1978) describe two different methods for measuring growth in individual students' writing, both calling for pretests and posttests in essay form and both drawing on detailed reader analysis of each student's performance on those tests. Metzger's instrument uses three indexes of student performance: a count of words per t-unit (an independent clause and all of its attached modifiers) and a count of deviances from standard English, both determined from the student's essays; and a score on a separately administered measurement of anxiety about writing.

Hake's more detailed instrument provides information on four dimensions of a writing sample: "(1) organizational coherence of the essay as a whole, (2) coherence within and between para-graphs and sentences, (3) mechanics and usage, and (4) punctua-tion" (1978, p. 48). A grader reads each paper twice, first making judgments about the first dimension, then recording errors in the other three. Finally, the grader makes a holistic judgment that the essay passes or fails. Using two kinds of judgments allows the pro-gram to measure both what individual graders feel is proper and what they, collectively, find fault with. Based on this information, too, the program can rate its graders on a scale of leniency and use that rating in a statistical formula to adjust raters' scores and in-crease the uniformity of the collective judgment.

This instrument requires computer assistance; all essays for evaluation are written on paper with a specially printed margin for raters to mark as they read. A computer then scans the marks in the same way that it reads the answer sheet from an objective test. This complex instrument gives students detailed information about their writing problems and the areas they most need to concentrate on as well as allowing them an index by which to measure their progress from the beginning to the end of the semester. It also enables students to enroll in a section of the course designed for students who share similar difficulties. As for the instrument's ef-fect on the program, Hake concludes: "Despite the humanistic an-tipathy generated by competency based learning, we have found it productive to teach to our test. Even though a testing format can be limited by the skill and imagination of those who employ it, it provides us with a rigor too often lacking in composition programs. The approach is mainly a refined self-conscious application of what most good teachers have practiced willy-nilly. By systematizing the criteria for students and calibrating graders, we have systematized our common sense. The difference between willy-nilly common sense and a systematized approach lies in stating our expectations about what we are to teach and what students are to learn and then devising a means to measure the performance of those expecta-tions" (p. 55).

Even after a program has adopted testing procedures, there are no clear and easy ways to establish what constitutes "minimal competency," no available standards of measurement that can be applied across the country. The faculty of each institution must agree on a standard they can endorse, and in so doing, they must take into account a number of requirements: (1) that students who meet the established minimal standard should be able to transfer to a sister institution without need for further remediation; (2) that minimal competence for student writers, and freshmen at that, must not be the same as the minimal competence required of a graduating senior or of a professional writer because writing is a skill that changes and grows throughout the productive life of the practitioner; minimal competence for freshmen writers must, however, constitute performance that is assured not to impede the rest of their academic work; and (3) that nonnative speakers of English are unlikely to perform like their native-speaking counterparts regardless of the intensity of their training, for many features of their writing, such as the use of idioms and prepositions, will improve through increased acculturation; thus their work must be judged by appropriately altered guidelines.

The CUNY Task Force on Proficiency in Writing convened in the fall of 1977 to select and implement an assessment procedure that would regularize the goals and products of writing programs across its seventeen colleges. Although administering an objective test would have been simple and economical, the Task Force, drawn from the English faculty at many CUNY branches, unanimously rejected use of an objective instrument for two major reasons. First, the Task Force echoed what seems to be a profession-wide distrust of objective measures of writing ability, despite clear correlations reported on a number of campuses between several different objective measures and essay readings used for placement purposes. The Task Force decided that only by sampling students' writing could faculty know with assurance that students apply their mastery of concepts to their writing.

The second reason for opting to administer and score a writing sample rather than an objective test reflected a concern for the effect that an objective test of isolated skills would have on teaching, specifically, that faculty would tend to ensure their students' success by emphasizing skills needed for the test rather than teaching broadly applicable writing skills. Requiring a writing sample, by contrast, would maintain or increase the quality of instruction by demanding the generalized application of particular skills to any written work.

Procedures for eliciting and evaluating the mass of sample essays that result from administering a university-wide written examination have been summarized by Diederich (1974), Lloyd-Jones (1977), and Mellon (1975). Their preference, as well as that of the California State University and Colleges' massive advanced placement testing procedure (White, 1973–1979), for holistic scoring led the Task Force, too, to opt for a holistic procedure. Other widely used methods of evaluating writing, such as error counts, type-token ratios (Finn, 1977), and t-unit characteristics (Hunt, 1970), require tedious time-consuming scoring, making them impractical.

Holistic scoring, by contrast, is quite practical for evaluating large numbers of essays since readers, once trained, can score an essay in two minutes. Cooper (1977) sets forth a variety of holistic scoring procedures, of which the CUNY procedure, detailed earlier in this chapter, might be identified as *general impression marking* or scoring in which raters match their overall impression of an essay against a graded series of essays. Cooper endorses such a procedure for summative evaluation since it yields a judgment about where on a ranked scale a piece of writing falls. It is less useful for diagnosis than primary trait holistic scoring, which directs the rater's attention to particular features of the writing sample, such as its vocabulary, structure, or tone, and asks for a score based on a holistic assessment of the chosen feature or features.

A reliable, valid evaluation procedure provides important information to a range of interested parties. It can indicate the success of a program to an institution's governing board, which will want reassurance that it should continue to fund and endorse the program. It can offer a department the opportunity to consider, articulate, and adhere to the standards that it may have previously held only informally and with a good deal of unacknowledged variation; for the individual faculty member, external evaluation of students' performance at the close of a term can indicate more objectively than his own sense of the course how well he has served the individuals in the group. For the students whose work is evaluated, the process represents the institution's accountability to its students; it signifies that the college respects the students' right to emerge educated rather than their ability to slip through an irregular screening process. This need for accountability to students must be a central motivation for evaluation of growth in writing, for as students can display their growth toward and beyond minimal competence in writing, faculty, departments, and trustees will, in turn, find their roles regarding their writing programs justified.

Evolution of a Writing Program

Because basic writing is a new problem—or at least a problem newly conceived—administrators and faculty have been forced to create new wings on existing departments or entire new departments charged with the task of providing basic skills instruction. Two administrative models have evolved: the English department model, in which basic writing courses are an extension of the freshman composition course under English department jurisdiction; and the skills model, in which a separate department of basic educational skills is created with responsibility for all skills instruction. For both models, the objectives are largely the same: to provide a framework of courses and support services for underprepared students. Advocates of the first model insist that since the goal is to help these students enter the mainstream, they should be part of that community from the start. Opponents cite their success in providing a full service department to meet *all* the needs of unprepared students, personal as well as academic.

Experience has also given shape to writing programs. For colleges contemplating new programs or revision of existing ones, the arduous, sometimes painful experience of one college—Hunter College of the City University of New York—may provide some insight.

The writing program developed over a period of four or five years, in several stages. During an initial compensatory period, the college chose not to identify open admissions students, on the assumption that to do so would be detrimental to their self-esteem (Decker, Jody, and Brings, 1976). Underprepared students took courses building on their strengths and interests, and the required curriculum, where possible, was modified in an effort to relate college to outside work. After a short time, the college realized that the real detriment to students' success was lack of skills rather than a need for relevance. The college changed its policy, modifying grading procedures to permit students more time to demonstrate competence and to explore new subjects without penalty. Support services were provided in the form of tutoring and counseling.

When these measures also appeared inadequate, a single, one-semester, pre–freshman composition course was created, taught by interested and talented staff from the English department—mostly poets, writers, and playwrights. After a year of this plan, it was clear that the new students were far more handicapped than originally realized and that compensatory measures did not meet their needs. The college then modified testing and registration procedures and established an optional writing lab and an academic advisory office to assist students with their myriad academic and social problems. Two years later, the English department, in conjunction with the advisory office, launched a three-course developmental writing program. A year later, the college senate voted to mandate that all students—both freshmen and transfers from community colleges—take placement tests and that those failing be required to enroll in developmental writing courses and other skills courses while other academic work be curtailed pending instruction in basic skills. An effort was made to recruit special staff to teach skills courses and to establish clearly defined criteria for each level of instruction. A parallel sequential program was created for students whose first language was other than English.

Later, the college added additional courses for ESL students and students at the lowest level of basic writing. In a move toward upgrading standards, it considered the issue of granting credit for remedial courses, taking into consideration both the real motivational value of credit to students and the strong pressure from the faculty to protect the college's degree status. A compromise was agreed upon which permits students to use a small number of remedial credits to fulfill requirements for the degree.

Most recently, the English department and the administration, in response to diminishing resources and continuing concern about students' writing performance, have taken steps toward engaging *all* faculty in the teaching of writing. This new "model," now gaining wide currency among colleges and universities, is one that has emerged out of the kinds of experiences described here and is a result of colleges' defining the problems, confronting them, and systematically seeking solutions.

These efforts, as earlier pages of this chapter suggest, have produced a substantial laboratory of teaching methodologies from which teachers can select those modes and pedagogies which best suit their own style of teaching. All these approaches emphasize constant practice in writing thoughtfully supervised by trained teachers, not only of English but of all subjects, including mathematics and science. Hechinger (1979), reviewing some recent books on writing, notes that "if the demand for good writing is confined to English classes, it will be driven out by the bad writing practiced in all other subjects."

And what is good writing? We still know precious little about how people learn to write or what writing is, but we have much to learn from an interchange among faculty in other disciplines, for what is good writing in a history paper may be inadequate in a laboratory report. English faculty must study the language of the social scientist and the biologist to find ways to strengthen the curriculum of writing courses to reflect the specialized lexicon, rhetorical modes, and content of other academic disciplines. They must also venture into other fields—into learning theory, discourse analysis, and psycholinguistics—in search of fresh insights about the behavior of writing. At the same time, faculty outside the English department must undertake to learn the writing skills necessary for their own subjects and agree to making writing an integral part of their curriculum.

Finally, both students and faculty must perceive writing "not only as a necessary skill in college and an advantageous skill in work but the most accessible way people have of exploring and perfecting their thoughts" (Shaughnessy, 1977b, p. 293). Daily practice and attention to writing at every stage of learning may yet save what Hechinger (1979) calls "the endangered skill." Although that may require the commitment of the resources of the entire academic community, the benefits of more and improved writing should be felt across the curriculum in improved student learning and performance.

2

Margaret M. Waters

Reading

✳ ✳ ✳ ✳ ✳ ✳ ✳ ✳ ✳ ✳ ✳ ✳ ✳ ✳ ✳ ✳ ✳ ✳

If one skill is needed in college, it is reading. Students know how to avoid mathematics, and they can reduce writing to the barest necessity; but reading is something they cannot avoid. The sheer amount and variety of required reading shocks many freshmen; even the least demanding course requires some reading in textbooks, monographs, and journals. Reading this material is only the first step; assignments often call for evaluating, comparing, contrasting, extrapolating, and generalizing.

The reading process has two facets: first, the reading material itself, which has difficulties and differences inherent in the structure of the material; and second, the reader, who brings specific skills and experiences or lack of them to the printed page. A reading program must address itself to these two aspects of reading. To appreciate the problems of college-level reading which arise from the diversity of materials, consider three typical passages, difficult in different ways. The first comes from a college-level basic mathematics text (Hecht and Hecht, 1978, p. 434):

> Measurement is a form of comparison. To measure *time,* we must compare with some definite unit of *time.* There are many such units, and while some are more convenient than others, any of them will do the job. However, inches and pounds have nothing to do with time. They measure entirely different things. This is why comparing time with inches doesn't make sense. To make the comparisons involving measurement, we must compare with a unit of the *same kind.* If we're measuring length, we compare with a unit of length, like the inch, foot, meter, or mile. If we're measuring weight, we compare with a unit of weight, like the pound or ton.

Because students often find the subject of mathematics forbidding, the authors of this passage have reduced its difficulty to a minimum level; they have simplified the vocabulary and sentence structure and chosen familiar illustrative examples, and they present the ideas systematically at a rate appropriate to student understanding of meaning.

The second passage comes from a science text with tightly packed ideas typical of "encyclopedic" writing (Parsegian and others, 1970, p. 85):

> The polar characteristics of water molecules cause them to form boundary layers around particles, thereby keeping the particles separated and maintaining the mixture as a colloidal suspension. Among the most important phenomena in biological systems are those associated with protein molecules and other molecules at *interfaces* between liquid-liquid systems, especially when one liquid is water and the other an oily substance. The long protein molecules having portions that are lyophilic and portions that are lyophobic, the molecules readily form membrane-like interfaces at the water-oil interface. Such interfaces give a clue as to what may be the organization of membranes that surround the cell, the nucleus of the cell, and other organelles as well.

The highly technical vocabulary of this passage presents a challenge, but its treatment and style are straightforward. Once the terminology has been mastered, the meaning of the passage should be relatively clear.

The third excerpt (Percy, 1975, p. 186) differs greatly from the other two:

> For it has become more and more evident that our main emotion, when confronted by both Freud and Skinner, say, is not partisan feeling—for both are "right" in their way—but rather epistemological embarrassment. Both men put forth dyadic models, one for invisible "forces" interacting within a psyche. The question now is not which approach is right, but how both can be right at the same time.

With one or two exceptions, its vocabulary is simple, in contrast to the second excerpt. But the passage is more difficult than either of the others not only because of the complexity of its sentence structure but also because its author predicates a wide background of reading in philosophy and the existentialist movement, assumes an understanding of the works of Freud and Skinner, and asks an intellectual reconciliation of their divergent approaches.

The background of reading and understanding required to comprehend this third excerpt illustrates the second facet of the reading process: that relating to the skills and experiences which the student reader brings to the specific material. For example, three students in a social science class were asked to read aloud the same passage about ethnic culture among Italians in Boston. The first student, an Italian-American, read without error, gave back information from the passage, and related the material to his own experiences, because he had a ready frame of reference in which new information could be interpreted and evaluated. The second student, who had some problems pronouncing certain words, could retell the specific facts contained in the material but could draw few inferences and make few connections with his own experiences except when asked penetrating questions by an examiner. A third student read the passage in a word-by-word fashion without obvious error but remembered little of what she read and, even when asked probing questions, was able to express no connections between her own experiences and the material she had just read.

From this comparison of differences in comprehension among these three students we can infer that students receive varying information from a passage, depending on their skills and backgrounds. The teacher of reading at the college level has therefore a very complex set of skills to teach.

Levels of Reading Skills

The reading skills needed to handle passages such as those presented are normally part of a developmental process extending from primary grades through college. Basic skills learned in the early years are gradually honed through wide reading at the secondary level. Vocabulary expands, understanding becomes deeper and more analytical, and students finally reach a point where, if not actually prepared for college-level reading, they are at least on the threshold. So great is the range and complexity of reading skills required in college, however, that many colleges, including the most prestigious, have always offered help with reading and study skills as part of their freshman orientation programs. These reading courses and programs were part of the developmental process of taking students with acceptable reading skills and exposing them to the more sophisticated reading and study skills needed in college. In the early 1970s, when community colleges developed on a vast scale and even senior colleges found themselves admitting new, nontraditional student populations, the need for this assistance to students in reading skills changed both qualitatively and quantitatively. Far more students required help, not merely in the development of college study skills but also in basic reading. The reading programs initiated at that time were essentially remedial in nature, in both content and emphasis.

Within the population needing reading help, it proved useful to identify several remedial instructional levels. The poorest students—at the basic level—were those who had made their way to college with minimal word recognition skills. Their comprehension skills were limited to factual recall of the simplest materials. A step up from the basic level are readers at the intermediate level who can decipher a passage, word by word, but have difficulty with the smallest measure of complexity or nuance. They require explication of the implications of function words like *however* and *nevertheless*. Devices like the shading of positive statements through the use of double negatives, as in the sentence "He was not without honor in his own country," are incomprehensible. When confronted with new words, these readers are not quick in making informed guesses based on the context or internal structure. Instead they either ignore the word, guess wildly, or slavishly look up every word in the dictionary, even when a word occurs only in passing.

A third group of students needing reading help are those who see reading as a passive, rather than an interactive, skill. To them, reading is not a personal and total response to the thoughts and opinions of the author, but is merely a mechanical, word-by-word procedure. In their concern for avoiding errors, their reading is sometimes painfully slow, and they reproach themselves for miscues (for example, reading *house* for *home*) even when these miscues have little effect on the meaning of the passage. In making notes on their reading, they underline too much, take too much for granted, and never think of questioning the author. The art of skimming is alien to them; they rarely read prefaces, introductions, or summaries, nor do they appreciate the use of charts, figures, and tables. Some students in this group may have problems with vocabulary, not only the specialized vocabularies of their various courses but even the basic service vocabularies of college texts. Far more serious for their intellectual growth is their view of themselves as passive receivers of information rather than as protagonists in the complex process of reading.

Thus, there are three practical problems to be resolved in setting up remedial programs for college students. The first is to identify the reading skills needed for working with college texts and related materials. The second is to assess the level of reading skills already possessed by the entering college student. The third, to be solved in light of the other two problems, is to define the criteria for identifying those students who will benefit from a course in remedial reading.

Diagnosis and Placement

As the passages quoted earlier would suggest, determining the level of difficulty of college material is not simple. College reading materials often contain writing patterns which are complex and often subtle; materials are structured differently in different disciplines, and labeling of materials by level of difficulty is at best a dubious practice. Readability formulae have evolved for use in developmental programs, but, as Fry (1977) indicated, they have limited usefulness at any level. Much college reading is "subject specific"; motivation, specialized vocabulary, and knowledge of the discipline play an important role in the skill and ease with which students can read the material. Thus, students interested in the field of biology may be able to negotiate a far more difficult level of discourse in that field than they could in a philosophy text.

Nor is the assessment of a student's reading level a simple task. A traditional criterion of reading ability has always been the high school record, which should reflect the student's ability to negotiate a demanding college curriculum. When all college-bound students took a standard, fairly rigorous college preparatory sequence, no further assessment of reading was needed. Now, with the many options available in the high school curriculum, it is almost impossible to ascertain the quality of the courses listed on the transcript. A student who has completed a course in European history may be presumed to have some skills in reading history, at least in terms of coping with a text. But the caliber of reading assigned in a mini-course entitled "Wit and Humor" is not as easy to assess. Therefore the use of high school records as a basis for reading placement should be a cautious one. Many colleges now administer standardized survey tests in reading to gauge students' reading ability.

The complexity of the reading process makes reading experts loath to depend exclusively on the scores of a reading test to determine level of ability. Yet it seems to be the only way to survey the skills of large groups of incoming students. Those who use these scores must be aware of their limitations. Critics of standardized survey tests in reading point out that most instruments test vocabulary in isolation, whereas students need to understand it in appropriate context. They question whether a student's skill at selecting synonyms or antonyms is indicative of that student's ability to distinguish subtle variations of meaning in different contexts. Critics also wonder if success on the short reading comprehension passages can predict the student's ability to sustain comprehension of the broader ideas to be found in serious, lengthy texts. Students who do well on standardized tests may nonetheless lack the analytical skills needed to cope with abstract concepts often found in course materials. Conversely, because most standardized tests place a premium on speed, they penalize the competent reader who happens to read slowly.

The above criticisms of standardized reading survey tests point out some of the misleading notions which have arisen concerning what these tests can do. The results of a standardized survey test indicate only how the group tested behaves in a particular kind of reading situation when compared with the norms specified by the testers. Test scores do not tell us too much about how a student will perform in specific college reading situtations. The limitations and criticisms notwithstanding, the survey test remains the most efficient way to test large groups of entering students.

The final decision in reading placement concerns the setting of the cutoff score—the score below which students will be placed in a reading course. In choosing a standardized test, administrators should select one with norms which are suitable to the group being tested. All standardized tests state in the test manual the norm groups on which raw scores, grade levels, and percentiles were based. For tests which have many different norm groups—for example, high school seniors, seniors who are college-bound, and community college students—it is important that the norm tables which are used be as close as possible to the type of student being tested. Thus a test for freshmen at a four-year college should not use high school senior norms or community college norms. Once the appropriate test and norms have been chosen, setting a particular cutoff point for reading placement is at best a perilous procedure. If set too low, it excuses students who are genuinely in need of remediation; if set too high, it may waste vast resources of time and money. Sometimes at the start of a program the faculty may define a cutoff point by a process of judgment and educated guesswork and then, after a year or two, may refine this guesswork through follow-up studies of student performance. In effect, this ad hoc procedure enables a college to base its norms on its own experience with its own population. Some colleges, however, are forced by financial conditions to use a far more pragmatic criterion; they change the cutoff point each semester depending on considerations of space and budget. This method of determining placement might be necessary but is certainly not desirable.

Even with the careful choice of a test, with the sensible setting of a cutoff point, and with the use of additional criteria, errors of placement are inevitable. To keep such errors to a minimum, some colleges use additional and more sensitive placement criteria: personal interviews or a second test, either an alternate standardized test (one with a greater diagnostic component than the first) or an "in-house" test. The "in-house" instrument has the advantage of having been designed by the reading faculty themselves to directly assess reading skills in light of the needs of the particular institution. An example of such an instrument is Bowles and others' *Comprehensive Reading Program Competency Examination of College-Level Reading and Study Skills* (1976), which requires students to read a chapter from an actual college text. Prereading skills and outlining of the text are required subskills. The vocabulary assessment is based on words taken from the passage. The vocabulary items involve both connotative and denotative meanings. The comprehension questions, in addition to some specific detail questions, ask for inferences and analyses of comprehension over the scope of the entire chapter. This test thus closely approximates the actual reading experience in a typical college assignment. Because each exam must be scored individually, the test cannot be easily administered to thousands of students, but it is quite helpful in adjudicating those questions which arise when students request a retest because they do not wish to take a remedial course.

Once a student has been identified as being in need of reading remediation, he must be suitably placed within the reading program. Most reading programs make provision for classes on at least two and often three levels of ability. Table 1 shows the typical placement in reading, including cutoff scores by percentiles, student characteristics, skills taught at each level, and the types of academic programs suggested for students at those levels.

Within the reading classes themselves, teachers usually use additional evaluative techniques to understand more fully the strengths and weaknesses of individual students. Robinson (1975)

Table 1. Initial Placement in College Programs.

Level	Reading Test Cutoff Points	Student Characteristics and Skills Needed	College Program
Recommended Advanced	50th percentile down to 25th or 35th percentile	Has all basic skills. Needs confidence for flexibility of rate. Ready for college materials. Needs sophisticated study skills.	Some take remedial writing, others freshman composition; twelve academic credits.
Mandated Intermediate	25th or 35th percentile down to 10th or 15th percentile	Needs vocabulary help. Finds college material difficult, needs pattern practices. Not ready for speed.	Some take remedial writing, others freshman composition. Some take remedial math; six to nine credits.
Basic	10th or 15th percentile and below	Poor decoding skills, lack of vocabulary, poor knowledge of affixes and roots. Poor comprehension of high school–level materials.	Most take basic remedial writing, noncredit math; no more than six academic credits.

lists some useful methods of informal assessment. He states that observations of student reading behaviors are sometimes helpful, revealing the subvocalizer who reads slowly, moving lips and head, visibly struggling with the printed word, and the daydreamer who stops often, easily distracted by private thoughts or by outside distractions in the environment. Teachers may also evaluate a student by asking a student a series of questions immediately after he has read a selection aloud. The instructor judges the processes used by the student in comprehending and organizing the material. Criteria for evaluation include the way the student treated an unfamiliar word, the student's purpose or focus of attention, and the importance of the ideas he chose.

Such a strategy helps teachers understand how the student approaches the reading task. Another procedure for informal evaluation is the informal reading inventory. Students are given a passage from a text, chapter, or article and then are asked to respond to questions which reveal the quality of their reading and study skills. The teacher can elicit information about the students' knowledge of vocabulary in context, their ability to locate information, and their summarizing and outlining skills. In written form, such a test can be administered to an entire class.

The cloze procedure, in which every nth word is omitted from a passage, has also been used as an evaluative tool for placement. (This testing strategy is discussed in detail later in this chapter.) The analysis of the words chosen by the student to fill in the blanks can provide some indication of the reader's experiential knowledge of the field and ability to use the flow of language as a tool for comprehension. These informal assessments together with the standard test scores and the high school transcript furnish the reading faculty with sufficient information for determining placement and providing the proper course of instruction at the higher levels of reading placement. Those students who score in the bottom decile should take a battery of diagnostic tests that will provide an even more thorough analysis of their strengths and weaknesses. Since these tests are specialized and need trained personnel to give them, they will be discussed later in this chapter, in the section on support services.

Instructional Models and Course Content

Because college students have such varied backgrounds, the college reading program cannot be simply a developmental one. In addition, the very complexity of the reading skills needed for college work calls for instructional models that address all the elements involved. Only by understanding the complexity of the reading process can faculty develop appropriate instructional models and course content.

In the process of reading, the reader begins by looking at the words in a passage, expecting to grasp their meaning. When the reader knows the words and the sentence or passage fits into his prior knowledge and experience, he can comprehend the text. What the reader understands thus depends not only on what he sees on the printed page but also on the extent to which his experience contributes to his understanding. When this process happens smoothly, reading takes place, meaning is acquired, and the reader is unaware of the reading process as such. When the reading process is slowed down by uncertainty of any sort, when errors in meaning, ambiguities of meaning, or unknown words appear, reading is impaired and meaning is not clear. The loss in comprehension can be due either to the reader's lack of skills, to lack of experiential background, or to the inherent difficulty of the material.

In the usual reading of a passage, the reader uses all available decoding skills to give meaning to the print; some words are so familiar that the reader automatically recognizes them; these sight words are perceived as wholes. If the reader finds unfamiliar words, his pace of understanding is slowed and he summons a variety of decoding skills. He will use the context of the sentence as a clue to meaning and pronunciation. However, context may not help, as with the word *telebinocular* in the sentence "He used the telebinocular machine." Here the sentence provides no clues beyond the indication that whatever the word means, it describes some kind of machine. The reader can also use an alternate strategy, searching for pronunciation help and meaning in *tele, bi,* and *ocular.* If the reader has a knowledge of the common morphemes he can assign some meaning: *tele*=far, *bi*=two, and *ocular*=pertaining to the eye. Using these fragments and the context, a reader might be able to understand the word. If the reader does not recognize the morphemes, he may try to pronounce the word, sound by sound, hoping the blending of phonemes will echo a word already in his oral or listening vocabulary. If none of these strategies helps, then either the reader skips over the word, losing some degree of meaning, or he interrupts his reading to consult a dictionary.

As each word is decoded, the reader simultaneously undertakes the more abstract task of assigning a precise meaning to it. Here vocabulary skills are needed. Each subject area has its own specific terminology; for example, chemistry has its *catalysts* and *reagents*, biology has its *mitochondria* and *endoplasmic reticulum*. These terms are precise and must be learned specifically for the subject area in question. Other more generally known words acquire specific meanings when they become part of the lexicon of a particular subject area, for example, the term *work* in physics. However, a reader need not know every word in a passage if the grammar and semantic cues in the rest of the sentence provide sufficient information for general understanding. For example, in the sentence "He tried to clarify the passage, but his explanation only served to obfuscate it further," the reader can guess the meaning of the word *obfuscate* if he knows the word *clarify* and the implications of the structure *but . . . only*. The reader infers that the meaning of *obfuscate* is opposite to that of *clarify*.

As the reader assigns meanings to words in a passage, he sees relationships among phrases, notes specific details, abstracts main ideas, and makes generalizations. Comprehension is complete only with this total understanding of the passage. When a reader's comprehension is poor, his problem is often, if not a lack of decoding skills and vocabulary knowledge, then a lack of experiential background; the reader does not have a ready body of ideas and concepts to relate to the reading material at hand. This analysis of the reading process begins to explain the phenomenon of students who claim to have read their assignments, yet cannot remember or discuss the material. Reading the same material two or three times does not bring them greater comprehension because, although they read individual words correctly, they do not grasp the complete meaning of the passage.

Various theoretical models seek to explain the cognitive processes involved in reading. A hierarchy of skills and an information processing model yield two general approaches to organizing the reading programs at the college level. The hierarchy of skills model (see Figure 1) invites a systematic sequential teaching of skills until mastery is reached. The information processing model encourages a holistic methodology where emphasis is placed on processing meaning and the necessary skills are taught in passing (see Figure 2). There are advantages and disadvantages to each approach and in practice many instructors combine the two approaches.

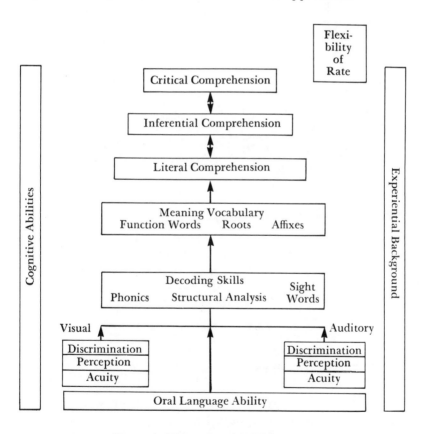

Figure 1. Hierarchy of Skills Model

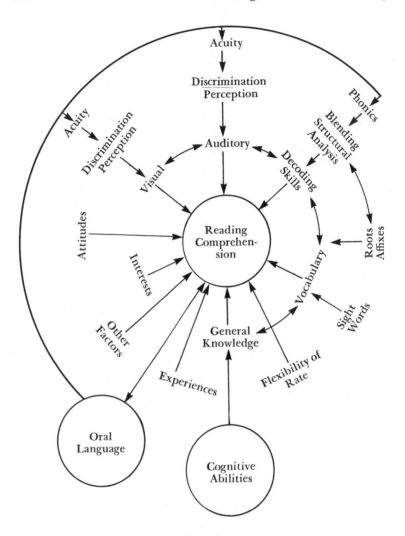

Figure 2. Holistic Model

Hierarchy of Skills Paradigm

In the hierarchical approach, students with the same instructional needs are grouped together and taught a sequence of basic reading skills. Thus students who need help in word recognition skills and vocabulary development are placed in the same class and progress together through a curriculum with several sequential levels. Materials of increasing difficulty are introduced at successive levels; at the highest level students work with the traditional college-level materials. This model comes closest to the developmental reading models of the lower grades. It presupposes either that students have not previously been exposed to basic reading skills in a systematic way or that they need a refresher course which is systematic in nature.

The systematic hierarchical approach seems best for those students in the basic level reading course. This approach enables students who have had poor reading instruction, minimal reading practice, and lags in earlier developmental skills to approach the subject anew. Students can now systematically learn the skills and integrate them into their cognitive system; students' reading practices can be integrated into patterns of rule-governed behavior. One disadvantage to such an approach is that those students who already possess some of the skills will be bored by the class. Another disadvantage is that if skills are taught mechanically, students may not be able to adapt from isolated drill practice to actual reading materials.

At this basic level, students' skills and proficiency profiles indicate extensive instructional deficiencies, not only in reading but in writing as well. Typically, their high school programs have emphasized vocational or business training and excluded those classes (literature and history) that require the development and practice of communication skills. Such students come to college with poor experiential backgrounds and very limited vocabularies; their prior experience has in no way prepared them for the difficulties of college reading materials.

Students at the basic level need a structured program to develop their reading skills. The basic reading course should develop the following set of skills:

1. Word attack: skills for pronunciation and meaning, making use of context, structural analysis, syllabication, and dictionary skills
2. Word meaning: skills in dealing with multiple word meanings, figurative language, denotative and connotative meanings

3. Sentence meaning: use of punctuation, interrupters, pronoun references, and word order
4. Making judgments: making comparisons, distinguishing between facts and opinions, recognizing assumptions and relationships, and recognizing an authority
5. Understanding generalizations: finding the central idea and supporting details, recognizing writing patterns such as comparison-contrast, cause-and-effect relationships, and simple listing.

While the student is learning or reviewing these skills, class exercises will be brief and practice will be specific to the skills being taught. Usually the student will also be enrolled in an intensive writing program and so the receptive-expressive relationship of language skills will be reinforced. Underlying these activities is the broader goal of effecting a change in the student's basic attitude; he will see reading not as the verbal processing of written symbols but as a thinking process, as an interaction with the text in which the reader searches and questions as he reads. At the end of this course, students proceed to the intermediate level of courses.

Students entering at the intermediate level or progressing from the basic level have mastered basic word recognition skills, know common morphemes in words, and understand the semantic structures of expository writing. Intermediate reading courses should help students develop four groups of skills:

1. Vocabulary: multiple meanings and subject-specific vocabularies
2. Comprehension: further practice in comprehension skills, skills of sequence, predicting outcomes, and drawing conclusions
3. Critical evaluation: understanding rhetorical patterns, inferring underlying hypotheses, recognizing bias, propaganda, irony, half-truths, exaggerated claims, validity and completeness of ideas
4. Inspectional reading: skimming and prereading.

Most intermediate students are enrolled in some college-level courses and can work with college-level materials. The instructor selects reading passages from college materials and appropriate professional magazines; these readings parallel typical college reading assignments and may be actual reading assignments from other courses. Students also read research works and practice more sophisticated study skills. The goal of work at this level is to produce competent analytical readers who have been taught that reading requires ongoing personal interaction with the text. Analytical readers can cope with the college-level articles and texts assigned in other courses.

Most colleges require that students take reading courses when their reading skills indicate need for instruction at the basic or intermediate levels. Successful achievement of intermediate skills is usually mandatory for all students, while advanced course work in reading is optional at most institutions. At freshman counseling sessions, students who could benefit from the advanced classes are strongly encouraged to take them, but enrollment is usually optional. At this advanced level, students are given the opportunity to learn the skills of the mature and sophisticated reader. Students at this level show some specific strengths and weaknesses: they have an adequate vocabulary and most of the analytical reading skills of the intermediate level. However, many of these students lack flexibility of reading rate. They tend to read all materials at a fixed rate of speed, regardless of style, content, or level of difficulty. Their powers of comprehension are adequate, but their reading skills need to be expanded to meet the heavy demands of college reading.

Course objectives at this level are best stated by Adler and Van Doren (1972). Students in advanced classes will have all the inspectional and analytical skills taught at lower levels. Now the student must learn to see the reading materials not merely as assignments to be read carefully but as the means to answer broader questions, either posed by the professor or chosen personally by the student. Students strengthen their abilities through the following activities:

- Examining texts to find passages relevant to a particular topic
- Constructing a neutral terminology for a topic through a reading of many authors

- Defining the issues relating to the chosen topic
- Making hypotheses or propositions about a topic
- Presenting an ordered discussion for class or for a paper
- Reading at a rate determined by the reader's purposes, skimming and prereading for an initial encounter with a book, careful reading of selected books or passages at a rate determined by the text's difficulty and the reader's goals.

Students who are reading at this level of proficiency will usually be taking a typical college program. The course allows them to attempt new and better ways study and read: students learn to synthesize material for presentation in a paper, examination, or class discussion, and they grasp the real purpose and meaning of the reading process. They are encouraged to try the new skills under guidance before they risk them in regular college credit courses. In this way, the college can meet its responsibility to produce a complete syntopical reader—that is a reader who, given a topic, can examine a number of titles and read only those pertinent to the immediate goals.

Holistic Reading Course Paradigm

For those students who already possess word recognition skills, adequate vocabulary, and literal comprehension skills, an alternate approach to course structure has been developed. Most students in these courses can work with college-level materials, and so the skills they are taught are directly relevant to their needs. This approach is best for students whose reading scores fall between the 15th and 25th percentiles on the college norms for a reading test. In these courses, specific reading skills are taught through the content of a general academic area.

There are two types of holistic reading courses. First are classes where reading is taught as a separate subject with content taken from a range of college material. Such courses have titles like "Reading and Study Skills in the Social Sciences," "Reading Skills for the Humanities Student," or "Reading Skills for the Natural Sciences." These courses are attractive to students who see in them the immediate relevance to their major area of concentration at college. Teachers can assign reading in appropriate texts, journals, and original sources. Students may be required to prepare bibliographies, write reviews of the literature, and answer essay questions based on their reading.

Second are classes in reading directly related to the content of a specific credit-bearing course. There are two ways to organize these classes: one section of the reading course may be linked in a general way to a half-dozen sections of some entry-level course, or the reading section may be tied to a single particular section of an academic course and the two courses, called "back to back" courses, are scheduled in successive time periods. In the first option, the students in the reading section receive general help with the material from the academic course. The reading instructor must meet a variety of demands, since the students are enrolled in several sections differing with respect to instructor, pacing, and emphasis. Students, however, may profit from discussion of the different approaches taken in the various sections. The "back to back" option, which pairs particular sections and their teachers, encourages the reading instructor to often attend the academic instructor's lectures; the reading instructor can then directly relate assignments to those lectures. For example, lecture notes taken by the reading teacher may be compared with those taken by the students. Within the framework of the academic course requirements and text, students learn to take essay examinations, to do library research, and to approach general reading problems associated with extended thematic content.

In these "back to back" courses, the teachers of the academic courses should teach the content in the usual way, while the reading instructor consciously isolates and examines the skills needed to successfully meet the requirements of the course. For example, the humanities teacher offers the standard lectures on a work of literature. The reading teacher conducts a class discussion on basic note-taking techniques and distributes outlined copies of the humanities instructor's lecture notes. The reading instructor then conducts individual conferences to review and discuss students' notebooks. Before examinations, the reading class discusses preparing for and taking an essay examination, and again, individual confer-

ences are held. After examinations, group and individual conferences are held to discuss the results.

The function of reading personnel in such specifically coordinated courses is *not* to conduct a satellite tutorial enabling students to meet the particular demands of the academic course.
Reading teachers should not be given a reading list of the academic
course texts and assignments in the hope that they will coach their
students merely to read and understand these materials. The reading course has its own objectives; the emphasis in the reading
course is always on the demonstrated acquisition of skills rather
than the assimilation of specified academic content. For the reading teacher's purposes, the academic subject is primarily a vehicle
for teaching reading skills that will serve the students' needs in all
current and future courses.

Mini-Courses

Another instructional paradigm which has been used successfully at several CUNY colleges is a reading course paired with a
one-credit academic mini-course. For students needing help in
reading, the mini-course is of particular interest because its content
is limited, its focus is sharp, its duration is short, and, since it carries
only one academic credit, its requirements are minimal. An example of such a course is one offered at Brooklyn College entitled
"Documentary Films of the American Indian." In this course, given
jointly by the Anthropology and Film departments, students are
required to attend a series of six films, read a text, and write a
paper. In this instance, the reading students already possess many
of the needed learning skills; namely, oral and visual literacy in the
viewing of films. The concomitant reading component stresses
the use of primary source materials and techniques for writing
papers. Class discussions by the reading teacher, utilizing the students' visual and oral literacy, illuminate the reading and focus the
choice of topics for the paper.

A related example of innovative course structure was a
three-week seminar on the works of Aleksandr Solzhenitsyn, a non-
credit course given by the reading program after Solzhenitsyn received the Nobel Prize. A member of the department of modern
languages agreed to give an informal talk to students. All available

library materials on Solzhenitsyn and his works were gathered in the reserve section of the library. The reading laboratory prepared multiple copies of magazine articles and book reviews. Paperback copies of the author's works were obtained, and students were assigned readings in preparation for the seminar. At the seminar, students had the opportunity to relate their readings to issues raised by the speaker. They were able to approach the works of the author through their reading of both the original sources and critical reviews. The seminar, although it granted no credit, was well attended, and students who participated found it helpful, since it gave them added assurance in discussing a popular campus topic and contributed greatly to their experiential background. For students who had fled from oppression abroad to this country, it was an opportunity to relate their personal experiences to the literary experience.

Summer Reading Programs

Several units of CUNY offer intensive summer remedial programs for entering students. Such programs usually include an integrated language arts program emphasizing reading and writing, research techniques, and skills needed for writing term papers. To make the program more attractive, it is offered in conjunction with either a credit-bearing course or an athletic program. Such an intensive program (often requiring six class hours daily) is valuable in that it allows students to become acquainted with their classmates, the campus, and its services before the pressure of regular classes are upon them. For those who administer remedial programs, the summer program spreads remedial instruction across the year, decreasing the need for adjuncts in the fall when there are usually more students needing remedial classes. Reports of these programs show them to be effective: the grade-point averages of freshmen who participated are significantly higher than those of students receiving help only in the regular remedial programs. However, some of this difference must be attributed to the fact that these summer students are a highly motivated group. They come voluntarily, spending many hours each day developing skills whose value might not be immediately apparent to them.

The preceding paradigms offer a variety of approaches to

teaching reading skills. Their use allows administrators of reading programs to match instructional methods and learning styles to a great degree.

Instructional Methods

The decision as to appropriate methodology for teaching the specific skills of reading is one which each teacher determines. Some methods work best for some teachers, other methods are more appropriate for a particular student's learning style. Smith (1971) believes that current instructional methods are probably sufficient for teaching reading. So many instructional methods have been tried, and so many succeed, that further changes in methodology are unlikely to produce great reading gains. Greater understanding of the reading process will help the teacher to choose those methodologies most appropriate to the needs of individual students.

Once the instructor decides upon a general approach, he can then select strategies to improve specific skills: word skills, comprehension skills, and study skills. Techniques for improving word skills focus on decoding, structural analysis, vocabulary, signal words, and context clues. Teaching comprehension skills requires techniques for improving the students' understanding of connected discourse. The methodology for teaching study skills includes techniques for teaching critical reading, syntopic reading skills, study strategies, and tactics for developing flexibility of reading rate.

Word Skills

Word Recognition Skills. The ability to decode printed symbols is basic to the reading process. Many students who come to remedial reading in college have a large sight vocabulary (words they recognize at a glance). However, these same students might not have the skills necessary to decode new, strange words. Problems in decoding arise because in the English language some sounds (phonemes) are represented by various letters of the alphabet (graphemes). For example, the sound f is represented by the grapheme *f* in *fish,* by the graphemes *ph* in *phone,* and the graphemes *gh* in *laugh.* The study of the generalizations regarding phoneme-grapheme relationships is called *phonics* (as distinguished from *phonetics,* the study of speech sounds, their production, combination, and written representation). Phonics should be taught systematically in developmental programs.

Reading teachers might be tempted to teach students the phonic skills they had missed previously. Experience dictates the contrary. Even if students are taught and learn the isolated phonic elements, they do not sufficiently carry over those skills into their regular reading to make separate work in phonics worthwhile. It is far more helpful to teach phonics incidentally as part of a larger program. In learning phonics, college remedial students have found these generalizations particularly helpful:

1. Vowels when they are long say their own name in a word. Base vowel sounds are more varied and can be taught in minimal contrast pairs and through spelling patterns. Fries (1963) gives lists of vowel sound patterns which instructors may find helpful in developing specific exercises for practice.
2. Syllables are either open or closed. Syllables are open when they end in a vowel. The vowel in an open syllable is long. Syllables are closed when they end in a consonant. A single vowel in a closed syllable is usually short. Examples of open syllables are *ba*-by and *a*-pron. Examples of closed syllables are *hap*-pen, *ap*-ple, and *In*-di-an.
3. Prefixes are separate syllables: *pre*-fix and *re*-turn.
4. Words may be split into syllables between double consonants: *ap-ply* and *suc-cess.*

All other phonic generalizations, such as the "silent *e*" rule and the rules for inflected endings, are best left to individual teaching for those students who need them.

Knowledge of the general rules for prefixes and suffixes can help students understand a word, even if they cannot pronounce the word. The word *economy* and its derivatives *economic, economical, economize,* and *economization* exemplify the shifting of accent and vowel values which result in minimal pronunciation changes. A student's phonic decoding might be incomplete in this case, but he will know the meanings of the words since the derivatives all resemble the base word.

Vocabulary Skills. Students' ability to correctly pronounce a word does not guarantee that they will know the meaning of the word. For example, decoding *prefrontal* and *prefulgency* may seem equally difficult. Some students pronounce both words with the correct sounds but no meaning. The student who knows the meaning of *prefrontal* continues to process meaning for the rest of the sentence. This student might also be able to correctly pronounce the word *prefulgency,* but not know the meaning of the word. This difficulty is analogous to that of a reader who can pronounce the words of a foreign language learned in high school and yet not remember their meaning. At this point a vocabulary meaning skill is needed.

How best to teach vocabulary skills at the college level is a controversial issue. One faction maintains that vocabulary should be taught in context; another, that vocabulary should be taught through the study of the etymology of words; and the third, that vocabulary is acquired in an order roughly comparable to the frequency words are found in literature and so can be learned from lists in a systematic, sequential manner.

The context school says that when confronted with an unknown word, the student should inquire whether the surrounding sentence or sentences give clues to the meaning. The student should look to see if there is a prefix or root which guides him to the meaning, and then, if neither strategy helps, the dictionary can be consulted as a last resort. Using this approach, the instructor selects reading passages from college-level materials for vocabulary practice. In class, the instructor reviews key words, or the students ask for help with difficult words.

A second group believes that vocabulary can be taught directly and systematically through careful attention to common elements of the morphology of English words. Brown (1971) developed a system of teaching vocabulary through programmed materials which utilize the common prefixes, suffixes, and roots. He selects fourteen words to illustrate how a knowledge of these could be used to unlock the meaning of over 14,000 words. Although his book has been used widely in college reading programs, it has the disadvantage that students need some knowledge of Latin or a Romance language to utilize the strategy fully. For example, in the word *transfer* the root morpheme *fer* resembles the Latin *ferre*, to carry, and the morpheme *trans* means *across*. In the word *translation*, however, although *trans* again means *across*, *lat* is derived from *latus*, the past participle of *ferre*.

While morphemic structure can be helpful, there are several problems which the teacher using this method should consider. Some words appear to begin with a common prefix, but the initial syllable is not a prefix at all. An example of this particular problem is the word *malacoid*. It apparently begins with the prefix *mal-* from the Latin *malus* (bad), but it actually comes from the Latin *malac* (soft). Here the student who assumes that the letters *mal* mean *bad* will be led astray. Other prefixes have become absorbed or bound, such as the *per-* in *persuade*. Still others are Old English prefixes rarely mentioned in vocabulary books, the prefix *be-* in the word *beyond,* for example. Students who are inclined to literally translate roots and affixes are better served if they are instructed to use morphological elements to get the "sense" of an unfamiliar word.

A third system of vocabulary development is that advocated by O'Connor (1948). He analyzed the words known by people who took his aptitude tests and hypothesized that words are learned in a sequential order which is roughly the same for everyone. Therefore, he listed words to be learned on the basis of the order in which the population in general learned them. He observed that individuals know precise meanings for those words which are in their personal lexicon. At the other extreme, there are words they do not know or recognize at all. In between are what O'Connor calls *frontier words*, words whose meanings are vaguely known and are easily confused with words which are related and similar in meaning. The pair of words *disinterested* and *uninterested,* for example, is often confused. O'Connor concluded that each person learned best, and most easily, those words which were at the frontier of that person's word knowledge. His method of learning vocabulary depends on an initial identification of known words, followed by the systematic study of words which are half-known, or easily confused, and ultimately study of those which are unknown.

Vocabulary needs also vary from one academic discipline to

another. The task of the reading teacher is not only to help students acquire a general reading vocabulary but also to teach students to isolate and interpret the important specialized terms of various academic fields. Adler and Van Doren (1972), in addressing strategies for teaching specialized vocabularies, distinguish between the author's vocabulary and the author's terminology. The author's general vocabulary is not associated with a particular subject (Wood, 1978). A history text may talk about *progressivism* and *rapacious* landlords. The author's terminology here is the word *progressivism*. *Rapacious* is more generalized vocabulary that could be found in any area. In learning a specialized vocabulary more than a dictionary definition is needed. Specialized vocabulary will differ in nuances of meaning from instructor to instructor and from text to text. Only when readers can understand the terminology, or "come to terms" with the book, will they comprehend the author's meaning.

In the natural sciences, reading materials contain not only a specific vocabulary of technical terms but mathematical symbols and formulae as well. The reader sometimes needs to interpret graphic illustrations in order to comprehend a particular term. In an explanation of DNA, for example, an illustration of the form of a double helix presents the concept more clearly than a definition. For complete comprehension of specific terms, the student must understand the illustration and the accompanying statement.

In the social sciences, the student again has special vocabulary problems. Words such as *role, drive,* or *rent* assume particular meanings within the framework of their disciplines. Other words present difficulty in the social sciences not because of their literal meaning but because of the connotations associated with them. For some readers the term *socialism* connotes *communism*. Yet, when the political scientist states that "a policy tends toward socialism," he is describing a policy of government control of certain industries, nothing more. The teacher must help students sift out special definitions, connotations, and emotional associations so that they can understand the essential information in a passage. When terms carry strong emotional associations, the reader must not let these color the author's precise definition.

The reading teacher's job is also to teach nuances of meaning. Pearson and Johnson (1978) give excellent examples of exercises that develop the students' awareness of synonymy and connotation. Categorization exercises ask students to cluster similar words: buddy, pal, and acquaintance are all _____. Differences in connotative meaning become clearer as students discuss a set of similar, but not synonymous, words: walked, trudged, skipped, strolled, ambled, sneaked, and strode. Sensitivity to nuance increases as students discuss a family of synonyms: ailment, poor health, illness, sickness, and disease.

The reading of literature presents additional problems: imagery and other forms of figurative language change and heighten the meaning of the printed words. The language of poets, fiction writers, and essayists includes irony, satire, metaphor, similes, and hyperboles. For students unfamiliar with these terms, the task of understanding meaning in the humanities looms large. The introductory reading course can only begin to help students develop skills for understanding how imaginative, figurative language is used.

As we have seen, decoding and vocabulary skills are necessary subskills, but only when the student integrates these and other interpretive skills into a working system for comprehending connected discourse does the reading process actually take place.

Language Structures. In addition to decoding and vocabulary strategies, which address themselves to the meanings of particular words, students can be alerted to other aids to meaning that are derived from a study of sentence structure, semantic patterns, and other lexical signals. These structural aspects of language are essential to understanding longer discourse.

Understanding the function of common connectives is a vocabulary skill learned at the beginning of the reading process. These connectives must be mastered, because they are important signals of meaning. Robinson (1975) lists five types of meaning signals which these connectives give:

1. *Go signals,* the coordinating connectives, express equivalent ideas: and, in addition, also, furthermore.
2. *Caution signals* tell the reader to pay attention to the next point: thus, therefore, in conclusion, in brief.

3. *Turn signals* warn the reader that what follows presents a different or opposing idea or a change in the direction of the discussion: but, on the contrary, conversely, despite, however, on the other hand, nonetheless, yet.
4. *Stop signals* say pay careful attention to what follows, for it is especially significant: significantly, undoubtedly, absolutely.
5. *Relationship signals* indicate relationships of time (soon, finally), space (there, here), cause and effect (because, since), degree (many, less), and condition (if, unless).

Brown and Adams (1968) propose two additional types of connectives: *summary connectives* (finally, therefore, for this reason, as you can see, in conclusion, in short, consequently) and *exception words* (although, though, while, to be sure, it is true, true).

Systematic exercises as well as individual aid given incidentally are helpful in teaching the implications of connectives. After initial instruction has been given, wide reading in a variety of materials will ensure reinforcement of the skills, for these words can only be learned well when they are in context.

Students should also learn the conventions by which authors signal the presentation of definitions of technical terms. Some authors identify precise word meanings through the use of footnotes or by reference to glossaries. At other times, they place the meaning of special terms in parentheses, make a statement in apposition, or even give a simple definition in the text. Words such as *or* and *that is* signal that the succeeding phrase defines the term. In the following sentence, the use of an appositive structure, signalled by *that is* and the commas, indicates that a definition is being given: "Dyslexia, that is, a dysfunction in the reading process with no clear etiology, is found more often among boys."

Other ways in which authors convey specific word meanings are by giving examples, using synonyms, describing experiences, making comparisons, and offering similes or metaphors. In reading the phrase "as enigmatic as the smile of the Mona Lisa," the student's visual memory of the portrait helps him understand the word *enigmatic*, although he may be unable to supply its precise meaning. The student may also infer the meaning of an unfamiliar word used in contrast to a familiar one. In the sentence "John, a parsimonious man, does not get along with his generous brother," the reader infers that meaning of *parsimonious* is opposite that of the word *generous*.

One of the strengths that students possess is their innate knowledge of language and their ability to function within its framework. Students can be assisted by the reading teacher in using their innate knowledge of syntax and structure to comprehend meaning. English word order gives some clues, inflectional endings also give information, and knowledge of noun, verb phrase, and clause markers promote understanding. Fries (1963, pp. 105–106) notes that in the nonsense phrases "a diggle was" and "two diggles were," the determiner *a* and the number *two* signal that the succeeding word, *diggle*, is a noun or name marker. The *-s* signals the plural of the noun, as does the verb *were*. In the sentence "A woggle diggled another woggle," the verb is signaled both by its position after the noun and by the inflectional ending *-ed,* which also signals the past tense. In the phrase "this woggle is digglier than," the *-er* signals a comparative adjective and *than* also indicates a comparison. The marker for adverbs is *-ly,* as in the sentence "This woggle diggled another woggle diggly." Fries' examples indicate the importance of readers' using grammatical structure as well as lexical meaning.

Two sentences given by Algeo and Pyles (1966, p. 244) demonstrate vividly the differences and relationships between lexical and grammatical meanings:

> Oll considerork meanork, ho mollop tharp fo concernesh bix shude largel philosophigar aspectem ith language phanse vulve increasorkrow de recent yearm engagesh sho attentuge ith scholarm.
>
> In prefarbing torming, we cannot here be pretolled with those murler dichytomical optophs of flemack which have demuggingly in arsell wems exbined the obburtion of maxans.

At first glance neither sentence means anything. The first sentence seems to be about language, philosophy, and recent years.

The second sentence gives more meaning; readers can deduce the following propositions (p. 245):

- that, whatever an optoph is, there are more than one of them;
- that the optophs we are concerned with are dichytomical ones and more murl than other possible optophs;
- that an optoph is something we might be pretolled with;
- that optophs are things and not people;
- that the obburtion of maxans can be exbined by optophs;
- that the exbining we are talking about took place in the past.

In the first sentences, we have some idea of the subject but not what is said about it. In the second the reverse is true: although we do not know what optophs and maxans are, we do know what is being said about them. Thus, both grammar and lexicon convey meaning.

A knowledge of word order, endings, and function words also aids students in determining meaning. An exercise based on these features of structure that can be used to develop vocabulary skills is the cloze technique.

Regular exercises using the cloze technique will help students develop a schema which utilizes their already developed semantic and linguistic abilities. Giordano (1977) advocates eliminating every tenth word in a paragraph in the original form and then using an unaltered paragraph. With practice, students will be able to read the altered and unaltered passages with comparable understanding. The following excerpt has two paragraphs, the first with cloze deletion and the second as originally written:

> Man's third major distance receptor, besides seeing and hearing, _____ smell, or olfaction, the sensitivity to odors emanating from distant _____. Man's sense of smell is not nearly as sensitive _____ that of many animals and insects. Male moths, for _____ , can smell female moths several miles away.
>
> Smell requires that appropriate molecules enter the nasal passages, where the olfactory epithelium is located. Figure 15.15 shows the lateral wall of the right nasal cavity. The epithelium is about 2.5 cm^2 and contains millions of hair cells, each with up to 1,000 hairs per cell [Communications Research Machines, 1970, p. 283].

The most important advantage of the cloze technique is that the comprehension of meaning is kept as the primary focus of decoding. Giordano emphasizes that "students are not required to achieve proficiency in graphic, phonetic, etymological, and orthographic decoding as the condition of reading" (1977, p. 150). Another advantage of the format is that it is emotionally well-suited to the maturity of college students.

No matter what basic strategies for word recognition or vocabulary development are emphasized, all must be taught. Instructors must guide students through careful analyses of many reading passages, applying the various skills, and finding the correct nuances of meaning to fit a particular context. Then, students must be encouraged to take a final step in understanding word meaning. Goodman (as cited by Singer and Ruddell, 1970) calls reading a psycholinguistic guessing game, a selective, tentative, anticipatory process. Skill in reading comes from more accurate first guesses and the relation of perceptual cues to syntactic, semantic, and phonological ones. Multiple strategies can only be used if the reader can cope with the uncertainty inherent in psycholinguistic guessing. Robinson (1975, p. 64) says mature readers need to learn to suspend judgment and live with uncertainty beyond a particular word in the search for meaning. This process is not an easy one and must be repeated with help and supervision, often enough, in a variety of texts, to arrive at the habitual use of many and multiple vocabulary strategies to deduce meaning. An excellent example of an exercise that requires the application of phonics, structural analysis, and vocabulary knowledge to a specific passage is given in Courtney (1960, p. 45). He presents a brief excerpt from Whyte's *The Organization Man* and selects certain words (here italicized) for discussion:

> It is a *churlish* critic who would *gainsay* people the *solace* of fairy tales. Current slick fiction stories do not do this; the tales are not presented as make-believe; by the use of detail, by the *flagrant* plainness of their characters, they proclaim themselves realistic slices of life. . . . The *verisimilitude* is superb . . . from the frayed cord on the bridge lamp to the *askew* hair of the young mother, the detail is almost photographically faithful to middle-class reality.

The words *churlish, gainsay, solace, flagrant, verisimilitude,* and *askew* are those which many students will find difficult. *Solace, flagrant,* and *verisimilitude* are from the Latin but not from the more common morphemes. Some students, however, may relate *solace* to *consolation* and thereby guess its meaning. The words *churlish* and *gainsay* are Anglo-Saxon, while *askew* is Middle-English. Before going to the dictionary, the student is encouraged to use context as well as other clues. *Churlish* has an unfavorable sound when used with *critic.* The word *verisimilitude* is defined in the text itself by the phrase "photographically faithful," a meaning reinforced by a root that echoes *similar* and the context, the vivid detail of the rest of the sentence. *Askew* if related to *frayed* would take on sufficient meaning; some students will know *skew* from geometry. *Gainsay,* although a compound, yields no help in either of its parts. Substituting other verbs does not help since the opposites *forbid* or *permit* might both fit. The dictionary *must* be consulted. *Flagrant plainness* is an unusual combination, and equally difficult since the words are dichotomous. Again, the dictionary is needed. Of the six words, the dictionary is needed for three.

Comprehension

Word recognition and vocabulary skills prepare the student for instruction in comprehension, the ultimate aim of reading. Students need to understand what they read, respond to the ideas, and apply the knowledge so gained. Each methodological approach to the reading process discusses comprehension within its own theoretical framework. Each reading manual for the college student organizes practice exercises in comprehension differently.

Manuals such as the one by Levy (1969) guide students from reading words to sentences and then paragraphs. Brown and Adams (1968) focus on the students' understanding of the variety of writing patterns found in the various content areas and thus differentiate comprehension skills according to the natural sciences, the social sciences, and the humanities. Wallen's (1972) approach to the comprehension process focuses on the students' ability to answer questions about the material. He develops a two-way classification of comprehension skills to organize the teaching of reading for comprehension (see Exhibit 1).

Exhibit 1. Classification of Comprehension Skills.

	Content Areas			
	Narration-Exposition Continuum			
Skills	*Literature*	*Social Science*	*Science*	*Mathematics*
Recall				
Interpretation				
Extrapolation				
Evaluation				

Wallen's classification proceeds from a simple recall of information found in the material through an evaluation of information, a more sophisticated skill. The other axis of classification is the range from narration as found in some literature to exposition in the abstract field of mathematics.

Pearson and Johnson (1978) present another theoretical framework. They list discrete comprehension skills, recognizing that for the sake of instructional convenience such an analysis is helpful. But they make the plea that comprehension is a unified process.

Faced with this multiplicity of approaches to the teaching of comprehension skills, the instructor must select those strategies that suit the material and utilize the strengths of the students. The following techniques represent strategies that are most useful in working with a wide range of college students. Several methods can be combined in the teaching of a particular passage or assignment.

Cloze Technique. Cloze procedures, which are used extensively to *test* comprehension and to teach vocabulary in context, can also be used to *teach* comprehension. The reader who uses past experience and knowledge of the topic and of syntactic structure to supply the missing words is developing a habit of contextual analysis. The cloze procedure consists of taking a suitable passage and deleting every seventh or tenth word, or deleting particular words at the teacher's discretion. The student is asked first to skim the paragraph as it stands, with deletions, and then to reread it, supplying an appropriate word for each deletion. The process requires the student to provide meanings during the actual process of reading.

It is radically different from the traditional technique for eliciting evidence of comprehension, whereby students answer questions after having read an entire passage. This cloze method might be indicated for those students who sacrifice comprehension to speed, racing through material whatever the level of difficulty. Moreover, it encourages students to use context as a clue to words and their meaning.

As an example of the kind of thinking that the cloze process requires, consider the following passage: "Only fools follow fashion. Wise men know that fashion _____ with the weather and what's popular _____ may be out of favor _____." One set of meaningful and grammatically correct choices consists of the words *fades, here,* and *there.* The original text has *changes, today,* and *tomorrow.* Discussion of this exercise would focus on the word *weather:* which is more appropriate, to say weather *fades* or it *changes*? This approach entails a search for meaning on many levels; it comes closer to being the obverse of the writing process than the traditional method of assessing comprehension.

The maze procedure is a less stringent use of the cloze technique. Here a choice of three words is given; one is correct, and the other two are distractors: Lewis and Clark _____ the northwest territories (founded, explored, went). A discussion of why some answers are correct, and others wrong, provides insight into the students' thinking processes and their ability to use syntactic and semantic clues. Modified cloze techniques use some letter clues to make choices easier. Students complete sentences like "They rode in the t __ x __ ," "They rode in the t _____ ," and "They rode in the _____."

Utilizing a Taxonomy for Meaning Skills. Wallen (1972) says that because reading comprehension is a complex intellectual process, the best indicator of the reader's comprehension is his ability to answer questions about the text. Wallen presents a taxonomy of meaning skills: recall, interpretation, extrapolation, and evaluation. For any reading material, the instructor may ask four types of questions to determine a student's level of comprehension. *Recall* questions include both identification and reorganization of specific information. *Interpretation* questions invite the identification or summary of major ideas, both explicit and implicit. *Extrapolation*

questions ask the reader to draw inferences from the causal relationships expressed in a passage. *Evaluation* questions require the
reader to make judgments, subjective or objective, about the
soundness of a passage. These four question skills are both sequential and cumulative. Thus, the thinking skills involved in recall are
utilized in each of the higher skills; evaluation requires the use of
recall, interpretation and extrapolation. The four question skills
are taught with materials along the narration-exposition con-
tinuum. Recall questions are used in literature, social sciences, sciences, and in the abstract field of mathematics. Theoretically, then,
the most difficult questions to answer are those of evaluation in
mathematics.

Wallen (1972) suggests that instructors use four basic teaching principles to teach these meaning skills:

1. Vary the exercise.
2. Vary the selection.
3. Vary the context.
4. Give informational clues.

These four teaching principles enable reading teachers to modify
their teaching techniques until the students' comprehension is
adequate. The four teaching principles are not steps but alternatives and may be used in any order or combination.

The first principle, vary the exercise, suggests that if a student is having difficulty understanding a passage, then the instructor should provide a less demanding exercise based on that passage. For example, a student has read a paragraph on the cause of
the Civil War, but cannot answer the question "What was the principal cause of the Civil War?" The teacher should then ask a less
demanding question, a multiple-choice question that states the
correct response as one of the choices: "Was the principal cause of
the Civil War states' rights, slavery, or foreign intervention?" This
second question, which provides the correct choice among two distractors, is significantly simpler than the first question, which calls
for a free response. Open-ended questions are the most difficult
kind of questions because the student must recall, organize, and
give back the information. After the students have mastered the

easier questions, the instructor should ask the more difficult types of questions until the students are able to answer recall questions about a variety of exercises and reading materials.

The second teaching principle is to vary the selection. Here the reading teacher may use two approaches. The first is to provide an analogous selection on a lower reading level. If biology students are having a problem with a passage classifying parts of the body by function, the teacher can give some a simpler exercise about classification and function, such as the following: "What general topic includes pliers, hammer, chisel, screw driver, and tool box?" After practicing such exercises, of varying degrees of difficulty, the students will eventually be able to provide the required response at the original level.

Another way to vary the selection is to change the content to one which is more familiar. If students are reading a passage in *Macbeth* concerning Lady Macbeth's influence over her husband, and are unable to see the relationship of subtle dominance by the woman, then the instructor might suggest an analogy. Discussing the more familiar biblical example in which Eve influences Adam may help students grasp the relationship in *Macbeth*. After mentioning more familiar analogous relationships, the class is prepared to address the less familiar selection from *Macbeth*.

The third teaching principle is to present an alternate context that involves the same concepts. College students may find that viewing a film clarifies the reading material. In mini-courses and back-to-back courses, the reading teacher can augment the context by films, trips, and discussions. Combining such activities is an example of an effective use of this teaching principle at the college level.

Closely related to the above principle is the fourth and last teaching principle: to give informational clues. If a student cannot get the correct answer, the teacher may provide it, along with an explanation of how it was arrived at. The explanation may help the student to proceed independently in subsequent reading.

The application of these four teaching techniques may be illustrated by the following passage taken from the introduction in a laboratory manual on food microbiology (Seeley and Van Demark, 1972, p. 147).

Like water and eating utensils, food can be sources of disease caused by microorganisms. Also, the growth of microorganisms in food can bring about changes in it, either undesirable—constituting spoilage—or beneficial—producing a more easily preserved food or one having a more desirable flavor. Although the subject of food microbiology is broad, the principles used are merely applications of the basic microbiology described in earlier sections of this manual. For example, food preservation entails asepsis to prevent contamination, as well as the use of environmental extremes, such as acidic surroundings or heat, to inhibit or destroy the microorganisms in food. Microbial spoilage of a food is an example of selective and enrichment culture, with the pH and the chemical composition of the food primarily determining the form of the spoilage.

The remainder of the passage discusses a series of experiments on milk and fermented foods such as sauerkraut, buttermilk, and cheese.

The paragraph lends itself to a question like "What is asepsis?" If the student cannot give a free response to this question, the instructor may replace it by asking whether asepsis in food (a) causes spoilage, (b) is expensive, or (c) prevents contamination? If the entire passage proves difficult, the teacher might refer to the textbook, where the material is explained in greater detail. Alternatively the discussion might be limited to the experiments with milk, since most students are familiar with the souring of milk. Finally the teacher might provide background information by demonstrating experiments or showing films.

Practice Techniques for Reading Assignments. The ultimate aim of instruction is to prepare the student to successfully complete the typical assignments given in college courses. Brown and Adams (1968) state that the efficient comprehension of materials requires that students adapt their reading style to the nature of the material and to their purpose in reading it. Each curriculum area has its own logic, body of data, vocabulary, and concepts, and therefore its own characteristic writing patterns and structures. Students must learn to recognize and understand such patterns. In order to understand the general patterns of a discipline, readers may adapt their reading styles to the particular materials. Students find that their comprehension increases if they follow three steps: preparation for a particular assignment, analysis of the content and structure, and synthesis, a process by which the reader makes the passage personally relevant.

When preparing to read a text, the first step is to explore. Brown and Adams (1968) offer such suggestions as:

1. Read the introduction or foreword quickly to see the rationale for the book, what it purports to do, and how it may differ from previous editions.
2. Look at the table of contents to see what important ideas and topics are covered, their relative importance (as indicated by the number of pages devoted to each), and the order in which they are covered.
3. Check the copyright date to ascertain how recent the book is. This is especially relevant in the natural and social sciences, less so in the humanities.
4. Investigate the format of the book. Do the chapters have summaries? Are typographical aids such as bold type used to highlight concepts? What are the functions of marginal notes or subheadings?
5. Look for special study aids. Is there a glossary or bibliography? What materials are included in the appendices? Examine the index. Check some of the concepts that seem important.

These five suggestions are suitable for the initial exploration of an entire book; however, they also apply to weekly or daily reading assignments. The student should have an overview of a particular reading assignment before beginning to read.

The second step is to analyze for the content. In this step students learn to read the material carefully. Whereas the first step applies to all written materials, this step is specific in its application to subject areas. Materials in the social sciences, the natural sciences, and the humanities differ sufficiently so that distinctive writing patterns can be identified and analyzed in each area as an aid to comprehension.

In the social sciences, the following characteristic writing patterns are found: (1) Details, illustrations, and examples are used to support a major idea. Students must learn to subsume the minor details under the major headings. (2) Definitions, often quite complex, are essential to the development of the thesis. Students must learn to recognize both the extended definition (when an entire chapter is devoted to explaining one complex term) and the specialized definition (a particular use of an old term or the coining of a new one). (3) Comparisons between two sets of circumstances are used to better explain the relationship of one to the other. (4) Cause and effect patterns are introduced to convey the underlying sense and order of events. This pattern requires careful reading since the relationship of cause to effect may not be directly stated, but left for the reader to infer. Sequences of events are important aspects of this writing pattern. (5) Complicated arguments incorporate reasons and generalizations, along with their exceptions. In this sophisticated writing pattern, the individual points of the discussion are as important as the conclusion. Complicated arguments make extensive use of connective phrases, prepositional phrases, and adverbial phrases to signal equivalences, contradictions, summaries, and exceptions. (6) Mixtures of fact, interpretation, and opinion are presented to increase the reader's understanding of the information and the author's opinions. Students need to distinguish fact from opinion.

In the natural sciences, Adams (1970) has identified five important writing patterns: (1) A classification pattern in which the subject of a discussion is divided into parts, signaled by subheadings. (2) A process-description pattern in which the separate steps are presented in order or sequence to describe a process and how it works. (3) A factual-statement pattern which combines facts, interpretations, and opinions. (4) A problem solving pattern which recounts problems and their solutions. (5) An experiment instruction pattern, important in laboratory work, which guides the experimenter-reader to discover the purpose, necessary equipment, order of steps, and results of the experiment. A good deal of writing in the natural sciences combines several of these patterns in a complex matrix. Thus, a passage may begin with a fact description, move to classification, and then to a discussion of a process.

In the humanities, comprehension tasks are quite different. In literature, tasks differ according to whether the student is asked to analyze imaginative writing, a novel, or expository critical prose.

The different forms or genres of imaginative literature set different analytic tasks. The reader must consider character, setting, plot, point of view, style, and theme as important aspects of a work. Literal questions ask the reader to analyze the specific details of what happens: who? what? and when? Questions on a critical level are concerned with the whys and hows of a story. The most personal response to literature is elicited by questions in the affective domain, questions which ask the reader to examine his feelings for the material or to explain likes and dislikes. These three types of questions may be asked about any work of imaginative literature—short story, novel, play, or poem. Expository writing in the humanities, which seeks to explain or evaluate any of the preceding genres, uses many of the same writing patterns as the social sciences.

Synthesis, the final step in comprehension, is the process by which students make what they read more significant. It utilizes the preceding steps and depends greatly on some of the study skills which will be described in the next section. Students internalize texts, or make them relevant, through critical thinking. They now review the content and organize it for assimilation, retention, and future use. They compare the material with other sources, class lectures, previous knowledge, or other books and materials on the same topic. A certain amount of rereading may be done for the sake of clarification. Harris and Sipay (1975) indicate that a very important component of comprehension is this ability to synthesize or weave ideas together. As the printed word yields meaning and stimulates the reader to think, the comprehension process is complete and the reader can use the reading material as a tool for further knowledge. The decoding process is no longer the focus for the learner. That process becomes subsidiary to thinking and organizing the reading materials. These study skills are the mature processes by which learning is organized; the next section of this chapter will discuss those skills.

Summary. The foregoing description of methodologies, organized so that they seem systematic and sequential, belies what actually takes place in a reading class. In a typical class, the teacher extemporaneously chooses methods and practices as they are needed in the immediate reading situation. The instructor might move from a critical evaluation of a passage to a discussion of vocabulary relating the interpretation of the meaning of a word to the evaluation of the passage, and then end the class with a review of certain affixes. Or, the teacher might focus discussion of an article or passage through the use of questions covering the range of comprehension skills from literal recall of items to critical evaluation of the author's tone. Such a discussion might conclude with an exploration of new material for the next assignment. This style of teaching is eclectic in that the instructor picks and chooses what seems best at the time, using highly structured programmed material at one time and then, when appropriate, conducting an open discussion to relate a text to the students' particular background. In all decisions about methodology, the teacher's basic goal is to provide the most meaningful reading experience for the students.

Study Skills

As students master the basic reading skills, they become aware of a need to further improve their study skills. Three particular skills help students become more efficient and productive in their assignments: flexibility of reading rate, syntopical reading, and systematic study skills. Once students acquire the basic reading skills, they can concentrate on using these skills in the acquisition of new knowledge. The skills outlined here can and should be taught at every level.

Flexibility of Reading Rate. Speed reading is one of the reading skills most popular with students. Overwhelmed by the amount of reading they must do in college, students are anxious to increase their reading speed as one way to improve their study skills. In comparing slow and fast readers, Holmes and Singer (1966) found some interesting differences. They determined that the abilities needed to improve the speed of a moderately fast reader differ greatly from those needed to improve the speed of a slow reader. The fast reader uses highly organized subskills so that reading functions as a unified process. The slow reader has not organized the subskills so reading is more analytical and the mechanical aspects claim attention. Reading speed is also dependent on the store of information possessed by the student—the greater the amount of previous reading done, the greater the diversity of life experiences, the easier it is to read.

While students often complain that their speed is poor, a reading teacher should never encourage students to increase their speed unless they are clearly ready for it. To emphasize students' reading speed before they have adequate decoding, vocabulary, and comprehension skills is to invite frustration and failure. Students who read slowly because they have poor word recognition skills or poor comprehension must first develop these basic reading skills.

Some students have sufficient reading skills but read slowly because they are inflexible in applying the skills that they possess. These students tend to read at the same rate whether they are looking at scholarly journals, reading an assignment for a class, or diverting themselves with some easy recreational reading. For such students, group or individual work on flexibility of rate should produce great dividends in overall reading power. Adjusting one's reading rate to one's purpose is an appropriate skill for instruction at any level.

Techniques for increasing rate involve the use of timed passages and various mechanical pacing devices for controlling reading rate. However, rates derived from such exercises are meaningless without an accompanying comprehension score and an evaluation of the level of the materials read. In any case, students may not transfer the greater speed achieved on these exercises to the assigned reading that they must do on their own.

Rather than concentrate solely on reading speed, remedial programs would do well to stress flexiblility of rate. Harris and Sipay (1970) provide a list of four reading rates and the purposes appropriate to each. (1) Skimming a text is useful when the student wants to get the gist of the material, to find a reference, to locate new material, to refresh his memory, or to answer a specific question. (2) Rapid reading is appropriate when the reader needs to get a general idea of the content, to find specific references, to locate material, or to review familiar material. (3) A normal pace should be followed when the student has to get details, grasp the main idea, read new material, solve a problem, or answer a complex question. (4) Careful reading, at a slow pace, is required when the reader proposes to evaluate the material or raise questions about it, to outline or summarize, and to analyze the thoughts presented.

The sheer difficulty of some material may also determine the reading rate. Thus a student reading a poem, a mathematics problem, or a philosophical passage may need to read it aloud to himself. This subvocalization process is entirely appropriate to some demanding materials. However, subvocalization retards reading speed. Students who subvocalize inappropriately or excessively should be made aware of their problem and given individual help.

In general, flexibility of reading rate will be a by-product of a good reading comprehension program and should not be the main focus in a remedial program.

Syntopical Reading. Adler and Van Doren (1972) use the term *syntopical reading skills* to describe the skills needed for reading two or more books on the same subject. First, students must realize that one text alone may not do justice to the topic; often other sources are equally, or more, relevant. In deciding which books to read, students should check copyright dates and currently popular authors. When writing a paper or researching a topic, students should be encouraged to skim through a book or read it superficially before settling down to a careful study. At this point they should use the table of contents, index, charts, and tables in order to significantly cut down the time they spend in choosing material for careful reading. Once the student has chosen the books that appear most important, he is ready to follow the five steps in syntopical reading:

1. Find the relevant passages: Read not just to have read the book, but to serve immediate specific needs. Read only to secure the information required.
2. Establish the terms: Identify the key terms and note whether the authors redefine traditional terms to suit particular intentions.
3. Put the questions clearly: Establish hypotheses relevant to the reading. Consider both the questions originally asked by the authors and new questions that arise from reading their texts.

4. Define the issues: Note where authors disagree, reach incompatible conclusions, or state inconclusive results.
5. Analyze the discussion: Organize the materials, analyze them, and present an ordered discussion of the results of the entire process.

These steps must be taken if the student is to write term papers, answer examination questions, or participate in class discussion, for real learning takes place only when the reading of material becomes interactive. No amount of comprehension is worthwhile unless the student can communicate clearly the fruits of the reading.

Procedures for Systematic Study. To improve the quality and efficiency of their studying, students should first examine their study habits: the physical conditions in which they study (time and place) and their motivation for studying. Students often complain that although they spend many hours studying, they have little to show for their effort and time. Better study habits can be developed if students are taught how to analyze their present habits. Students who need to make better use of their time, for example, can first determine how they currently use their time by keeping a chart of a week's work and noting how much time is actually spent studying. When students see how many interruptions they allow, and the extent of each, they are encouraged to replan their time, perhaps by replacing social hours in the cafeteria with study hours in the library. Sometimes students find that they work willingly in courses that interest them but leave more difficult or less absorbing subjects for the last minute. This habit may be changed by establishing a scheduled study time for each course.

Many students underestimate the effects of the physical conditions in which they study. College freshmen insist that in high school they always studied with the radio or television blaring at them and nonetheless received good grades. Some students can tune out distractions and study in noisy places. But for the majority, the more serious college-level studying requires optimum conditions. Most residential colleges have evolved rules or customs for the maintenance of quiet study areas. In commuter colleges, students whose homes may lack the necessary quiet and privacy should be encouraged to study in the library—where quiet usually reigns.

Good study habits are different from good attitudes toward studying. Attitudes are more basic and involve motivation, drive, and curiosity. The psychology of motivation is complex; motivation often reflects the student's ability to set and reach realistic goals. For example, some students find that their motivation lags because the goal of a college degree is so far away. Such students need to set short-term goals to keep them going—read this chapter, write this paper. Other students can work consistently with long-range goals—get an A in a course, earn a B.A. degree. Negative motivations such as text anxiety and fear of failure can hinder achievement, while self-confidence, drive for achievement, and curiosity promote study.

After reviewing their study habits and attitudes, students may find that they need to refine certain study techniques. Many students come to college with outmoded notetaking rituals learned in high school. They take too many notes, getting down all the specifics and none of the general questions. The style for lecture notes should be an in-class jotting down of the important ideas. Often the teacher's lecture differs from the assigned readings and the student who cannot abstract the important ideas common to both is at a disadvantage. Hodgins (1970, p. 20) defines good lecture notes by saying "Whatever else notes should be, they should be functional—aids to jog the student's memory. In style, notes should resemble an economical telegram sent to a moron."

Students also need to take notes on the assigned texts. Here students usually underline the important ideas. Anyone who has ever bought a second-hand text has observed the differences in the underlining skills of previous owners. Some students underline little, while others seem to underline everything. The goal of underlining is somewhere in between—to help students to identify important ideas, both in the original reading and when they come to review for examinations.

More important than either of these skills is "making a note," the jotting down of ideas, thoughts, feelings, hunches, and questions that come to the reader's mind. It is in this process of note-making that the reader develops a firm grasp of the broader questions of the discipline. These notes reflect the fleeting ideas whose direct relevance is sensed by the student, but not yet made explicit. They are the questions the reader poses: "Is *this* the result of *that*?" "Is this why it happened?" "What is the relationship between these two ideas X and Y?" Notes like these, made in the margins of texts and notebooks, perhaps not directly related to the content at hand, represent the seeds of creative, critical thinking.

Notes taken on lectures and texts may be supplemented by model study guides, prepared at first by the instructor and then by the students themselves, as a pattern for their own study and analysis of the course readings. Study guides focus a student's attention on the material, raise questions about relationships and definitions of words, examine writing patterns, and lead a student through the delineation of a particular point being made by the author. They sometimes indicate which less important sections can be skimmed. Study guides tell students to look for certain information and then ask them to analyze, interpret, or evaluate that information. By practicing with such study guides, students can move toward independence.

A more specific skill which is helpful is systematic cramming *at the proper time*. Most teachers warn students against the practice of postponing study until just before exams and then cramming. However, cramming at the beginning of the term, as a way to get an idea of the entire course, can be an excellent study technique. Hodgins (1970) describes an exercise in which students are given a half-hour to "read" and compare two books, Wylie's *Village of the Vaucluse,* a sociological view of life in a French village, and *The Navaho,* by Kluckhohn and Leighton, a study in cultural anthropology. The students are asked to spend eight minutes with the first book, looking at the child-rearing practices and nothing more. Then they are given three minutes to make notes. Next, the students are asked to determine what the government is like and to relate child-rearing practices to government. There are two more eight-minute passes at this book, one spent searching for economic behavior and the other on a topic of the student's choice that weaves the earlier topics together. When the second book is introduced, the students are given four more eight-minute periods, this time to make comparisons. At the end, they take an examination dealing with the similarities and differences between the two sources. The results, which are often surprisingly good, give the students confidence in their ability to deal with the pertinent ideas of the course.

Figure 3 illustrates the usefulness of the cramming method. The circles represent the areas of the books concerned with child-rearing, government, and economics. Where the circles overlap, the ideas and events described reveal important aspects of the structure of the society. Other areas are proportionally less valuable. This organization can be very illuminating to the student new to the material and unaware of priorities. Areas labeled in order of importance are:

1. Vital—labeled 1—that which all experts in the field are expected to know.
2. Importance—labeled 2—material which is necessary.
3. Relevant—labeled 3—convenient if mastered.
4. Conditionally superfluous—labeled 4—material not necessary to the topics but sometimes the source of surprises in examinations.

This exercise in cramming thus encourages students to study with the larger questions of the course in mind.

One other technique to help students focus their efforts in studying is the *SQ3R* method developed by Robinson (Harris and Sipay, 1979). This procedure asks the student to do the following:

1. Survey the material to be read, to get a quick overview.
2. Question to guide careful reading; turn heading and topics into questions.
3. Read the material to answer the questions.
4. Recite the material by underlining, note-taking, or recall.
5. Review, either immediately or at intervals, to aid in long-term memory.

The *SQ3R* method is appropriate for students who can already select essential ideas and synthesize material.

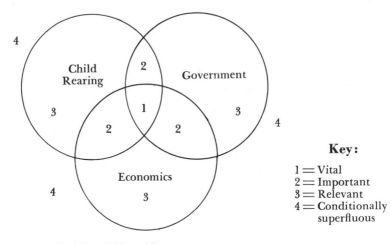

Source: Hodgins, 1970, p. 15.

Figure 3. Overlapping Frames of Reference

Support Services

As colleges have developed programs in reading, a variety of support services have proved helpful to faculty and to students. Services most useful to reading programs include reading laboratories, tutoring programs, counseling services, special library orientation sessions, and diagnostic testing. These services are necessary adjuncts to reading classes, providing both individualized academic and personal support.

Reading Laboratory

Most reading programs include a reading laboratory, which provides a variety of materials to supplement the classroom teacher's work. The best laboratories are those which offer eclectic materials chosen from a broad range, rather than housing only a few machines or other resources. Because students vary in their learning styles, multisensory materials—filmstrips, cassettes, and workbooks—are particularly valuable. In vocabulary study, the visual presentation of the word coupled with the correct pronunciation helps students who have never heard some of the vocabulary words. Many laboratories have reading pacers, machines which present visual materials at a set rate of speed, that can encourage students to increase their speed without sacrificing comprehension. However, students cannot use such audiovisual resources without direction and supervision. Ideally the student arrives in the lab with a definite prescription based on the teacher's diagnosis of individual need. This diagnostic prescriptive approach considers a student's particular needs that cannot be met in class and utilizes the specific learning strengths of the individual student.

While class reading sessions are the usual setting for teaching a skill, in the reading laboratory, reinforcement of that skill takes place through the individual prescription. In the lab, a particular skill can be applied to a variety of content materials, or an instructor can indicate extra skill practice for students who need it. Students who have been absent for the initial teaching of a skill can make up the work. Students who have mastered a particular skill and need no further practice can be given an alternate assignment more appropriate to their individual progress.

The focus on individual prescription and progress in the reading laboratory points to the need for the laboratory staff to develop a detailed catalogue of the available resources. Such a catalogue allows the teacher to provide a variety of choices for particular skills, levels, and interests.

Tutoring

One support service of particular value to a reading program is the availability of peer tutors. Tutors are usually chosen from capable upper-division students, particularly those who are doing well in their own academic majors. However, most tutors, whatever their merits, need a training program if they are to succeed. Training sessions may emphasize the needs of reading students and the design of the program. One successful strategy is to have prospective tutors bring in one of their own papers. By analyzing these papers, they discover how word meaning can be deduced from context, and how they themselves use vocabulary, function words, prefixes, and suffixes. They perceive their own formal and logical strengths and weaknesses, and thus learn to see reading as a thinking process that entails more than the mere decoding of written words. Having come this far themselves, they are ready to consider methods for sharing strategies and techniques with the remedial student.

Above and beyond this, tutors who have successfully completed several courses in their major field are in a particularly strong position to help the reading students with materials in that field. While the reading instructor, whose students are enrolled in many academic courses, may not be able to satisfy individual needs, the tutor can provide individual help with assignments in the particular academic area. Tutors can also help to supervise the diagnostic prescriptive assignments set for students in the reading laboratory.

Counseling

With the inception of open admissions, counseling for the new student population became a top priority. Supportive counseling units were structured to help students with questions about financial aid, registration procedures, grading, and so on. In addition to these counseling programs, some colleges have tried to have counselors work more intimately with reading teachers. Sometimes students ask for counseling help when in fact it is reading help that they need. Students who complain that they cannot cover the work or cannot concentrate may need specific help in taking notes or in organizing study time. Other students may actually need counseling sessions to assess their attitudes toward their work and education. In both cases, the counselors need to know about the reading skills required in courses commonly taken by freshmen. Reading instructors can provide counselors with this information and correlate it with the skills possessed by the student. Thus a counselor will be able to plan an academic program for a student that will be commensurate with the student's ability and will not overwhelm him.

During counseling sessions, a discussion that begins with a

student's problems with course work may in fact reflect the student's deep personal need to communicate to a supportive person. When the counseling and reading programs are mutually supportive of one another, a coordinated program can be set up, in which reading materials for class are taken from counseling materials discuss problems. Such coordinated programs can be team-taught with great benefit to the students, who receive reading instruction in class and individual counseling in private sessions with the counselor on the team.

Library Aid

An unusual but very helpful support service is the availability of a special librarian for remedial students and their instructors. Faculty can call upon the librarian for student tours and for orientation sessions on the use of library facilities. These orientation sessions are more detailed than the usual library orientation. In addition to pointing out the features and use of the library materials, the librarian gives the students actual practice work with task cards and worksheets. The lessons in library work include using card catalogues, indexes, abstracts, and specialized dictionaries. Students also learn to use microfilm and microfiche files, readers, and printers.

The aid and support given by the library service is particularly important to students whose previous library experiences have been minimal. Quick tours tend to overwhelm the students; far more valuable is the opportunity to return for help from the librarian as needed during the semester. This remedial services librarian is available to students who are preparing research papers, as well as to faculty who need particular help in choosing materials for a topic to be taught. The librarian may also serve students taking mini-courses on writing term papers.

Screening and Diagnostic Services

Another support service needed by reading programs is a clinic that offers the specialized diagnostic tests that assess perceptual acuity and screening tests that provide a highly specific profile of a student's reading skills. These services are usually available at colleges that offer a clinical training program in reading remediation. If a college does not have such a program, a minimal set of screening procedures should be available to support the reading program. Students referred for such services include those who score at the lowest levels on the placement test (usually the 10th percentile or lower). A thorough series of diagnostic tests is needed to isolate these students' strengths and weaknesses. Most reading experts agree that students whose test scores are so far below the norm should be screened for perceptual problems.

Loss of auditory acuity, the ability to hear sounds at different intensities and frequencies, can cause the student to miss specific sounds in conversation and in lectures. Auditory perception, sound blending, and auditory closure skills are necessary to organize auditory sensory data into language. To assess the student's ability to discriminate auditory data, tests such as the Wepman Auditory Discrimination Test (1973) or the Goldman-Fristoe-Woodcock Test of Auditory Discrimination (1970) can be administered. If these screening procedures indicate problems, the student should be referred to a specialist or to a clinic.

Visual defects are another correlate of reading failure. Kirk, Kliebhan, and Lerner (1978) indicate the conflicting evidence with regard to reading failure and visual problems. Farsightedness is found more frequently among disabled readers than average readers, and eye-muscle imbalance is related more significantly to reading failure than are acuity factors. Still other studies say there is no direct relationship between reading problems and visual defects. The Keystone Visual Survey Test measures visual acuity at normal distances and visual function at reading distance. The test evaluates overconvergence, underconvergence, and fusion—three measures of the ways in which the eye muscles function together. Based on the results of these tests, students may be referred to an eye specialist. Students who complain of fatigue while reading, or who say they fall asleep at their books, may have focusing problems. These students may have forced themselves into visual accommodations which hinder comfort and ease in prolonged reading. Reading becomes an uncomfortable process and these students do not read of their own volition. Lower standardized test scores can be one manifestation of such problems.

For some students, such auditory and visual problems are the underlying cause of reading disability. Other students lack visual motor skills and visual memory skills. The Bender Visual-Motor Gestalt Test (1946) has been found helpful to trained reading diagnosticians in assessing visual motor skills. Poor visual motor coordination, while not a definitive cause of reading disability, is another indication of vulnerability in the reading process.

There are also a number of diagnostic tests which evaluate basic reading skills. Reading diagnosticians should routinely administer a test of the student's decoding skills. Often a student may have amassed a large sight vocabulary, but he has little or no ability to decode an unknown word. A useful group test of decoding ability is the California Phonics Test. This is a criterion-referenced test; students who do not meet the criterion may be given an individual diagnostic test such as the Bryant Decoding Test. Because the Bryant Test uses nonsense syllables rather than real words, students cannot guess or use familiar sight words; they must rely solely on their decoding skills.

Once the specific reading profile of the student has been assembled, a course of instruction is planned. A number of students who have been referred for these diagnostic services are found to have some type of learning disability which had gone undiagnosed at lower school levels. As more and more students with learning problems present themselves for college educations, colleges must begin to meet their needs much the same as do special education classes in the elementary and high schools.

Conclusion

This chapter has addressed the tasks of those who would organize a reading program at the college level. A remaining question, rightly and simply asked, is "Are reading programs worthwhile?" The answer to that question is not a simple one. To college administrators, worth can mean that the students learn to read well enough to meet standards set on tests with particular national norms. For these administrators, the worth of the reading program is based on the number of students who meet the criterion at the end of instruction. Most reading instructors would disagree with such a simplistic expectation. Yes, many students will meet the criterion; however, many others will not. Progress is not always immediately manifested on standardized tests.

Any evaluation of the worth of a program needs to take into consideration the many variables that influence the reading process. When a recent college graduate was asked what were her most valuable college experiences, she singled out two teachers and two skills they had taught well; the first was an instructor of literature who taught the student to read fiction and the second was a political science teacher who taught the skill of reading nonfiction. Because she learned these two skills, the student felt the four years of college were worthwhile: a lifetime of learning was now available to her.

3

Linda Ann Kunz

English as a Second Language

❋ ❋ ❋ ❋ ❋ ❋ ❋ ❋ ❋ ❋ ❋ ❋ ❋ ❋ ❋ ❋ ❋

If asked, teachers at seventeen colleges of the City University of New York could probably open classroom doors that would show an observer every variety of adult English as a Second Language being taught and learned today. The observer might see a class called English for the Foreign Born resembling the one in which H*Y*M*A*N K*A*P*L*A*N first came to grips with his second language, as well as an open classroom where students' name tags hang on pegs which indicate the language-learning activity they

Note: I am grateful not only to my coauthors in this book for their steady feedback and encouragement during our project but to my friend and colleague Ann Raimes of Hunter College, whose clear, eclectic voice is so present and so appreciated in this chapter, especially in its methodology section. I am also indebted to the CUNY ESL teachers who painstakingly gathered and wrote up the data that resulted in an organized goldmine of information about CUNY ESL programs: Wolhee Choe, Linda Barker, Gay Brookes, and, again, Ann Raimes.

have chosen for the time being: controlled composition, picture composition, small-group work with a tape recorder, aural-oral practice with colored rods or any of a dozen or more individual, paired or group tasks. One teacher might be the center and initiator of all communication in the classroom, another a prominent part though hardly saying a word throughout the class period, a third not prominent at all but moving around the classroom talking to individuals and groups in an amiable, seemingly informal way. The observer might hear students' native languages and translation being used in the teaching—this in the most traditional and in the most experimental classes. He might see students ranging in age from seventeen to seventy, representatives of as many as fifteen different cultural backgrounds in a single class and an equally wide variation in the students' economic status and educational experience. One ESL class would have true beginners in it, people learning to say "My name is Sonia" or "Take two green rods." Next door a class in writing for bilingual students might be discussing the use of narrative in an essay, as exemplified by Orwell's "Shooting an Elephant." At some colleges, students nearly as beginning and nearly as advanced could be found together in the same classroom.

It is gratuitous to say that the main feature of a college English as a Second Language (ESL) program is diversity. Yet when a teacher or department faces a spectrum of students who range from a middle-aged, well-educated diplomat's wife, whose only need appears to be the mastery of spoken English, to an eighteen-year-old who has spent a good part of his life moving back and forth between a Caribbean island and a New York City ghetto and has had little experience with any of the basic school skills, educators must ask a fundamental question: "What do they have in common besides the fact that they are more fluent in another language than in English?" And there are many related questions: "Can they learn together? Who has the best chance of succeeding in college work? Is ESL even a 'remedial' or 'basic education' area in the first place?"

The ESL experience of the City University of New York (CUNY) has shown, at the very least, that any nonnative speaker of English of college age or above can go to college to learn the language. A factory worker can take an ESL course in a continuing education department and not be concerned with matriculation or customary admission requirements. A foreign student heading for a Ph.D. degree in mathematics can, if he needs to, learn the names of the numbers in English in the same school where he will earn the first of his several degrees. A skills-deficient bilingual student can study reading and writing taught from an ESL point of view. Colleges can accommodate the diversity among ESL students and their needs and college teachers can teach the very basics of English with a realistic hope of seeing many of their students progress rapidly within the college community or outside in the larger community.

CUNY has come up with no ESL formulae. If anything, it has proved that formulae are impossible if an ESL population is as diverse as that of New York City or any other large, metropolitan area. The following pages describe what has happened in ESL at CUNY, particularly during the past decade, since the beginning of an open admissions policy. The experience is rich but in no way complete. The mistakes and failures, as much as the successes, suggest something of what to look for and what to avoid in an ESL program and show what good reason there is to welcome the wide cultural experience ESL students bring to the university setting.

ESL Students

Paul Goodman once said in a talk at Teachers College, Columbia University, "If we taught people to speak their native language the way we teach them to read, half of them would stutter, and many wouldn't speak at all." This may be a harsh judgment, but it makes a point: we *don't* formally teach people to speak their native language, yet they *do* speak and comprehend it perfectly well for the social milieu in which it was learned. This is a most important commonality among ESL students—whoever they are, they have already mastered in their first language at least two of the communications skills they need in English. They do not need to learn to speak and comprehend; they need to learn to speak and comprehend *English*. If they can read and write in their first language, those skills do not evaporate; they have to be applied to English reading and writing. This competence is all too easy to overlook if a person cannot express himself to a placement tester, adviser, or teacher, and ESL students are often the most talked-down-to students in a college population. ESL teachers and other professionals correctly note that ESL is not a remedial field and that ESL students, with no more exceptions than in any random college sampling, are not "learning disabled" or in any other way less able to meet the demands of college work than their native English-speaking counterparts. ESL students do need more time to meet language skills requirements and usually more attention; their numbers do include skills-deficient students. But their abilities, aspirations and past successes are as wide-ranging as those of the larger population, and they should be met just as individually.

There are three groups within a college ESL population: visiting foreign students, foreign-born American residents, and American-educated bilingual students. Each group has a counterpart among native English-speaking students, and it might be useful to teachers or administrators with limited exposure to ESL students to see them in relation to students they already know.

Until 1970 and the advent of an open admissions policy, CUNY had two main types of students studying English as a second language: foreign students and the foreign born. Although these terms have a touch of the ridiculous about them since one would have to be foreign born to be a foreign student, they do refer to two rather different groups still present not only in New York but all over the United States.

The most precise use of the term *foreign students* refers to those persons studying in the United States on a student visa, but it has been used more generally to mean people who have come here to study (usually in a specialized field) with the intention of returning to their own countries on completion of a degree program. Foreign students are usually, though not exclusively, of college age and have come to the United States on the basis of academic excellence in their home countries and/or substantial economic means. ESL teachers tend to anticipate that these students will be cultured, well-educated, highly motivated, and diligent. Although cultural differences, homesickness, and critical views of America and Americans may make for difficulty in adaptation, a fairly high level of self-esteem and a clear sense of identity among most foreign students favor their academic success. Their only native English-speaking counterparts in the United States are British, Irish, Canadian, Australian, and New Zealand foreign students. This *whole* group is often felt to be one of the most desirable from a faculty viewpoint.

What distinguishes the foreign born is their intention to make their permanent home in the United States. Typically they are persons of all ages who wish to learn English not only to study but to work and live in this country. Most have jobs and have therefore appeared in the largest numbers in evening classes sponsored by departments of adult or continuing education or a school of general studies program. Although most learn English through free programs offered by the public school system, religious organizations, and various service agencies, sizable numbers have chosen to enroll in college, many beginning as nonmatriculating students hoping to earn a degree at a later time. Their native English-speaking counterparts are any adult learners who see work and study as a feasible, perhaps necessary, combination in their lives. Financial means, educational background, and language skills proficiency vary enormously among the foreign born, but, on the whole, maturity and seriousness of purpose bring them well-recommended to the ESL classroom.

The open admissions policy brought a third kind of ESL student to the University, and sheer numbers forced major changes, including the mingling of students with quite different backgrounds, attitudes, and purposes in newly expanded ESL programs. This third group, once included among open admissions students because they did not meet earlier CUNY admissions standards, are recent high school graduates who have had all or most of their education in this country often having learned English and their first language simultaneously. Like their native English-speaking counterparts in reading and basic writing classes, many have met more failure than success in school thus far. In some cases inadequate English is the only reason for such failure; often, however, there is the same combination of skills deficiencies, prejudices and preconceptions, and other personal and sociological factors which make college life difficult for nearly all such students, no matter what first language they speak. Whatever the reason, it

takes courage for them to enter college. Family and financial problems may be severe, self-esteem low, and notions of college work
vague. There may be a cultural tradition pulling a student in what
seems to be the opposite direction from his or her college aspirations. These are students who have taken on great odds to get a
college education, and that should be respected.

Of the more than 5000 students in ESL classes at CUNY
approximately 60 percent are speakers of Spanish. The community
colleges tend to have the higher proportions, senior colleges lower,
but none has fewer than 35 percent Spanish-speakers in its ESL
program. The next largest language groups are French-speaking,
ranging from 10 to 35 percent, and Chinese-speaking, ranging from
3 to 20 percent. As many as a hundred other languages are represented in the student body, but only Italian, Greek, Korean, Russian, and Rumanian are spoken by sufficient numbers of students
to form small language communities. And this matter of language
communities is important: a student who has friends and
classmates who speak his first language has the benefit of social
support but the academic disadvantage of speaking English only
with his teachers and a few slight acquaintances.

The length of time that an ESL student has been in this
country is an important variable, but one that is hard to use predictively. It is certainly *not* an accurate generalization to say "the
longer, the better." Yes, bilingual people who were born here or
came at an early age are likely to speak and comprehend English
with ease, but they may have had little or no chance to learn to read
and write without dealing with a language problem at the same
time. Recent immigrants, in contrast, may have tremendous difficulties with everyday English, but the majority are literate, often
quite skilled, in their first language.

It is hard to say how much the variables just discussed have
to do with ESL students' success or failure in university work. No
matter what his background and previous education, the individual
ESL student has to respect the English language and English-
speaking people and their culture enough to invest himself
wholeheartedly in what he is learning. An ESL teacher should want
to look as carefully and honestly as individual students will allow at
attitudes and experiences which may have some bearing on their

learning of English. Class discussions, conferences, and writing assignments are appropriate means of learning more about students as long as students can avoid revealing more than they want to. Teachers should ask questions like these about each student: (1) What brought this student to the United States; was it a matter of choice or of political, economic, or familial pressure? (2) Have her experiences in learning English been largely positive or negative? (3) Does she feel at home in this country? (4) Does she plan to stay here? (5) Does she have American friends? (6) How does she feel English and American culture compare with her first language and culture? (7) Does she like speaking English? (8) Does she see her treatment in this class, this college, this city, as fair?

Concern and understanding might increase if teachers ask themselves similar questions about their own feelings, for example: What brought me to this classroom, and was it a matter of choice or of academic or economic pressure? Have my experiences in teaching English been largely positive or negative? Do I feel at home in this field, with these students? ESL teachers need this understanding because, although they are not counselors or advisers, they are often the only college personnel that ESL students talk to. ESL students often do not know about, or are reluctant to seek out, the help of college counseling and advisement services. Furthermore, since ESL classes are smaller and meet more regularly and for more hours than most other courses, they encourage interpersonal involvement. If an ESL teacher does not show that he is willing to step beyond the customary college boundaries of impersonality if the student wishes to, the student is not likely to take such an initiative elsewhere.

Research on motivation among ESL students has shown quite conclusively how great the effect of attitude is on language learning, but it has not yet shown whether inquiry, understanding, and kind criticism can change negative attitudes and feelings of alienation or superiority so often hidden under extremely civil and cooperative exteriors. Whether it is the student alone or teacher and student both who are hiding such feelings, whether the data are complete or not, one should look beyond academic matters to find out why there is such a high rate of failure among ESL students. Generally speaking, CUNY ESL teachers rarely expect more than 60 percent of their students to pass a course on the first try, and there are students who have been in an ESL sequence for as long as five years. The fact that any one of these students may have the same language background, academic preparation, number of years in this country, and even English fluency as another student who took those courses four or five years ago and is now in graduate school should encourage teachers, as much as possible, to know their ESL students personally and individually.

Diagnosis and Placement

Like reading and basic writing, ESL programs aim to integrate matriculating students into the college mainstream with skills equal to those of students who place directly into freshman composition. Freshman composition, then, is the meeting place, the testing ground, for accuracy of placement and for effectiveness of basic skills programs. Figure 1 shows ten different courses in a fairly extensive language arts program in which an incoming freshman might find himself. It should also suggest the enormity of the placement task. (Each dot, of which there are eleven, indicates a possible starting point.)

The ESL programs at CUNY vary greatly in number and level of courses, but most agree on several things: that oral language fluency must precede a heavy emphasis on reading and writing, that students should be able to skip levels, and that a minimum of three course levels is needed if students include beginners in ESL.

One of the major disagreements—or, at least, variants—is the point at which ESL students should join their native English-speaking counterparts. Though the majority do so at the freshman composition level (Model 2 in Figure 2), two alternatives have been tried. The dotted line in the figure indicates the point at which integration occurs. The reasons for such variation seem to be more administrative and economic than pedagogical; factors considered include the size of the ESL staff and whether or not the English department approves an ESL version of freshman composition. No significant difference in students' subsequent achievement has

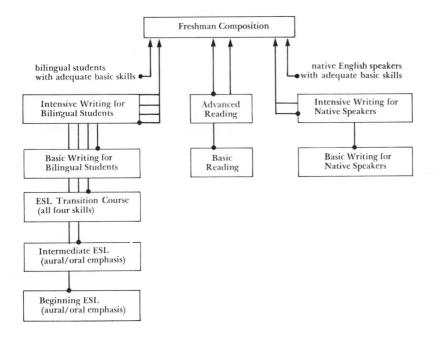

Figure 1. A Developmental English Sequence

been reported though some colleges note that their ESL students have expressed a preference for earlier integration with native English speakers. This issue requires further study.

Special Problems of ESL Placement

Accurate placement in reading, basic writing, and math is difficult enough; however, only one skill area is involved in testing each of these. In ESL there are *four*—aural comprehension, speaking, reading, and writing—and they may be highly disparate in a

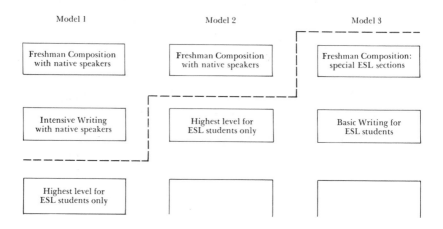

**Figure 2. Models for Integration of ESL and
Native English-Speaking Students**

given student. To illustrate: One student is placed in a beginning
level course because she does not speak English. This *is* an appropriate level for her, but at the same time, she may have a good
educational background and a high degree of literacy and writing
skill in her first language. A second student, American-born or
educated mainly in the United States, places two, even three, levels
higher than the first student because he speaks English fluently, yet
he may be close to illiterate in *two* languages and speak a nonstandard dialect or both. Furthermore, he may not even know how
inadequate his English is for college work because he has gotten
along with it all or most of his life. Does the first student need five
semesters of ESL? Can the second student hope to learn standard
English, reading comprehension, and formal writing skills in two
or three semesters?

Even if existing placement instruments and procedures were
to determine varying skill levels in each student—which they do
not—it would indeed be a prodigious undertaking to offer the

tailor-made course sequences that would be necessary to meet the needs of all ESL students. Some colleges have tried to solve this problem through modular programs and mini-courses which avoid lock-step sequencing and allow students to concentrate on the skill areas they need most. The majority of programs, however, have had to rely on teachers' recommendations for course-skipping and mid-semester transfers and an elaborate grading system to allow students who need the most help to repeat courses without penalty.

Placement Procedures

If a college ESL population is small, a placement interview with ESL faculty or bilingual students' advisers is highly recommended. Unfortunately, most colleges cannot afford this luxury and rely instead on a questionnaire to identify ESL students and a combination of tests to place them.

Questionnaires to Identify ESL Students. The key items on a questionnaire to spot possible ESL students are these: (1) Where were you born? (2) What was the first language you learned? (3) How long have you been living in the United States? Place of birth identifies students who should, even if they are bilingual, be placed among native speakers of English for purely social reasons. Not all teachers agree on this point since an American-born bilingual student's English may indeed show first-language influence, but unless such influence is so great that a student really needs ESL instruction, he is likely to learn better among the kind of classmates with whom he has shared all his educational experience. The second question identifies ESL students but also native speakers of English from Guyana, Panama, the West Indies, and other countries where English is spoken widely if not exclusively. Some of these students may exhibit what appear to be ESL problems but are in fact dialect-related and should be treated differently. The third question is most useful in conjunction with a writing sample and, where necessary, an oral test. Here is where various "mismatches" show up—for example, a person who has lived in this country for many years and has English fluency but little or no writing experience, or a person who has just arrived and can understand and speak very little English but can write a formal essay because of years of traditional instruction in the language in his own country.

Objective Tests for Screening. Almost every CUNY college used some kind of writing sample for the ESL placement even before the Writing Assessment Test was instituted in the spring of 1978, but the large number of students being placed justified the use of a screening instrument as well. This most often took the form of an objective test, whose scores indicated which writing samples should be read. In 1974 the CUNY ESL Council, composed of ESL coor- dinators and teachers from all the colleges, recommended the use of the Michigan Test of English Language Proficiency as most ap- propriate although some colleges found that their ESL populations scored too low for such a test. Bronx Community College, which has only two ESL levels, placed students whose scores were less than 70 in a lower-level course and those with scores between 70 and 85 in an upper-level course. Essays were read where test scores fell into the marginal area between 65 and 75. Any student scoring above 85 on the test was told to return at a later time to take the tests for native speakers of English.

Essay Tests. Prior to 1978, CUNY writing samples varied from a fifteen-minute, 75-word paragraph to a fifty-minute, 250-word composition. Topics for the shorter samples tended to accommo- date the particular thoughts and experiences of ESL students, for example: "Describe your experiences on arriving in the U.S." or "Why did you come to the U.S.?" Longer samples sometimes drew upon ESL experiences as well, but more often tended toward im- personal, expository topics: "All men are created equal. Agree or disagree" or "More and more divorced fathers are taking custody of their children. What are some of the difficulties involved?" These are not recommended topics. Some of them are downright deadly, and CUNY teachers might be the first to admit that if they knew what kinds of topics would appeal to students, test their skills fairly and produce essays that would not bore readers, they would be glad to assign them.

Of the several approaches to placement essay reading tried at CUNY, the most efficient seems to be a holistic reading by a single reader (an ESL teacher) backed up by an in-class essay during the first week of the semester. Holistic reading requires the reader to take only a couple of minutes to read an essay and immediately assign a number or course level on the basis of an overall impression of coherency, content, correctness, and style. Some colleges, before a six-point scale was introduced officially, preferred a numerical rating, especially if readers were new to the college's ESL sequence, but if readers were experienced, assignment directly to course levels precluded an additional reading. There is probably no way—and perhaps no need—to avoid what is happening at CUNY right now: as readers grow accustomed to using the six-point scale, they begin to associate it with the course levels at their own colleges, the result being that one-step placement is still possible.

Some colleges prefer an error count over a holistic reading and are even administering a second placement test after the mandatory Writing Assessment Test in order to retain their local procedures. Error analysis of various kinds is gaining popularity in ESL testing, but there has not been any systematic research on its effectiveness in the CUNY setting as yet.

Oral Tests. Students who have scored very low on an objective test and failed to produce an intelligible writing sample are notified that they must return for a short oral test. One such test used at CUNY is the John Test, so named because it consists of a seven-picture sequence depicting a day in the life of a boy named John. The test takes approximately ten minutes to administer and has three parts: comprehension questions about the pictures, connected discourse (a retelling of John's day as if it happened yesterday), and a series of questions that the student must form on instruction (for example, "Ask me his name," and "Ask me what he'd like to do when he finishes school."). The highest possible score is 100, and although the test has no standardized norms, it has been used with adults and college students over a period of eight years and has proved adequate for beginning and intermediate placement.

Re-Sort Essays. During the first week of the school term, students in all but the lowest ESL levels write a second essay, which their own teacher reads to determine whether everyone has been placed correctly. If the teacher wishes to suggest a change of level, she gives the essay to the ESL coordinator to read; if the coordinator agrees to the change, the student may shift courses by the second or third class meeting. Simultaneous scheduling of different levels facilitates such transfers.

In addition to its use as a placement check, the re-sort essay can serve a second, diagnostic purpose for the individual teacher. At this point, also, error analysis may prove manageable and useful.

Figures 3, 4, and 5 illustrate three models for ESL placement. All three derive from knowledge and experience gained in CUNY ESL programs; there are, therefore, particular omissions and inclusions which reflect CUNY biases but differ from current practice in other college settings. The models presented here, for example, do not use those standardized objective tests designed for native English speakers. Although some CUNY colleges do use tests such as the California Achievement Test (CAT), Sequential Tests of Educational Progress: English Expression (STEP), and the Stanford Tests of Academic Skills, most ESL teachers assert that native speaker tests are not reliable for ESL students.

Neither do the models include tests of aural comprehension; such testing has not proved useful and is time-consuming to administer. All three models, however, include an oral test for lower-level placement in spite of the fact that such tests are just as time-consuming as their aural counterparts. Oral tests are not yet a common placement feature for this reason and also because there are few such tests available for adults, but the need for them will probably be felt more and more as colleges confront squarely the reality of students whose English proficiency levels are so low that written test results are either inadequate or unobtainable.

Model A (see Figure 3)—or, at least, its essay feature—most closely resembles CUNY's Writing Assessment Test. It aims at standardization of placement and exit testing among the colleges and reflects the bias of ESL and basic writing teachers in favor of an essay test as the most valid measure of writing proficiency. It is tremendously demanding of faculty and clerical time and requires careful training in the use of a six-point scale for holistic reading.

Further, such a scale loses its effectiveness if it is interpreted differently by different programs or colleges. The only way to assure standardized scoring may be to have central reading of papers by trained and paid readers.

Figure 3. Model A: Essay/Oral Test/Re-Sort.

1. Preregistration:
    Essay test administered to all entering freshmen
    Identification of ESL students through questions
    answered on essay booklet |

2. Separating of ESL essays from those of native speakers and reading of essays: two readers, one of whom is an ESL teacher; a third reader if there is a significant difference in the scores of the two readers

3. Placement into freshman composition and higher-level ESL courses |

4. Recall of students with lowest essay scores for an oral test |

5. Placement into lowest ESL courses

6. First Week of the Semester:
    Second essay administered
    in all but lower-level courses
    Re-sorting of some students
    among levels

CUNY simply does not yet have the data to recommend the use of so time-consuming a test, which needs a chance to prove itself (for that reason it will not be discussed in further detail here). Nevertheless, such a model deserves investigation by any large university system in which the numbers of students transferring from community college to senior college require placement compatibility. In the future, many colleges may change over to objective tests for ESL placement, and the reason may be especially good or especially bad: bad if it is the result of budget and staff cuts alone, good if one or more of the objective tests now being field-tested shows itself to be a feasible alternative to essay tests.

One such objective test is the Davidson Test of Ability to Subordinate (TAS), a fifty-item sentence-combining test which

Figure 4. Model B: Objective Test/Essay/Oral Test/Re-Sort

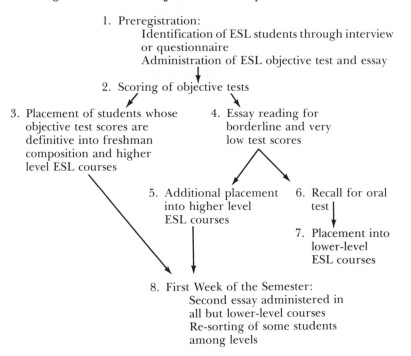

1. Preregistration:
   Identification of ESL students through interview
   or questionnaire
   Administration of ESL objective test and essay

2. Scoring of objective tests

3. Placement of students whose
   objective test scores are
   definitive into freshman
   composition and higher
   level ESL courses

4. Essay reading for
   borderline and very
   low test scores

5. Additional placement
   into higher level
   ESL courses

6. Recall for oral
   test

7. Placement into
   lower-level
   ESL courses

8. First Week of the Semester:
   Second essay administered in
   all but lower-level courses
   Re-sorting of some students
   among levels

measures discrete, significant grammatical elements of writing ability for diagnostic as well as placement purposes. Students are asked to complete a sentence frame using the information given in two kernel sentences. Here are three examples:

a. The doctor look at the leg. b. The leg had an infection. c. The doctor looked at _____ .

a. Why is he always complaining? b. We do not understand. c. We do not understand _____ .

a. They were satisfied. b. Their satisfaction was complete. c. They were _____ .

Another objective test developed at CUNY is the CUNY Cloze Tests, which originated at Queens College. These particular tests are not available commercially, but teachers have found it easy

Figure 5. Model C: Objective Test/Oral Test/Re-Sort

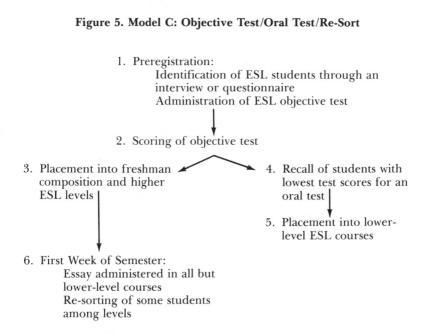

1. Preregistration:
   Identification of ESL students through an interview or questionnaire
   Administration of ESL objective test

2. Scoring of objective test

3. Placement into freshman composition and higher ESL levels

4. Recall of students with lowest test scores for an oral test

5. Placement into lower-level ESL courses

6. First Week of Semester:
   Essay administered in all but lower-level courses
   Re-sorting of some students among levels

to construct their own cloze tests. All one does is to select a passage of about 350 words which is close to the criterion style of student writing and omit every nth word. The sample following deletes every fifth word, but deletions up to every ninth word are also possible.

Fill in every blank with *one* word.

Tom never seemed to _____ enough money to pay _____ bills, so he always _____ money to the shopkeepers _____ the small town. Most _____ them were patient and _____ men and did not _____ to him very often _____ the money that he _____ them, but there was _____ who was not at _____ understanding and who loved _____ very much. Whenever he _____ Tom, he reminded him _____ the money that he _____ not paid him, and _____ did this in front _____ all Tom's friends.

Both the Davidson TAS and the CUNY Cloze Tests are easy to administer and score. Both have been found to correlate well with the Michigan Test and with placement essay scores.

	Correlation with Michigan Test	Correlation with Essay Ratings
Davidson TAS	.69	.74
CUNY Cloze Tests	.83	.70

These two tests are still quite new, and it is unlikely that ESL teachers will rush to discard essay test placement in favor of objective test placement without a good deal more data. Many teachers, furthermore, agree with Shaughnessy (1977b) that aside from placement and diagnostic purposes, it is *good* for students to write an essay so that they see writing matters in college. They feel they were placed in a course to work on what they were tested on.

Course Levels

ESL students can be placed into as many as five different course levels. These five should be taken as hypothetical, although there is nothing in their nature to make them unrealistic. CUNY is only now trying to establish some uniformity of these levels among colleges, and until that goal is achieved, a third-level student at one school might be a fifth-level student at another.

Levels One and Two: Beginning and Intermediate ESL

- *Objective Test Score:* under 65 on the Michigan Test
- *Oral Test Score:* under 40 on the John Test for Level One; 30–50 for Level Two
- *Essay Test Results:* a rating of 1 on a six-point scale for both levels; Level One students may not even have attempted to write an essay

Level One includes mainly students who have recently arrived in the United States and have little or no previous experience with English. Level Two may also include recent arrivals, but they are more likely to have had some English instruction. A second group may appear at Level Two; that is, persons who have lived in the U.S. for some time but have not needed to use English (for example, Spanish speakers who live and work with Spanish speakers). In all cases, the teacher should try to determine students' skills in their first language.

Here is a portion of a Level Two placement essay:

> People are lived all around the world. Each day many people born while others died. People's lives goes in circles. During this nineteen years, I always ask myself about three questions. I wonder where is the people go. What is truth? What is the value for people to live in the world? I was searching this answers for a long time.
>
> First, I wonder where is the people go. Where are they come from? When a baby was born other people will feel happy. Day by day he grows up. One day he will face the death, then he finished his whole life. Is that means life? I really dull about it.
>
> All of the three things, which I was wondered about for a long time are still can't find out by people. The life without truth, love and value is nonsense. What people searches for are true lives and value. This kinds of things can't find in this world. It is belongs to another world.

The complete essay from which this sample was excerpted was a good example of classical five-paragraph organization. The writer learned it in English classes in her home country. Her ideas manage to come through, but the main reason for level two placement is non-English syntax, which shows most in the verbs and word order. If an error count were used, it would show an average of one error for every three words.

Course Content. Both levels feature listening and speaking practice and integrate reading and writing mainly as a follow-up to what has already been taken up orally. Level Two may also include some writing which is not directly related to oral work.

Suggested Course Load. For both levels, fifteen hours of intensive ESL and no additional courses are suggested. (Colleges have different policies about granting credit for ESL courses. Some give no credit for any of their ESL courses, some give credit only for the higher-level courses, others give a fixed number at the end of the course sequence.)

Exit Criteria. Many colleges have established behavioral objectives for lower-level ESL courses and measure achievement solely on the basis of objectives reached. This is probably the best way to determine exit from Level One, but by the end of Level Two, students should be able to produce a paragraph of simple narrative or descriptive English in which the syntax is fairly coherent.

Level Three: ESL Transition Course

- Oral Test Score: 40 and above on the John Test
- Essay Test Results: a rating of 1 on a six-point scale

This is the first level at which students may have a considerable mixture of first and second language abilities. The only feature that places these students together is the fact that they can speak and comprehend English fluently enough to work on reading and writing but cannot write a coherent essay of any appreciable length.

Here are two excerpts from level three placement essays, the first by a student who has lived in the U.S. most of her life and scored 88 on the John Test, the second by a student who is a recent arrival with several years of traditional English behind her and a score of 46 on the John Test (where most of her errors were in comprehension).

Sample 1. There is person close to me who have her good and bad feature. That person is my sister. One of her best feature is, that she know what she's doing, nevertheless mom always is argueing with her, because she want to do everything on her way and mom dose'nt like that. Almost everytime they're argueing is about that.

My sister is a very good girl and dauter to mom. Mom dose'nt have complain about it.

One of her worse feature is, that she dose'nt like to help me in the house works. I'm fed up to talk to her about it. Sometime I do'nt wash the dishes waiting for her to do it, but, she dose'nt move a finger. When friday come we have to argue, because I have clean the whole house and she have not done a thing.

Sample 2. Today there are many workers in U.S. They are in different ages. Every kind of job must needs the skillful and experimental experiences. Most of people think that the older people get a lot of experience and knowledge. They work harder than the younger one. Therefore the young people cannot be able to find the job easily if the older people don't retire.

Most older people don't want to retire. Perhaps they get a lot of fun in their jobs. But on the other hand, the young people don't have a chance to get a job. Or some of the lower position workers cannot promote to a higher position. When the older people work for a certain time, their abilities must decrease, which is depend on their own health. Although some of them still have a good physical health, but their actions are slow down gradually.

Though the first essay sample is more idiomatic and the second more mature, both are riddled with errors but nevertheless coherent and "English-sounding" in structure. The first student can benefit from a course which combines all the communication skills because she will have a chance to use reading matter and conversation to achieve more depth and maturity of content; the second will derive the greatest benefit from hearing and using English vocabulary and idioms. Both can profit from a lot of writing practice.

Course Content. This level features free conversation, with or without simple reading matter, and a wide range of writing activities from controlled composition to original narrative and descriptive essays.

Suggested Course Load. Six hours of ESL writing and three of reading (combined or at least coordinated) in addition to freshman seminar and basic math, if needed, are suggested.

Exit Criteria. A 250-word narrative or descriptive essay in idiomatic English though major grammar or sentence structure errors may still be present.

Level Four: Basic Writing for Bilingual Students

- Objective Test Scores: 70–80 on the Michigan Test
- Oral Test Score: 65 and above on the John Test, if used
- Essay Test Results: a rating of 2 or 3 on a six-point scale

Students at this level have fluency in both speaking and writing but have a pattern of writing error in one or more major areas: sentence structure, grammar, diction, or mechanics. Here are two writing sample excerpts, which roughly parallel the two selected from Level Three in that the first writer has lived in the U.S. most of his life while the latter is a recent arrival who has had formal English training in her native country.

> *Sample 1.* Many people work in factories because they came from other countries and they can't speak English. That's why they work in a factory where the people are not consider and they have to make most of the hard work because the people who work their doesn't understand the language and if they don't work hard they think they are going to lose the job. It is hard to find a job because when you go out looking for a job they ask you if you have any experience with a machine how can you have any experience with a machine if they don't give you a chance to learn how to operate it.
>
> Married women who came from other countries and have never work because when you get marry, I don't said in any country is the same, but in some places women don't work because she have to take care of the house and if they have children is even worse.

> *Sample 2.* We are part of the living things, but we fight against them to survive. We are the only rationals on earth. This gives us the privilege to think first and act after and not only to act by instinct. We want everything in a profitable way for us until the point we will destruite the living things to get our purpose.
>
> The man is the perfect plant on earth. He can breath, nourish himself and move without help. But on the other hand, to be human being doesn't mean to be a perfection. He puts down trees, flowers, grace and plants to construct a road or a house. We love the nature and try to keep it alive on a "decorated" aspect. This is not enough. We have to respect it all the times.

Both writers comprehend everything they hear except vocabulary which is beyond them; both speak with ease and communicate clearly, the former in spite of nonstandard features, the latter in spite of missing or inappropriate function words and some incorrect idioms. The former will profit from rigorous editing of written sentence structure and inflection as well as increasing formalization of style. The latter needs to be less formal; she oversteps the boundaries of her command of English when she writes. Both need some formal grammar instruction and a wide range of free writing activities.

Course Content. This level treats the grammar of written English more thoroughly than any other level, but grammar should be taught in the context of full-length original compositions. For the first time, students move beyond narrative and descriptive writing into comparison, explanation, and basic argumentation.

Suggested Course Load. Six hours of ESL writing and three of reading, coordinated if possible, with a limited academic program are suggested.

Exit Criteria. Students should be able to write a 250–300-word expository essay with no major pattern of grammatical or syntactical error. For example, there should be no more than three verb errors in a paper of this length. Lesser errors—mechanics, misused prepositions, and content vocabulary—may still be present. The rudiments of organization should be present, but not necessarily at the paragraph level.

Level Five: Intensive Writing for Bilingual Students

Objective Test Score: 80–90 on the Michigan Test
Oral Test Score: not necessary at this level
Essay Test Results: a rating of 3 on a six-point scale

In its purest form, this level should include only students who are beyond grammar or any other basic writing problems and need only a review of formal writing conventions as well as an introduction to paragraph development and rhetoric. Realistically, however, Level Five takes in all students whose writing needs are simply not as great as those of students at lower levels. Thus, one student may have one major grammar problem left, another may write quite correctly but not entirely idiomatically, a third may write quite correctly but have difficulty organizing a whole essay under the pressure of time, a fourth may just write too simplistically. The first of the two excerpts below represents this last problem; the second is almost the exact opposite.

> *Sample 1.* There are several reasons why a person may lie. Lying is good sometimes because it makes some situations easier. I lie if I see that it can help me to accomplish something that I want. Here are a couple of examples of the benefits of lying.
>
> When I was a little boy, I used to love to go to the river. My mother never let me go, because it was very dangerous. I used to lie

to my mother to be able to go. By going to the river, I was lying to my mother. But, it was the only thing that was left for me to do.

Another example is my marital status. I am happily married, and I have a beautiful child. If I meet a girl that I like and I talk to her, she might like me, too. As soon as I tell her that I am married, she might don't like me anymore. The only thing that can save me is to lie to her. By doing this I am also lying to my wife, but I have no other choice.

Sample 2. Education does not merely consist in infusing knowledge, but its mental and moral training is the great consequences. Although ignorant people seem to live a more pacific and happy life than those who are educated, it is my firm conviction that it is nevertheless the latter ones who are in truth happier.

There is also the moral aspect of education is better than cheating and that doing good is a virtue notwithstanding the disdain of a society who scorns the good intentions of the do-gooders. In other words, in a society where the citizens are educated, there is more law and order, and so, if the community is in order, the citizens will be happier.

The first student knows what he wants to say and says it simply and clearly; the second gets terribly tangled in a kind of "pulpit parody." The differences in their educational backgrounds and pictures of themselves jump out of their writing, yet they might make a fine team for paired writing and editing: the one more sophisticated, the other more sincere. Both need to study the basics of style.

Course Content. The course is a catchall: a little grammar, a little rhetoric, a little style, and a lot of critical response to drafts and final copies of major papers. Paragraph development and vocabulary building, with good reading matter as examples, should also be a feature.

Suggested Course Load. Three hours of intensive writing, advanced reading if still necessary, and an unlimited academic program, except in English, are suggested.

Exit Criteria. Students should be able to write a 350-word expository essay which meets freshman composition entrance standards. The only allowance for students' bilingual background might be in the area of vocabulary and idiom.

Instructional Methods

Imagine that you are at an informal gathering of college and adult ESL teachers attending a national convention. You will probably be impressed by the enthusiasm and vitality around you, but you may be dismayed by what appear to be chasms of disagreement across which people talk when the subject is methodology. Here is but the surface.

You will hear much about the student-teacher relationship: initiative and control, freedom with restraints, knower-learner, counselor-client, the whole-person view of the learner. You will hear about motivation, instrumental and integrative; about verbal and nonverbal communication; about the classification of error, the cause of error, the treatment of error, whether error is error in the first place. Most of all, you will hear the learning process itself being discussed: the subordination of teaching to learning, receptive versus defensive learning, audiolingual habit theory versus cognitive code learning theory, centrally cognitive and centrally affective learning, learning without teachers, reflective versus productive performance. There will be more talk about the role of psychology in teaching than ever before in the eighty-seven years since William James brought American psychology to American teachers. Listening to those deeply interested in the affective domain, you will hear the projected questions of the learner being discussed: "Who am I?" and "How does what I am learning relate to who I am and where I am going in life?" (Rardin, 1976); "How am I related to others?" "What about me is like others and different from others?" (Weinstein and Fantini, 1970). Again and again the talk spreads far beyond skills, method, language alone. You may even hear reference to the assertion that language learning can become "a recovery of the innocence of our self, a return to our full powers and potentials" (Gattegno, 1972).

And all of this is coming out of only *two* of the fields on which college ESL is based! ESL and modern language teaching methodologies are the home base for ESL teachers, but the majority of those teaching credit-bearing courses for matriculating college students are teaching writing. ESL as a field does not have the academic history to suggest writing methods that go beyond sentence-level mastery (that is, correct grammar, syntax, mechanics) and writing for limited practical purposes. College ESL teachers have to draw upon methods in several fields for teaching native speakers of English (see Figure 6).

Is it any wonder that college ESL teachers have a lot to talk about and little to agree on? The sources and influences are many, while the experience, at least in prefreshman composition courses, is still of little more than a decade's duration.

Perhaps the best way to look at what college ESL teachers are doing in their classrooms and why is to take up each of the major sources of methods as it is and as it appears in these classrooms.

ESL and Modern Language Teaching

The teaching of ESL and modern languages in the United States has undergone two major revolutions in methodology during this century. The first was a post–World War II break from the traditional, or grammar-translation, method, and the second, twenty years later, was the proliferation of new, affectively-based methods and approaches which crowded, but did not supplant, the

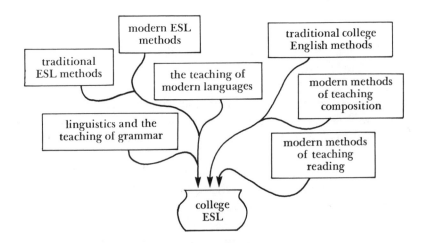

Figure 6. Sources of College ESL Methods

audio-lingual stimulus-response method which had ruled supreme since the war. Looked at simply, there was one method, then a different method, then many methods. But in fact, no method has disappeared altogether. The grammar-translation and audio-lingual methods are past the prime of their popularity, but they are still in use.

Grammar-Translation. The grammar-translation method does not intend to produce fluent speakers of modern languages. It was designed to provide part of a broad liberal arts background necessary to a well-educated person—that is, one who could read at least one foreign language. Students are taught in their native language, and the curriculum focuses on a sequence of textbook exercises which introduce new grammatical items, vocabulary, and idiom and ask students to translate, fill in the blanks, and write some cautious "original" sentences and sometimes a whole paragraph. Chapters of such textbooks begin with a reading passage, usually about the geography, customs, and culture of the target language country; poetry or short literary passages in the target language are sometimes included. Although some students fall by the wayside in the face of much memorization and translation, others do indeed learn to read well.

The grammar-translation method is still used in some high school and college modern language classes because school-age Americans have not had a burning need or desire to *speak* a new language. Although grammar-translation is no longer a principal methodology for teaching English as a *second* language in the U.S., it is still the primary means of teaching English as a *foreign* language in other countries. Students from Asia and the Middle East, in particular, who are now entering American colleges are very likely to have studied English for years by the grammar-translation method and may have a passive knowledge of the language that far exceeds their ability to speak and comprehend it.

Audio-Lingual Methods. Politics, scholarship, and psychology dovetailed in the 1940s in such a way as to produce the first revolution in language teaching methodology. In the armed services and in the field of diplomacy, there was a growing need for *speakers* of foreign languages; at the same time foreign scholars were flocking to American universities as European universities were being

closed by the Second World War. Linguists Kenneth Pike, Charles
Fries, and others helped to develop the audio-lingual approach to
language teaching based on structural linguistics and behavioral
psychology (Haskell, 1978). The times were ripe for such an innovation: sociologists and political scientists were still championing
the "melting pot" theory, and educational professionals viewed the
acquisition of English by foreign immigrants as necessary language
and culture replacement.

The audio-lingual method differs from grammar-
translation in that the target language is used exclusively in class
and both grammar items and communication skills are sequenced:
listening, then speaking, then reading, then writing. A lesson begins with a simple pattern, introduced by many repetitions by the
teacher, followed by many repetitions by the students, both chorally
and individually, then (again in a fixed sequence) expanded into a
dazzling array of drills: substitution, conversion, completion, question and answer. Meaningful drill alternates with mechanical drill;
dialogues are acted out and memorized; visual materials abound.
Teachers might grow hoarse, students dizzy with drill, but at least
people begin to *speak* the language they are learning.

"Classical" audio-lingual methodology is represented by the
Army Method, which is still used by the Defense Language Institute for military and diplomatic personnel; the Berlitz Method,
long a commercial success because of its popularity among Americans traveling abroad; and the Michigan Method, developed by
Robert Lado and Charles Fries at the University of Michigan to
teach college-level foreign students. The Michigan Method is still
used at many college campuses, often in modified forms. The
majority of ESL and modern language teachers who received
specialized training in those areas during the fifties or sixties use
some form of audio-lingual to teach the spoken language. Most
textbook writers in these areas, if they are not already committed to
grammar-translation, base their readings, dialogues, and exercises
on the carefully sequenced, controlled drill format of audio-
lingual. Even in higher level courses dealing primarily with reading
and writing, some audio-lingual influence persists as students are
introduced to written structures in a planned sequence and asked

to do exercises which require completion, conversion, and other drill-types popularized by audio-lingual methodology.

The number of college ESL and modern language teachers who defend the social and psychological bases of audio-lingual may be dwindling, but the number who simply use it and find it amenable to change is probably almost as large as when it was the queen of modern methods.

The Second Revolution. Beginning in the late 1950s, influences as diverse and powerful as those which had brought audio-lingual to its pinnacle challenged its reign. In linguistics, Noam Chomsky and others asserted that language was innate and the product of a thinking brain, not habit-formation; further, that language *performance* does not always accurately reflect language *competence*. In cognitive psychology, the notion of language learning as a passive response to outside stimuli was opposed by the theory that language acquisition takes place actively, if unconsciously, and passes through similar stages and strategies among speakers of all languages. In sociology, studies of dialect, particularly of what has come to be called Black English, challenged contemporary ideas of correctness and brought new emphasis to language variety and the need for affective models of education to meet students' emotional needs. In education, a respect was growing for ESL as a professional field, for ESL and bilingual teachers, and for the students themselves, no longer seen as needing to *replace* their native language and culture but rather to *add* English language and culture.

If there is any common thread among all these developments, it is the feeling that language learners need to be respected more. Learners were once seen mainly as recipients and respondents; the newer theories in the social sciences propose that learners are whole selves, with cognitive powers more extensive and complex than we knew, with feelings and attitudes more pivotal to learning ability than we wanted to admit, with lives and histories that bear heavily upon everything going on at any moment in the classroom. The term *whole-person approach* has become an umbrella term referring to research, methods, and materials concerning the need for deeper understanding of the learner. Many and varied as today's methods are, they share the whole-person concern. Two very different methods that emphasize learner investment and initiative are the Silent Way and Counseling-Learning–Community Language Learning.

The Silent Way. "Let the student work on the language; *you* work on the student." This advice is given to language teachers by Caleb Gattegno of Educational Solutions, Inc., in New York, who developed the Silent Way as part of a larger approach to the subordination of teaching to learning. He describes his primary concern this way (1974, p. 3): "When I teach a language, that language remains a secondary preoccupation of mine although it is the prime concern of students. My function as a teacher is to do all I can to make students find in themselves the powers required to be in the new language as they are in their native language. Since one is free to use the mastered language for expression of emotions, feelings, ideas, perceptions and so on, teachers have to aim at a similar freedom in the new language."

Five colleges in the City University of New York use methods based on the Silent Way, although none uses it exclusively. Right now it is used more with ESL beginners than with advanced students, more for listening and speaking than for reading and writing, more in programs for nonmatriculating students than in those for matriculating students. It is too early to say whether its greatest importance will come from the number of settings in which it appears or the effect it has on teachers' thinking. Certainly many college ESL teachers are giving it at least a sustained critical look. My own bias should be explicit here. I think any teacher interested in the learner as a whole person should know something of the Silent Way and consider what it has to say about teacher and learner, whether specific methods or materials are adopted or not.

Identifying features of the Silent Way are easiest to spot in a beginning lesson whose focus is on speaking. An observer would notice immediately that the students do 90 percent of the talking right from the outset; that the teacher seldom, if ever, repeats anything she has said; that periods of silence are part of the lessons; that mistakes, along with the hypothesizing and trials that generate them, are welcomed; and that for a time all the talk concerns a set of colored rods. The teacher points to and manipulates these rods while providing only that vocabulary which the students cannot arrive at through analogy or trial and error. Very quickly the students begin manipulating the rods themselves, generating whole sentences directed at one another and using the teacher to confirm the correctness of their sentences and guide their self-correction when they are wrong.

This is how a Silent Way first lesson at the beginner level often starts:

> Teacher and students are seated around a large table. The teacher has an array of colored rods before her and begins the lesson by picking up several different ones, saying, "A rod," for each. She then beckons to the whole class.
> *Students:* A rod.
>
> She motions to individual students to say the same thing in response to seeing a rod she points to or holds. If pronunciation is not accurate, she has the student try again, sometimes after hearing another student say, "A rod," again, but she does not repeat the word herself. When she is satisfied that students are approaching a good sound and are sure that each of the different sizes and colors is called "a rod," she points to a blue rod.
> *Teacher:* Blue.
> *Students:* Blue.
>
> The teacher holds up three fingers and points to them in succession; some students catch on to the idea that they should try to put "blue" and "a rod" together.
> *A Student:* A rod blue.
> The teacher signals to reverse the order of the words.
> *A Student:* A blue rod.
>
> Again individuals say the phrase as the teacher points to a blue rod. She repeats this process with several different colors, with each saying only the color itself but requiring students to put it into a three-word phrase. She then picks up two rods of the same color.
> *Teacher:* Two.
> *Students:* Two blue rod.
>
> If any student knows or hits upon the correct plural—which the teacher has not said—she may use him as a model for the rest of the class. If no one knows it, all may try; the teacher uses gestures to "pull out" the noun plural or cut off an adjective plural if it appears, and, throughout the lesson, a nod or shake of the head to affirm the correctness or incorrectness of structure and pronunciation.
>
> The teacher lines up single rods and pairs of rods and points to them with increasing speed, adding only the word *and* where it belongs in the oral list.

Students: A red rod, two blue rods, two white rods, a yellow rod, and two black rods.

The teacher pushes all the rods whose colors are known into the middle of the table and gestures "take."
Teacher: Take.
A Student: Take a blue rod.

The teacher signals to that student to say the same thing directly to another student. While she only signals who should give the command or, if unnecessary, does nothing but listen and correct silently, the students actually communicate with one another for the first time.

One of the first questions asked by instructors new to the Silent Way is, "Do you have to use rods?" Stevick (1974, p. 312) says: "For years I was skeptical on this point, preferring to use toy villages, or Tinkertoys, or real objects, and actively refusing to have anything to do with rods. I now prefer rods to Tinkertoys because they are more visible, less distracting, come in more colors, and do not roll off the table." He adds that the more important reason for using rods is that they invite imagination. They become people, houses, a clock, a whole neighborhood in a remote town.

Teachers also ask, "When do you get *away* from the rods?" and the answer is simply, "Whenever you want to." They are nothing but very compact, convenient visual aids, and some Silent Way teachers never use them, while others use them all the way up to the most advanced conversation levels.

Once the matter of rods, which attracts far more attention than it deserves, is somewhat clearer, teachers ask, "Do I ever get a chance to talk?," "When do the students read and write?," "How do you teach vocabulary?," and "Is there a textbook or structure sequence?" Sometimes the answers seem vague or ambiguous or at least not very helpful: the teacher can talk when she wants to so long as she does not say what the students are saying; students can read and write from the outset and anytime; the teacher does not *teach* vocabulary at all; there are charts and supplementary materials but no textbook, no syllabus or structure sequence. The structure is in the language itself and in the learning process. If teaching is really being subordinated to learning, then students initiate the talking, reading, writing; students ask for the vocabulary they want; the students themselves or student progress determines new items to be introduced on a day-to-day basis.

If the Silent Way is gaining popularity, which seems to be the case, these may be some of the reasons. First, it respects the learner's mind, his ability to figure things out for himself, and his previous knowledge and experience. In an aural-oral lesson, it allows students to volunteer, hold back, even drop out and come back later if they need to. Silences are honored. Second, the planning is careful, the standard of production high, and the whole process orderly and dignified in appearance, yet there is much freedom of choice for both the teacher and the learner. A student, for example, can introduce a wholly original topic, and if it is not hopelessly beyond him structurally, the teacher will generally follow right along. All kinds of expression—thoughts and feelings, personal and impersonal—are welcome. Finally, the Silent Way encourages students to try whatever seems right to their inner ear, to take risks, not to fear mistakes. If something comes out right, there is no patronizing "Very good!" or exclamation of surprise; the teacher *expects* students to do well. She also expects mistakes and treats them as the beginning of all new learning. In short, the Silent Way shows the target language to be sensible and systematic without grammar explanations and the learner to be far more capable than even he himself might have believed.

Both teachers and students have raised objections, often on the same points that others welcome the most: the lack of a text or sequence, the minimal interest in vocabulary, the wide-ranging student initiative. The Silent Way is not for teachers who are shaky in grammar or feel unsure about students' powers; it is not for students who prefer clear directives from their teacher. And if the learner is to be respected, those preferences should count.

Counseling-Learning and Community Language Learning. Counseling-Learning is a model for learning which grew out of Curran's 1972 study of the psychological dynamics of adult learning based on the therapeutic theories of Carl Rogers. Community Language Learning is an offshoot of Counseling-Learning designed to illustrate the possibilities for a union of language learning and counseling.

The theoretical underpinnings of CL/CLL are many and

complex. Some of the basic assumptions are that all final learning is value learning; that resistance is inherent in any adult learning situation; that human learning is whole-person learning; and that human learning moves through a five-stage process of internalization (Rardin, 1976). The model based on these assumptions presents a picture of an individual as the center of his own universe, resistant to outside influence unless that influence can be seen as trustworthy and nonthreatening. A learner does not simply add knowledge or skills to a stable core of himself but invests his whole self, consciously or unconsciously, into all learning. Counseling-Learning suggests a means of understanding the dynamics of that investment and using both the positive and negative constructively.

Only one CUNY ESL program which is part of the Tutoring-Counseling Service of LaGuardia Community College is using Counseling-Learning systematically with ESL students. Other teachers, however, are using some form of the so-called counseling response. To many this means simply a kind of skilled listening, a nonthreatening way to show a person that one is trying to understand what he is saying, thinking, and feeling. If, for example, a woman says poutingly, "Herbert would just *die* if he didn't have his Thursday night out with the boys," the listener may not judge ("That old toad!"), question ("What do the boys have that you don't have?"), or bring herself into the picture ("My Edward is like that, too"). She may only restate what she has heard ("So Herbert feels he has to go out Thursdays") or, at most, mirror the underlying feelings ("You're pretty critical of him for going off like that"). Counseling responses may be centrally affective—that is, aimed at an understanding of a person's feelings, as in the example—or centrally cognitive—aimed at verifying one's understanding of information being given. The possibilities for classroom use are many. Some teachers of beginning and intermediate ESL classes use counseling responses as a gentle form of linguistic correction. For example, if a student says, "I no feel good today," the teacher responds, "You don't feel well today" (Czarnecki and Ramos, 1975). Teachers of advanced students are using counseling responses to participate in class discussions and to improve students' listening to one another by having them give counseling responses as well. Some teachers have set up counseling contracts with students in conferences by saying, "If you'd like to say whatever you want to for about five minutes, I'll do my best to understand what you're trying to express." Students who take the contract may choose to hold closely to academic matters or take a more personal direction. In composition classes a teacher or student partner listens to a person read his writing aloud and responds sentence by sentence with how he thinks the spelling, punctuation, or grammatical inflections should appear on the reader's paper.

A Community Language Learning lesson is the purest application of the Counseling-Learning approach. Although CLL does not seem feasible in most college ESL settings because it requires the teacher to know each student's native language, a knowledge of the method can affect teachers' attitudes if not their methods. A Community Language Learning course shows the five stages of growth which the Counseling-Learning model asserts are necessary to all learning. CLL aims for "optimal regression" of the learner to a mental state of childhood or adolescence where dependency is permissible; then it allows him to assert himself—"grow up" in a sense—at his own pace.

CLL lessons can be as varied as those using any approach and can, in fact, incorporate most of the techniques used by other methodologies. There are, however, three distinct parts to early CLL lessons. First, students may say whatever they wish in their native language and then repeat and record it in the target language after the teacher, called the knower in CLL, has translated it for them. Second, knower and learners together analyze what has been said in the preceding segment. They listen to the tape, see the sentences in writing, and take up grammar points. Third, the learners express their feelings about what has taken place, and the knower gives counseling responses. For example, this is how a first lesson at the beginner level might start:

> Eight students, called clients, are seated in a circle with a tape recorder and a microphone. The teacher, or knower, stands outside the circle and waits for someone to start. There is some embarrassment and uneasiness, but finally one client takes the microphone (which is still turned off).
> *First Client: No sé que decir.*
> The knower moves behind her, touches her shoulder gently

and gives her the translation in a low voice. She switches on the microphone.

First Client: I don't know what to say.

She switches the mike off. Another client reaches for it.

Second Client: Ni yo tampoco.

The knower does the same thing with this client.

Second Client: Me neither.

Another client takes the microphone after it has been switched off again.

Third Client: Quizás debemos empezar con la identificación de ciertas cosas en la clase.

Some clients look at her, startled by the length of the statement; others comment on the suggestion in Spanish, but the knower does the same thing he has done with the previous two clients, this time breaking the translation into manageable phrases.

Third Client (with knower): (Perhaps we should start) Perhaps we should start (with the identification) with the identification (of certain things) of certain things (in the classroom) in the classroom.

Fourth Client: No quiero hacer eso.

The knower translates again in the same gentle way.

Fourth Client: I don't want to do that.

Fifth Client: Me neither!

This client looks very pleased with himself for having recalled this short utterance. He repeats it with the mike on.

Sixth Client: No me siento cómoda.

The knower approaches to translate, but the client glances at him sharply as she turns on the microphone and tries to start on her own.

Sixth Client: I no—I don'—(Knower: feel very comfortable) I don' feel very comfortable.

College ESL teachers who observe or participate in CLL demonstrations sometimes say, "I'm impressed, but I can't imagine this with my own students." Few teachers have seen CLL used with anyone but Americans, and many questions of the "translatability" of American psychology arise: Would ESL students be at ease with the lack of teacher-structuring? Would they take the initiative? Would they object to being touched, as the knower does when he translates for a person? Yet whatever questions and reservations teachers have about CLL as an approach, few teachers seeing it for the first time fail to be amazed at what happens when language learners are allowed to express their feelings. People who have said weakly, "I just never had a good ear," or "Languages aren't my cup of tea," begin to speak about things like anger, frustration, futility, and humiliation. And some feel understood and can learn better.

College students learning English as a second language have no choice as to their cup of tea. They simply cannot do well with their studies or their careers unless they do well with English. Yet many languish in basic education courses—barred, it seems, indefinitely from full participation in college life by their ESL difficulties. Nothing troubles a college ESL teacher more than a student who seems intelligent, highly-motivated, and hardworking—and spins in his tracks when it comes to English. Helping such students is one of the reasons for the continuing interest in Counseling-Learning and Community Language Learning in spite of problems of logistics and many as yet unanswered questions.

Eclectic Methods. Eight CUNY ESL programs use eclectic methods, meaning either that different teachers do different things; that ESL ranges from beginning all the way to advanced (composition courses), which no one method seems to span; that teachers know what they do but do not have a name for it; or that methods used are a selection of what faculty see as the best of the known methods and approaches. In some colleges, one philosophy or approach may prevail, but many techniques, activities, and materials are included that do not belong exclusively to that approach. This is the case at the College of Staten Island: "There is an eclectic approach to the selection of methods . . . though the Silent Way philosophy of subordinating teaching to learning is considered especially valuable. Teachers use varied and diverse methods individually suited to their students, including audio-lingual, situational-reinforcement, individualized instruction, show-and-tell, group interaction, discussion and debate, problem-solving, free writing, interviewing, group writing, acting, learning through songs, limericks and games, as well as the Silent Way. There is a continual attempt to prepare students to meet academic requirements as well as day-to-day language needs."

The list just given is a hodgepodge of everything from whole methodologies to grade school games and activities, the criterion for inclusion, perhaps, being simply "whatever works." And since "working," at least at beginning and intermediate ESL levels, means helping students improve their spoken English, there are few limits to the kinds of things teachers will try. For example, ESL teachers have always borrowed from the elementary and high school classroom to provide colorful and enjoyable materials and activities in ESL classes, whatever the age or ultimate goal of the students. So long as the students' age, status, and culture are respected, college administrators and fellow faculty should not be dismayed to hear songs being sung or to see pictures, colored rods, and a flannel board being used in an ESL class.

Learning arrangements such as team teaching, individualization, paired work, group work, and the open classroom are identified specifically neither with the lower grades nor with ESL, but ESL may have been one of the first subject areas to bring them to the college classroom. Individual, paired, and group work will be discussed later as part of a look at composition methods in ESL classes, but all three are used for aural-oral practice as well, the first, of course, with a tape or video recorder, as in a language lab setting. The use of elaborate audio equipment is not as popular as it was in the fifties and sixties, the heyday of the language labs, but cassette recorders and players are common.

One of the most interesting ESL experiments in CUNY was a combination of team teaching and open classrooms. Two classes with their four teachers met together regularly with an increasing number of choices offered the students as to what they would work on each day. At the beginning of the semester, choices were limited, but as students became secure in each activity, a new one was introduced until there were about a dozen different things students could do. Generally no more than four or five activities actually did go on at one time but more important than the numbers involved was the goal of having students learn how to make the wisest choices for their own learning. For example, a student might prefer to work alone and would therefore tend to choose self-paced writing tasks like controlled or guided composition as a regular activity. If, however, this student were gradually assuming some of what are traditionally teachers' responsibilities—assessing her strengths and weaknesses, trying to evaluate the benefits derived from one activity or another—she might choose to go against her inclinations and work, say, with an oral practice group if that could be seen as potentially beneficial. Twenty years ago with all kinds of visual aids, props, and regalia, students and teachers acted out everything from a barnyard to a banquet in the classroom, but large areas of adult involvement and responsibility were missing as teachers—often exclusively—planned, modeled, directed, corrected, assessed, and so on. If one of the earmarks of new methods and eclectic methods is less of the "show" seen not so long ago in ESL classrooms, this may be because ESL classrooms are gradually becoming more like the rest of the world.

ESL Writing. Ten or twenty years ago, ESL writing was largely a matter of having students record what they had already heard, said, and read. Most teachers felt that if students so much as looked at a sample of written English before mastering it orally, they would forever mispronounce it, or worse, they would always long for it to sound the way it looked. Although attitudes have changed a good deal, ESL writing techniques and materials still stop short of the needs of college ESL students aiming to enter freshman composition courses. ESL teachers can look to their own field for writing practice designed to improve listening, reinforce speaking, focus on specific grammar points or sentence patterns, and increase vocabulary or fluency, but they will find few techniques or materials that address the matter of formulating and organizing ideas in formal writing. From this point on, the former will be called *ESL writing* and the latter *composition*. The techniques and materials listed below are part of ESL writing.

Dicto-comp. Dicto-comp is a variation of standard dictation technique. The teacher reads a paragraph two or three times while the students listen, then asks them to reproduce the paragraph as closely as possible from memory, paying close attention to the flow of the main thoughts. Such exercises provide practice in following logical development of thought and writing coherent paragraphs.

Controlled Composition. Controlled composition is a series of writing tasks which ask students to copy and make grammatical variations on model passages, as with the following exercise from Brookes and Withrow (1974, p. 9):

Eyes of a Hawk
(1) They call him Mr. Hawkeye. (2) He is the world's fastest reader. (3) He works for a printing office. (4) He reads every single book printed in that office.

(5) Mr. Hawkeye waits at the end of a big machine. (6) Piles of pages continually move toward him. (7) After he picks up a page, he scans it. (8) He looks for printing and typing errors. (9) Sometimes he notices mistakes. (10) He uses a pencil to mark them.

(11) He doesn't smile or look up. (12) He is a very fast worker. (13) The company pays him very well because he is the most valuable employee in the office.

- Rewrite the passage, but change *Mr. Hawkeye* to *Mr. Hawkeye and Mr. Scanner.* You will write about two persons instead of one. Sentence 1 will be:
    They call them Mr. Hawkeye and Mr. Scanner.
- Pretend you are writing about a person who lived in the past. Sentence 1 will be:
    They called him Mr. Hawkeye.

The following sample of controlled composition for advanced students comes from Kunz (1979, p. 36):

Old is Beautiful

(1) When I walk down Third Avenue, I love to peer into the windows of the little shops that sell old and beautiful things. (2) Since I often take my walks after closing time, I cup my hands against the windows to get a small look at the treasures inside. (3) I see things that tell a story without words, bits of history, often something that is clearly one of a kind. (4) Some things look as if they have not been cared for deeply in a long time, but I know their beauty is still there.

(5) This is how I feel about old people, too. (6) I know their value, and it hurts me when others miss it.

(7) Most old people are treated badly by our society. (8) They are forced to retire in their early or mid-sixties because their experience and need to work are not given credit. (9) Often they are nudged into nursing homes by their own families.

(10) I was raised by my grandmother and given a deep sense of the value of experience. (11) My sister and I were taught to respect all people, regardless of their age, color or creed. (12) My grandmother was loved by all the people around her because she was known to be wise, kind and able to do things well even in her last years.

(13) Old people should be treated like fine gold. (14) They may be tarnished by age, but they can be polished by respect. (15) You might be surprised at their bright and shining qualities.

• Rewrite the entire passage, changing every sentence in the last three paragraphs to the active voice. The first sentence in your third paragraph will be:

Our society treats most old people badly.

• Rewrite the entire passage condensing the following sentences by using one of the forms of the words indicated to replace several words in each sentence:

antique/antiques (sentence 1)   discredit/discredited (sentence 8)
glimpse/glimpsing (sentence 2)   competence/competent
unique/uniqueness (sentence 3)   (sentence 12)
cherish/cherished (sentence 4)   luster/lustrous (sentence 15)

Controlled composition materials can be used regardless of course content. This material is appealing for several reasons. It is easy to use and easy to correct and lends itself to individual or class use. The exercises focus on major grammatical and structural points without using technical terminology. Students like the method, in part because they can produce whole compositions rather than lists or isolated paragraphs, and the volume of their writing encourages them.

The major complaint about controlled composition is that it is too controlled; it invites not a single creative or original thought on the student's part. Teachers should use it purely as supplementary writing practice, not in a real composition course.

The three most popular controlled composition texts are Brookes and Withrow's *10 Steps: Controlled Composition for Beginning and Intermediate Students* (1974), Kunz's *26 Steps: Controlled Composition for Intermediate and Advanced ESL Students* (1979), and Kunz and Viscount's *Write Me a Ream: Exercises in Controlled Composition* (1973).

Guided Composition. Like controlled composition, guided composition involves writing from a model. A little more choice and originality are involved in the latter than in the former, as can be seen in the instructions under Item D of the following example (Baskoff, 1971, pp. 17–18):

What Am I?
I usually go to work by subway. I get to work by 8:00 A.M. Before I start my job, I put on my uniform and look at myself in the mirror and make sure that I look neat. At 8:30 in the morning, I go on duty. I usually eat lunch from twelve to one and generally take a

ten-minute break in the morning and in the afternoon. At 4:30 in the afternoon, I go off duty.

I enjoy my job very much. I meet all kinds of people and talk to everyone. Many people ask me questions, and I give them the necessary information. I try to be very helpful. I never stay in one place long. On the contrary, I am constantly on the move. Most men take off their hats in my car. Sometimes I tell passengers to put out their cigarettes. Some people smile at me and others ignore me. My life is a series of "ups" and "downs."

Quotation

The test of a vocation is the love of the drudgery it involves.

—L. P. Smith

Composition Exercises

A. Comprehension Questions on Model Composition
   1. How do you usually go to work?
   2. What time do you get to work?
B. Common Expressions

to put on	on the contrary	by subway
to make sure	to take off	by bus
to go on duty	to put out a cigarette	by train
to go off duty	to smile at someone	by car
		to ignore someone

C. Questions on Common Expressions and Vocabulary
   1. What do you usually put on first in the morning?
   2. Do you always make sure you have some money before you leave?
D. Write a composition in the third person singular about someone's job. Try to follow the model and use the following questions as a guide.
   What is he or she (Mr. X or Miss Y)?
   First Paragraph: 1. How does he go to work?
                    2. What time does he go to work?

These instructions come from Baskoff's *American English: Guided Composition* (1971). Another popular guided composition book is Robinson's *Guided Writing and Free Writing* (1975).

Picture Composition. Picture composition moves one step further away from control by offering students a visual rather than a verbal model. Teachers generally use single or strip cartoons from newspapers or magazines, and although students may choose their own vocabulary and structures, they are still bound to the action and characters of the cartoon. Picture composition should not be confused with the far more sophisticated activity of students' interpreting and discussing visual material. In a later part of this chapter, visual materials which are meant to provoke thought and lead into real composing activities will be discussed.

Ten-Minute Writings. Ten-minute writings, which are used at all but the most beginning ESL levels, are at the opposite end of the spectrum from any kind of controlled or model-oriented writing. Students write without stopping for ten minutes, usually at the beginning of a class period and often with no suggestion of topic. Many find that they can write far more than they had thought they could, especially if no one is going to see what they have written. Teachers generally do not ask students to hand in these writings but may have one or two students volunteer to read them aloud or, if a topic has been used, invite the whole class to comment. Whatever the variations, ten-minute writings are popular because they tend to increase writing fluency and help students avoid that dreaded blankness that so many feel when they begin a real composition.

Sentence Generating. This technique is more word study and manipulation than actual writing. It is based on teacher-made lists of whole words, roots, suffixes, and punctuation marks. The teacher writes a list on the board, and individual students, using a pointer, tap out whole sentences combining items from the list, which their classmates then "read" aloud or write down. Here are three lists, which are roughly beginning, intermediate, and advanced.

List 1:		*List 2:*		*List 3:*	
a	–s	touch	–es	one	first
rod	and	he	–ed	friend	–er
red	it	she	has	last	–ing
blue	them	him	been	suffer	–s
take	her	her	by	love	–'s
give	me			mean	more
one	another			long	then
ones	more				

In all but the beginning lists, sentence generating is quite technical without the technical terminology. Students must deal with inflectional endings, word order, subject-verb agreement, and often various semantic subtleties. Arguments arise, for example, as to whether a sentence like "Last lovers last longer than first ones," makes sense. Obviously, some silliness is hard to avoid, but the discussion is usually lively, and no one is hurt in the attack and defense that goes on.

Sentence Combining. Strong (1973) introduced sentence combining to college classrooms. (This technique is discussed in detail in Chapter One of this book.) Since sentence combining exercises have proved popular among ESL teachers, there are now lower-level texts appearing with such exercises in them. One of the most recent is Gallingane and Byrd's *Write Away* (1977).

Linguistics and the Teaching of Grammar

ESL teachers have always drawn heavily on linguistics for their teaching of English and particularly of grammar. Some might say too heavily, perhaps, in that ESL has sometimes been taught as if it were a branch of applied linguistics. It is not that, but applied linguistics does indeed have a great deal to offer ESL teachers. The four areas of applied linguistics discussed here have made themselves felt in classroom practice and in teachers' ways of planning and evaluating.

Contrastive Analysis. Contrastive analysis is the examination of parallel features among two or more languages for the purpose of seeing how they are both similar and different. Here, for example, is a literal translation of a simple sentence in several languages besides English.

- English: Life is a dream.
- Spanish and French: The life is a dream.
- Russian and Polish: Life is dream.
- Chinese: Life dream.

ESL teachers have used contrastive analysis both predictively and instructively. That is, they might use contrastive information only to anticipate difficulties speakers of various languages might have, or they might share, or even acquire, such information with students as part of regular classroom practice. The information above, for instance, tells a teacher that speakers of Romance languages might tend to use too many articles in English (using a definite article with uncountable nouns like *life*), while speakers of Russian, Polish, and Chinese might tend to omit articles because their languages do not have any.

Thus, contrastive analysis is a useful method for determining the source of many students' errors. Some instructors feel its greatest value is that it can promote a better attitude toward error. As Rizzo and Villafane (1975, p. 63) point out: "A student appreciates knowing, when he finds he is committing some error, that he is not an inferior learner . . . but that he has simply been analogizing—the most respectable of mental activities—in a situation where, rather exceptionally, to analogize produces error." Lay (1975) suggests that students can collaborate in the task of determining why they make particular errors and that such ability is a sign that they can develop the habit of self-correction in the composing process itself.

Transitional Dialects. Contrastive analysis is predicated on the notion that ESL error derives principally from first language interference. This idea has been challenged by recent research in the area of interlanguage, or transitional dialects. Transitional dialect theory asserts that language learner's errors are rule-governed according to constantly changing and sharpening hypotheses he is making about the target language. Nearly everything that is customarily called "error," then, is not error at all (Dickerson, 1975, p. 406): "Nontarget performance should not be considered 'erroneous' but viewed, first, as a necessary part of the language learning process, and secondly, as important information about the character of the learner's changing language system." A native speaker of Chinese, for example, might say or write "This book belong Harry," in an early stage of learning, and later, "This book is belong to Harry." Both sentences have at least one error if error is taken to mean only what is not standard English. However, the second sentence is much closer to standard English than the first and shows that the learner is trying out auxiliary verbs—and not just randomly; at this stage, he may also say or write "It is depend" or "I am agree" and other constructions that suggest a pattern, a rule he is testing. Such a rule does not come from his first language; Chinese does not have auxiliary verbs. Rather, it is part of his transitional dialect, a promising representative of the systematic learning process he is undergoing.

Most of what has been written thus far in the field of transitional dialects is quite technical and difficult to read. Teachers who use Silent Way, Community Language Learning, or a method which draws upon a philosophy similar to theirs are already committed to welcoming and utilizing error and will, therefore, be likely to welcome what transitional dialect theory has to offer as well. Perhaps such insights are even more important at the advanced ESL levels, where most composition teachers admit they need to improve the way they regard students' written errors. No one has shown yet that transitional dialects occur in writing the way they do in speaking. Still, this is an area of research and potential application that bears watching.

Error Analysis. Error analysis, another new area of applied linguistics, differs from contrastive analysis and transitional dialect theory in that it makes no assumptions about the cause of error. Errors are looked at for their nature, not their cause, and are categorized in ways that can help a teacher establish some teaching priorities.

One of the most important distinctions that error analysis makes is between errors that cause miscommunication and those that do not. For example, the three errors in the sentence "I try for drive more slow" may affect a listener, but they do not impede his understanding. In contrast the question "Does your mother worry you when you drink?" sounds like good English, but it does not convey the speaker's meaning if the speaker meant, "Does your mother worry about you when you drink?" (Burt, 1975).

Error analysis also distinguishes global errors from local errors. Global errors affect overall sentence organization, while local errors (for example, missing or incorrect inflectional endings) do not. Global errors include wrong word order, missing or wrong sentence connectors, and various other missing or wrong syntactic clues.

Here is one example of how an error analysis classification

can be used in the classroom. Burt notes that most verbs which indicate a person's feelings or reaction, *psychological verbs,* have the person who experiences something as their subject and the stimulus as object or complement: "She loves that color" or "He's glad you're here." There are psychological verbs, however, which have the experiencer as the object and the stimulus as the subject: "This lesson bores me" or "The performance amused everyone." Such verbs must be used in the passive voice if the experiencer is to be the grammatical subject, but learners often overgeneralize a rule from the larger to the smaller category, saying, "He doesn't interest his classes." Many ESL students would be glad just to have a list of these verbs, which error analysis can provide. Better, perhaps, a teacher might discuss these two categories and have students practice using the two groups.

Even if a teacher does not apply contrastive analysis, transitional dialect theory, or error analysis to classroom practice, some knowledge of each should have a good effect on the way he sees students' errors. Whether he feels errors result from first language interference or transitional hypotheses or whether he is not concerned with cause at all but only with nature, he will at least be much less likely to think there is anything willful or stupid in their origins.

Sector Analysis. If ever there was a nature/nurture type of argument in the teaching of ESL—and basic writing as well—it is the question of whether to teach grammar at all. The only ESL teachers who do not have to deal with this tired issue are those who teach lower levels and use a methodology that takes a definite stand on grammar. At higher levels, there seems to be no agreement in sight. Most of the relevant research suggests that grammar teaching is not helping students speak or write any better than they would without it. Users of modern grammars insist that it is not grammar itself but the use of an archaic Latinate grammar of English that stands in the way of positive results. Yet there is no evidence that clearly points to modern grammars' doing what traditional grammar supposedly cannot.

Most ESL teachers teach grammar anyway. The majority use various adaptations and simplifications of traditional grammar, but some use sector analysis, a form-function approach which can be used to analyze any language and has been applied extensively to

English. Developed and taught through the sixties and seventies by Robert Allen of Teachers College, Columbia University, who was himself an ESL teacher for twenty years, sector analysis has two main features that recommend it to teachers. First, it shows English to be the sensible, systematic Germanic language that it is, and second, it has a classroom version that is constantly being revised and improved through use.

This classroom version of the grammar, which has come to be known as x-word grammar, is not a mini-version of the whole grammar. It is a practical combination of excerpts from the sector analysis of English, classroom teaching techniques, and student self-editing techniques. For example, the sector analysis of English posits one enormous sentence pattern made up of all the positions, or "sectors," that can be filled or left empty to make real sentences. With its levels telescoped, such a pattern would be symbolized by fifteen or more letters and stretch halfway across the blackboard. X-word grammar takes the idea of a fixed number and arrangements of positions and offers seven basic sentence patterns, which form the basis for over 95 percent of all sentences students write:

> T (Trunk):
>> Henry VIII had six wives.
> LT (Linker and Trunk):
>> However, he had a hard time getting an heir.
> FT (Front Shifter and Trunk):
>> Though Henry VIII had six wives, he had a hard time getting an heir.
> TE (Trunk and End Shifter):
>> Henry VIII had a hard time getting an heir though he had six wives.
> T+T (Trunk Plus Trunk):
>> Henry VIII had six wives, but he had a hard time getting an heir.
> T= (Trunk with Two Verbs):
>> Henry VIII had six wives but had a hard time getting an heir.
> TI (Trunk with Insert):
>> Henry VIII, who had six wives, had a hard time getting an heir.

If students can recognize the seven basic patterns in their own writing, they can do a fair job of punctuating as well. In the sample sentences above, the rules for the use of commas are simply LT, FT, T + T, and TI but never T = or TE. The semi-colon rule is T;T and the colon rule T:. 'T' means TRUNK; a trunk is the basic sentence unit, and it is the only construction type (as opposed to phrases, clauses, and other types) which can be turned into a yes-no question (for example, "Henry VIII had six wives" can be asked as "Did Henry VIII have six wives?"). Thus students can test their sentences. If they cannot make one whole yes-no question out of a sentence of theirs, they do not even have a sentence; it is a fragment. If they can make two whole yes-no questions out of a sentence, they need a semi-colon or comma and conjunction between the two, but not just a comma, or the sentence is run-on (the error that many teachers call a comma splice).

X-word grammar takes its name from the twenty words that begin yes-no questions in English: the *BE* family *(am, is, are, was, were)*, the *DO* family *(do, does, did)*, the *HAVE* family *(have, has, had)*, and the modals *(can, could, shall, should, will, would, may, might, must)*. These x-words are the core of English grammar . . . first because they are ubiquitous in English and form a unique and very tidy category, second because students already know them although they have never looked at them as a category, and third because many writing problems show up right around the x-words: subject-verb agreement, negation, word order, tense, missing or repeated subjects, verb forms and certain kinds of fragments. . . . The term "subject" is defined simply as "the position between the two x-word positions," which is easy to find just by making a yes-no question because the x-word moves from the right of the subject to the left. Every x-word has a subject it must agree with. Verbs, on the other hand, lose most of their grammatical meaning once their x-words are removed; they indicate neither number nor person nor tense without their x-words (Kunz, 1977, p. 68).

New grammars of English are descriptive instead of prescriptive. Sector analysis encourages bilingual students to test, experiment with, manipulate the language instead of always being manipulated *by* it. Although at the present time Allen, Pompian, and Allen's *Working Sentences* (1975) is the only sector analysis text available, four others are in process, and the demand for such material seems to be increasing.

Borrowing from the Natives

A colleague who had recently switched from teaching lower-level adult ESL to higher-level college ESL said, "Just a few months ago, I was some hotshot ESL teacher with all my flashcards and colored rods, and now I'm reluctant to admit to the people around me that I don't even know what rhetorical modes *are,* let alone how to teach them!"

ESL composition teachers have to borrow from any source that might give them what they need to teach the formulating, composing, and editing of ideas on paper; their own field does not offer enough. And rather than asking whether and what he can borrow, the ESL teacher should ask, "Is there anything I *can't* borrow?" and, "What modifications do I have to make when I bring something that was meant for native English speakers into my classroom?" The answer to the first question is, "Practically nothing." The answer to the second is a description of the differences between advanced ESL students—who should rightly be called bilingual students—and their counterparts in basic writing courses.

This final section on methodology covers some of the subject matter, techniques, and materials that ESL composition teachers borrow from basic writing. Each is discussed more fully in Chapter One of this book; the purpose here is to discuss adaptation for bilingual students.

Rhetorical Modes. Borrowing work on rhetorical modes, ESL teachers should keep in mind that students educated abroad are likely to have learned less obvious and linear patterns of organization and argument than their American counterparts. A comparison of argument in three languages can be represented schematically as follows (Kaplan, 1966):

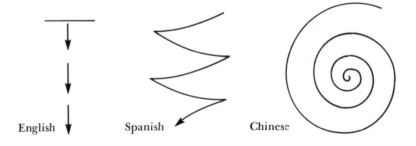

English   Spanish   Chinese

To many ESL students, the English-language way of developing a point is terribly unsubtle, if not downright crude. Generally, we prefer to start with a thesis or other generalization and proceed to supportive detail. More often, speakers of other languages tend to start with a question, an instance, some other type of detail, and lead up to a main point or thesis statement. This does not mean that an ESL teacher realizing this difference should not still teach deductive development; it simply means that the teacher should not assume that this approach is what comes "naturally" to students or that it is the best or only way. I have seen students visibly relieved when they were told they had a choice of inductive or deductive development.

Whether Americans are more opinionated than other people is a moot question. That most Americans will express an opinion on anything from astrology to zeppelins is less in doubt. Bilingual students often claim not to have opinions on topic after topic. Many are critical of the outspokenness of Americans with what appears to them to be flimsy bases for argument. Some seem consistently to take both sides of an argument in their writing or to cling to the raising of questions or citing of facts without drawing a conclusion or otherwise stating an opinion. The only problem is that the teacher or some of the more Americanized or outspoken students will have contempt for the person who does not readily venture his opinions. Perhaps the best way to avoid such bullying and coaxing is not to tell students how they should organize their thoughts but rather to examine ways that people, themselves included, do it.

Group Activities. Simulation games, paired editing, small-group discussion and writing, and other learning arrangements for composition work have been tried among CUNY ESL students with considerable success. ESL students, on the whole, will simply do what a teacher says more readily than American students, and this fact is both an advantage and a disadvantage. It assures that nearly every student will try a new arrangement, but it sometimes masks the strong disinclination a student may feel about working with one or more other people. ESL teachers should not assume that because their students usually cooperate there is any less potential for unhappiness and resistance than among other students.

Sometimes there is more, especially if what students are being asked to do encroaches on their territoriality (if, for example, a teacher says, "Pull your chairs in close together, knee to knee, so you can hear each other well") or ignores sex or age roles dictated by their culture.

Even if a teacher does not know what students' personal and cultural restraints concerning group interaction are, she should look for signs: visual cues like gestures, posture, and facial expressions as students work together; superficial or meager writing resulting from group work; or an overall decrease in completed work. New activities and working arrangements can be introduced but they should be introduced gradually and carefully with as much comment and criticism as students will give. Looking beyond (or behind) students' overt willingness can help prevent some of the discomfort and resentment that is often felt quietly in ESL classrooms.

Writing from Visual Stimuli. Culture influences perception as much as it does language. If a teacher is willing to look at the subtle variations, even in such seemingly straightforward things as spatial relationships, among his students, he will probably choose very explicit visual material at the outset and only gradually introduce schematized, and often culturally loaded, material like cartoons. Humor in particular is vastly different from culture to culture, and what we find hilarious can fall flat among bilingual students if adequate preparation and context are not provided.

Three Composition Activities: Art, Literature, the Opposites. Raimes' *Focus on Composition* uses Magritte's *Portrait,* that unblinking eye gazing out of the center of a slab of ham on a plate, as the basis for a composition activity that combines group work, drafting and developing a paragraph, and analysis of one's own and a partner's writing. All of this is part of what Raimes calls a core composition, the writing assignment in each of her chapters which introduces new syntactic and rhetorical structures. This core assignment asks partners to examine and discuss what they see in *Portrait,* then "repaint the picture with words" individually. When both partners have finished their paragraphs, they write answers to questions posed by the text: "What did you mention first? What did you mention last? Why did you choose to do it that way?" They discuss their answers with each other and, at this point, either or both may choose to rewrite the paragraph before handing it in. The teacher treats this paragraph not so much as a finished product but as a means to determine what the student needs to focus on. More than a dozen group or individual tasks follow the core composition; the teacher recommends those that best suit each student's needs.

I have used this activity many times, always with very satisfying results, first, I believe, because of the oneness of freedom and control skillfully and subtly incorporated into the task, second, because it uses real art. Though many students are nonplussed by the painting at first, they nearly always come to like it and write interesting things about it if given time and a chance to talk about it. I have sometimes asked them to write one paragraph that is as much as possible pure observation, another speculation as to the artist's state of mind or the meaning he wanted to convey, a third a combination of the two. These paragraphs are wonderful to read and easy to mark nonjudgmentally, at least to the extent that success in distinguishing perception from interpretation can take precedence over the writing being good or bad.

Magritte's *Portrait,* Grant Wood's *American Gothic,* Hopper's *Night Hawks,* photographs, cartoons, and film stills encourage students' feeling that they are writing in the real world, not the artificial ESL world that most textbooks and many teachers create. The Raimes text illustrates consistently that if students need any simplification, it should be in structure, not in content or interest level.

In a paper given at a statewide ESL teachers' conference, Edward Palumbo said: "In order for a pupil to feel the world is on his side, the diversity of the world has to be in the lessons and presented in such a way that the pupil feels the world is explaining his life in a friendly manner." Palumbo, who bases his teaching of bilingual students on the Aesthetic Realism of Eli Siegel, described using Leigh Hunt's poem, "Jenny Kiss'd Me," to generate discussion and writing.

> *Jenny kiss'd me when we met,*
> *Jumping from the chair she sat in;*
> *Time, you thief, who love to get*

Sweets into your list, put that in!
Say I'm weary, say I'm sad,
  Say that health and wealth have miss'd me,
Say I'm growing old, but add,
  Jenny kiss'd me.

The question students are asked to answer is: "Does this poem show that no matter how sad or disappointed a person is, if he can name one thing he likes, he is stronger?" Students like the poem and the question because both acknowledge the bad feelings a person can have, the fact that the world is not always nice, and, at the same time, suggest that we consciously look for what is good, what can honestly be liked.

Many ESL teachers are reluctant to use poetry with any level of ESL students. Yet poetry can reach deeply beneath layers of culture and individuality to touch a universal person. Certainly, not all teachers believe this, but that should not prevent anyone from experimenting with poetry with ESL students. Yes, it takes even more careful preparation and patience than using visual art, but students feel that their minds and abilities are respected by such study.

Like Palumbo, I am a student of Aesthetic Realism; I, too, am certain that the purpose of all education is to like the world, and I base my teaching on that principle. My best writing assignment for bilingual students is one that has them look at something in the world and at themselves in a way they have never done before—that is, in terms of pairs of opposites they share. We start very simply. Pairs of students take five minutes to list as many pairs of opposites as they can think of; no one ever has difficulty with this, so we talk about how people learn the opposites (if they are learned at all) and agree on them so widely in spite of cultural and individual differences. Then the class choose what they feel is the ugliest or the least interesting thing in the classroom, and we look at its opposites: ugly *and* beautiful, hard and soft, light and dark, surface and depth, and so on. Each student chooses some nonliving thing that he can describe in terms of three pairs of opposites it has. When that part of the writing is drafted, I ask them to describe themselves or someone very close to them in terms of the same

three pairs of opposites. Some students are surprised by this addition. They ask, "Hard and soft in me. . . light and dark?" But here
the thinking and writing become the most interesting, the most
creative. Very seldom does anyone choose to write about someone
other than himself; very few students write fewer than two typed
pages even though I do not set a word limit.

This section ends with a Chinese student's response to the
opposites assignment. We had not mentioned poetry, but he chose
to combine poetry and prose in relating himself to the wind.

> *I, Like the Wind*
> *I, like the wind,*
> *Can soar up, can plunge down*
> *As in my emotions.*
> *I, like the wind,*
> *Can rage strong, can go limp*
> *As in my passion.*
> *I, like the wind,*
> *As soothing as a summer's breeze,*
> *As irritating as the Arctic's freeze*
> *As in my mood.*
> *I, like the wind,*
> *As light as a warm front's tail,*
> *As dense as a cold front's gale*
> *As in my thoughts.*
> *I, like the wind,*
> *Omnipresent,*
> *Spanning across the Universe*
> *As in my love for you.*

Sameness and Differences

In the poem "I, Like the Wind," I compare myself with a
natural phenomenon, the wind. There are five stanzas. All of the
stanzas start with the line, "I, like the wind."

The first two stanzas have a set pattern or rhythm. They
consist of three lines each. The second lines of the stanzas consist of
two fragments. The two sets of fragments tell us that my emotion
and passion can go to opposite extremes like the wind. The wind is
very unpredictable. It can soar up to the limits of the sky and
plummet to the ground in a matter of seconds. The words used in
each line are opposite extremes. The first fragment is in a positive
tone, and the latter is in a negative tone.

In the third and fourth stanzas the pattern and rhythm are

elaborate. There are four lines instead of three. The second line has a positive tone and the third line a negative tone. The words that are used have two syllables as opposed to the first two stanzas. The words are also more descriptive and expand the visualization of the poem in view of the world. The comparisons of the feelings to the wind become more complex as in my mood and thoughts.

The last stanza is the most important one. The word structure is different from the preceding stanzas. The second line has only one word. That is because the word *omnipresent* needs no adjectives to describe or modify it. *Omnipresent* is a word that has connotative meanings with God's presence. The scope of the poem travels far to infinity with the use of the word *universe*. The last stanza is trying to convey to the reader that my feelings are boundless and eternal. The last line describes the feeling of love and reveals to the reader that the poem is written for a special person in my life.

—Charles Chin

Support Services

ESL programs draw heavily upon support services available to reading and basic writing students because higher-level ESL students' needs, as has been discussed earlier in this chapter, are quite similar to those of their native English-speaking counterparts. This section will not duplicate the descriptions of support services in Chapters One and Two, but instead will describe aspects of such services which are tailored to the special needs of ESL students. Where a CUNY ESL program has an innovative approach to support services which does not exist in just the same form for English-speaking students, that, too, will be included.

There are three factors which make support services even more essential for ESL students than for most others. First, nearly all ESL students need help and encouragement in social adaptation. Those who are new to the United States have to learn not only a new language but a new culture and lifestyle, or, at least, they must make their peace with the new setting if they are to do well in it. Second, even the most able and adaptable among lower-level ESL students cannot get enough listening and speaking practice in the classroom. Most speak their first language at home, many with their friends as well, so out-of-class practice, both formal and informal, is highly desirable. Third, there are ESL students whose needs are similar to those of native English-speaking students—personal problems and learning difficulties—but are exacerbated by linguistic and cultural differences.

Unless he is already adapted to, or integrated into, American culture, the ESL student who seeks out tutoring, counseling, or other support services is showing not only that he wants extra help but also that he is able to overcome his self-consciousness in order to get it.

A Comprehensive Program

One of the recurrent problems of support services is that it is difficult to coordinate them and not overlap services to various groups within the college population. Brooklyn College, CUNY, has a comprehensive counseling unit in which three counselors work full-time with students from a 285-person ESL program. Students receive academic advising and program approval at the beginning of the school term and nonacademic, as well as academic, counseling throughout the year. Early in each semester, the counselors hold group sessions for incoming freshmen on such matters as the rules and regulations of the college and the cultural differences in styles of education. Group sessions continue until students seem comfortable in the college.

Tutoring is also organized through this comprehensive program. Counselors arrange for peer tutoring using students in the program and work-study students. They have also helped set up an English club and encourage students who want to put on cultural programs such as plays or a spring festival.

Although their major concern is that ESL students not feel alienated from the social life of the college, the counselors have also initiated college-wide interest in the needs of the bilingual students. As a result, some departments offer several courses in Spanish, and others have designated sections of regular courses for ESL students. Brooklyn College is the only CUNY unit with so well coordinated a program of support services. The remainder of this section discusses each of its functions as they appear separately elsewhere.

Counseling and Advisement

Most CUNY colleges have at least two full-time bilingual counselors if their ESL population is over 200. Hostos College, where nearly the entire student body speaks Spanish, has five bilingual counselors who, in addition to counseling, are involved with an English club and other social activities. Where there are not enough regular counselors to meet the demand, peer counseling and faculty counseling have been found to meet most student needs. Peers have the obvious advantage of common experiences and empathy, and faculty generally cooperate willingly. In addition to peers and faculty, many colleges use CETA assistants for academic advising.

At Hunter College, the Office of Academic Advising and the Office of Student Services jointly offer a one-credit Freshman Seminar, which is required of all freshmen taking more than one developmental course. The content of the seminar encompasses general training in college skills. Group discussions focus on such topics as test anxiety, time management, note-taking, and strategies for participating in class. Students in this course say that they would take it voluntarily if it were not required, and although such a course should not be used as a substitute for individual counseling and advisement, it has the advantage of reaching all developmental students.

Tutoring

Tutor Selection. Certainly knowledge of ESL needs and approaches is valuable in any tutor. However, it seems that personal qualities, particularly respect for students' language and culture, are more significant than a tutor's preparation. Some of the best tutoring is done by undergraduates who have been through the ESL program themselves and will empathize but not commiserate with the students they are tutoring.

Kinds of Tutoring. Tutoring assistance can take many forms; tutors may assist teachers in the classroom, hold workshops for the entire class, or work with small groups and individual students. In the classroom, for example, a tutor could participate in a number of the regular class meetings, working with individuals or small groups, marking exercises or controlled compositions, or moving around the room as students work on an assignment. The tutor would be assigned to work with one class throughout the semester and would use his knowledge of what takes place in the class to tutor those same students outside of the class.

These tutors may also conduct workshops, with the teacher present, for the entire class or a large part of a class. During these sessions, planned by the teacher and tutor, the tutor is primarily responsible for lesson follow-up. This is often a good time for students to work on homework assignments and for the teacher to see students individually.

If two to five students have a particular need or problem, small-group tutoring can be even more effective than individual tutoring because of the interaction among students and the fact that a single student is not always "on the spot." Tutors and students express strong and widely differing opinions about group tutoring; it seems essential to ask students how they feel about it since the best tutoring cannot work if its format is objectionable to participants. If a student objects to group tutoring or does not fit into any group already established, individual tutoring is advisable. For both group tutoring and individual tutoring, a weekly one-hour meeting is standard, but more frequent meetings are recommended if budget and scheduling permit.

Tutors can also be assigned to work with students who have failed a course. In lieu of attending his regular classes, the student meets at least twice a week with a tutor in an independent study program. This special tutorial has proven successful because students know they must pass this time or repeat the course they have already failed. Teachers, glad not to have a student in class who is all too familiar with the material, give such students more conference time and encouragement than others might receive.

A Tutoring Model. Although it is often considered a luxury, a plan which brings tutors into the classroom is by far the most effective means of assuring close coordination of ESL teaching and tutoring. It is especially needed in lower-level courses where the teacher is introducing core structures for oral practice, and all or most follow-up work should arise directly out of that core.

Figure 7 illustrates a model for a tutoring program for the lower-level and writing courses of an ESL program of about 325 students. Such a plan needs six teachers and six tutors. Teachers' course loads would be fifteen hours, although those teaching lower-level courses might have two or four additional workshop hours with the advantage of having a smaller total number of students than teachers in higher-level courses. One teacher would have three hours' release time for a coordinator's job, and another would have the same release time to supervise tutoring since the administrative demands of this coordinated program are great. Tutors would also have fifteen contact hours with students though a third of that time would be spent monitoring in the lab rather than tutoring. One tutor would have a lighter load in order to take care of student sign-up for tutoring, day-to-day materials needs, and assistance to new tutors.

Tutor Training. If tutors participate in classes, the need for training is lessened by at least half. If they do not, a training program must acquaint them with the content and methods of the courses so that they can draw upon the course content for follow-up tutorial. Particularly if tutors work with lower-level students, they cannot rely on their own abilities as speakers and writers of English; the tutoring supervisor must teach them methods or, at least, the use of materials which they can use.

An ESL Lab

A lab is informal, open to all comers, materials-oriented, and minimally supervised. If a lab has a casual, social atmosphere (which might be inappropriate for other disciplines but not for ESL), so much the better if students feel they can walk in and chat with a sympathetic peer. This being the case, it is worth noting that lab monitors may be work-study students or other inexperienced persons if tutors are unavailable. Basically a lab monitor need only know where materials are and how to help students to use them.

A good physical arrangement for a combined lab and tutoring center is one large room where most materials and files are kept and several smaller rooms for individual and small-group tutoring. Materials which have proven useful for lab work include the texts

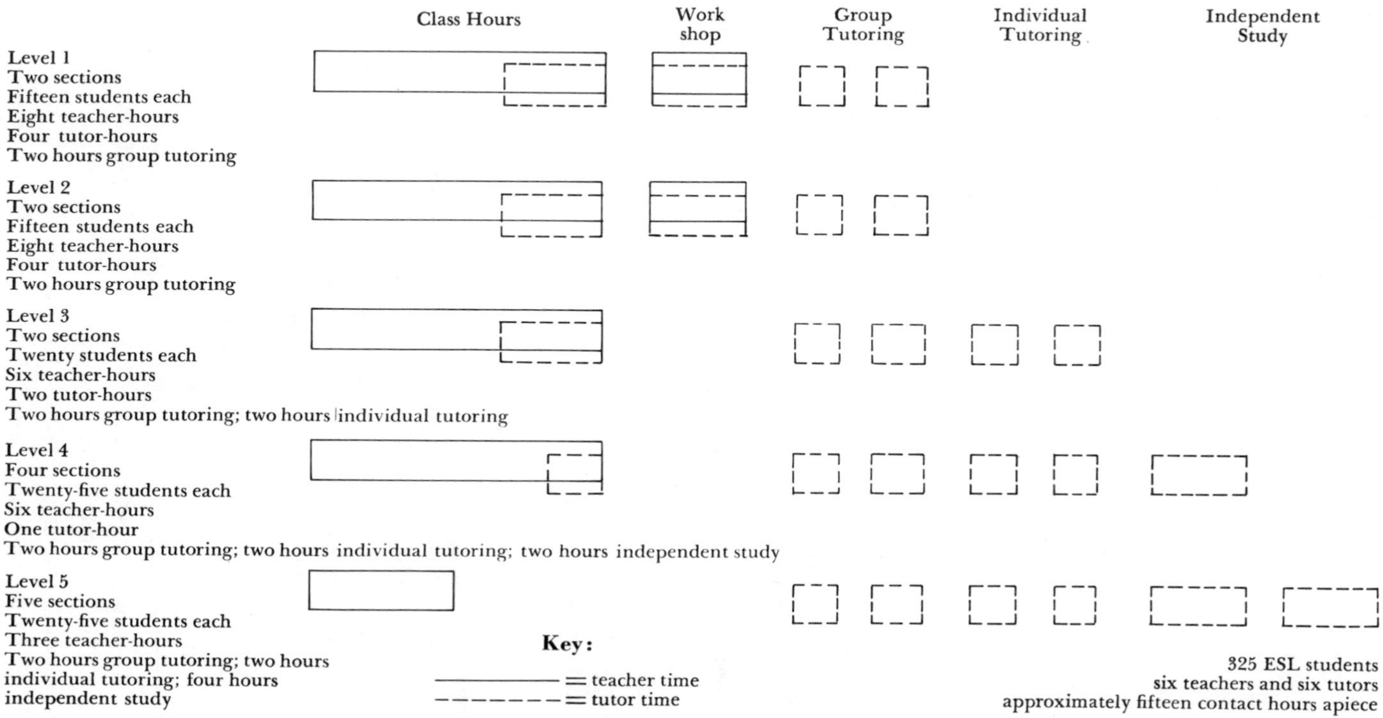

Figure 7. A Teaching and Tutoring Model

described earlier in this chapter (controlled composition, sentence combining, and picture composition); reference texts like Praninskas' *A Rapid Review of English Grammar* (1975), Crowell's *Index to Modern English* (1964), Yorkey's *Study Skills for Students of English as a Second Language* (1970), and some of the various texts of English idioms. Unfortunately, most of the recorded material for ESL use consists of remarkably boring grammar drills, but some ESL teachers have used songs and stories on tape to provide more interesting and realistic listening material.

Faculty Involvement

Although the counseling unit or other personnel may coordinate support services, there is no substitute for faculty-student contact outside the classroom. At the very least, ESL teachers should plan to spend one hour a week in scheduled conferences for every three hours in class. This is often a college requirement for developmental courses, and some colleges pay part-time teachers for these hours, but if they do not, faculty should view such time as essential to student progress. The majority of ESL teachers give conferences focused on skills, sometimes as many as three or four for each student over a semester, but the ESL teacher is rare who would back away from students' raising more personal issues. Some teachers trained in counseling-learning techniques use five to ten minutes to allow a student to say anything he wants to with the understanding that the teacher will simply do his best to comprehend through echoic responses. Other teachers have found their conferences turn into counseling sessions, and it appears that a lack of training on the teacher's part is compensated for by his familiarity with the student and his concern for the student.

Nearly all of the services described in the preceding pages—tutoring, labs, English clubs, bilingual courses, and special sections in other departments' courses—have been set up entirely by the faculty at many CUNY colleges. Ambitious faculty members also have acquired grants for additional services and special programs throughout the University. For example, the director of the Queensborough College Writing Lab received a New York State Council of the Arts grant in 1975 to work with a group of ESL

students on a slide and sound show. The ten students who participated used cameras and tapes to record their own and their
families' and friends' experiences on coming to this country. In
1974, two faculty members, also at Queensborough, received a
grant from the Vocational Educational Skills Administration to establish a writing center for students in career programs. The center
has a full-time director, assistants, and instructors who prepare
materials for sound-on-slide machines and sound-page machines.

La Guardia Community College recently received a grant to
develop support services in humanistic education. This three-year
grant, funded at $122,000 for the first year, will enable the Basic
Skills Task force to hire four new full-time counseling-tutors, who
will be trained in Counseling-Learning procedures and will work
with all developmental skills students.

4

Miriam Hecht
Geoffrey Akst

✷ ✷ ✷ ✷ ✷ ✷ ✷ ✷ ✷ ✷ ✷ ✷ ✷ ✷ ✷ ✷ ✷

Mathematics

In reading and writing remediation, objectives are relatively well defined; the immediate problem is how to attain them. In mathematics, the "how" of remedial instruction has not lost its importance, but it is preceded by several other questions: what should be taught, to whom, and why.

Viewed in the aggregate, the content of remedial mathematics is not a single subject; it is a network of related subjects. To extract from this material one "best" remedial curriculum for all students is virtually impossible. Literature majors may need arithmetic but not algebra; nursing students may need algebra but not trigonometry; technology students probably need as much mathematics as they can get. Even if we accept the rather narrow definition proposed by Roueche and Wheeler (1973, p. 223) that " 'Remedial' implies the remediation of student deficiencies in order that the student may enter a program for which he was previously ineligible," it leads us to different courses of study for different populations.

As a rule, remedial mathematics courses, apart from their arithmetic content, cover material selected from the traditional academic high school sequence. Typically, this sequence consists of a year of elementary algebra, a year of plane Euclidean geometry, and a year of "eleventh-year" or "fusion" math, providing additional topics in algebra along with some trigonometry and analytic geometry. Before 1970, this preparation was required for admission to many colleges, including all branches of the City University of New York (CUNY). However, it must be borne in mind that this substantial curriculum was designed for a preselected, academically oriented student body. To expect it of today's underprepared open admissions population is unrealistic.

Moreover, the dimensions of the problem are cause for the greatest concern. A 1978 survey of two-year colleges conducted by the American Mathematical Society found that 44 percent of all math enrollments were in arithmetic or high school algebra. In mandated proficiency tests administered to high school students or entering college freshmen, it has been common for between 30 and 50 percent of all students to fail in mathematics; when CUNY began using such tests in 1978, nearly twice as many students failed mathematics as reading.

It is tempting to speculate on the reasons for these deficiencies, but the answer may be simply that mathematics has never been an easy subject. For some students the content is hopelessly abstract. "I don't know what you're talking about," they protest, and they are telling the literal truth. Piaget claims that a considerable degree of intellectual maturity is needed to cope with the level of abstraction inherent in mathematics; possibly a number of high school and college students are not yet ready. Moreover, mathematics has a large component of sheer technique; to develop this technique may require more practice and drill than students are willing to give to it. The cumulative nature of mathematics also poses a problem; within a given branch, each topic builds upon the previous ones. This means that learning must be thorough; a student who is floundering halfway through the semester may be drowning by the end. Finally, mathematics, in contrast to reading and writing, is very much a "school" subject; very little learning or reinforcement takes place outside of class.

To design a remedial program in the face of these constraints involves a number of complex decisions. In language remediation, it is reasonable to work toward maximizing learning; there is little question that "more is better." In mathematics, faculty must first select content, justify it, and match it with students for whom it is appropriate. Only then can they ask "How do we go about it?"

In what follows, we will turn our attention to these issues. First, however, we would like to indicate what we mean by the term *remedial mathematics.* Because it seems impossible to produce a comprehensive definition which can be used unequivocally to characterize courses which colleges themselves designate as remedial, we will rather tentatively suggest a few characteristics which can serve as guidelines: (1) *Content:* By and large, the content of remedial mathematics courses is taken from arithmetic or the traditional high school curriculum described earlier. However, there are exceptions: thus, some calculator mathematics or a few topics from statistics may be introduced. (2) *Credit:* If a course carries reduced credit or none at all, then the college itself probably views the course as remedial or partly so. (3) *Placement:* The college has usually developed a uniform placement procedure to identify students who can benefit from the remedial program. On some campuses all incoming students are evaluated in this way; on others, only those in specific, mathematics-related curricula. (4) *Enrollment:* Typically, students who have been identified as in need of remediation are strongly urged, or even mandated, to take the remedial courses. Even when the course itself is optional, mastery of the content may be a condition for graduation.

We recognize that this handful of clues is very far from a formal definition, but perhaps it will serve to get us started. Ultimately we are concerned with defining the term *remedial mathematics* not by any cursory statement but by an examination of remedial programs, the problems they face, and the solutions that have been found.

Objectives

In principle, at least, the development of a remedial program should grow out of its objectives. But in mathematics remediation, objectives themselves are a subject of lively controversy.

In general, program objectives fall into four areas: (1) those based on the value of mathematical content such as definitions, algorithms, techniques, and theorems; (2) those based on the value of mathematical patterns of thought such as logical inference or abstraction—patterns sometimes referred to as "processes" to distinguish them from the content mentioned above; (3) those based on cultural considerations; and (4) those concerned with affective growth—the outlook, attitudes, or personality of the student.

Content Objectives

On the face of it, one excellent justification for mathematics remediation is simply to teach students the content of the course; the assumption is that they will need it, if not in subsequent college work, then in the outside world. This point of view leads to several clear-cut, pragmatic objectives.

Preparation for Next Course. Probably the most widespread objective of mathematics remediation is to provide the skills needed for subsequent coursework, in mathematics itself or in related fields. Thus Ablon (1972, p. 1127), describing a remedial program at Staten Island Community College, writes, "The program is aimed at our technical (pre-engineering, science, and technology) students. We have only one objective: *to prepare these students to enter our regular precalculus courses as quickly as possible.*" Similarly, an arithmetic course may serve as preparation for statistics, and so on.

The reasoning behind this objective is irrefutable. A student must take a certain course, he lacks the prerequisite material; therefore, he needs remediation. This approach, however, may be criticized for its narrowness; it identifies the smallest possible remedial population and offers it the smallest possible amount of mathematics.

Open Options. A second objective extends the above point of view; we may call it *open options.* The issue here is that many students arrive at college with no clear sense of their ultimate curriculum or career goals. By the time they finally decide, they may find themselves shut out by the mathematical requirements of the field. Thus a student deciding to major in biology may belatedly discover that the course of study requires calculus—which in turn must be preceded by a year or more of mathematics remediation.

Similarly, a prospective business administration major may be shocked to learn that the curriculum includes linear programming and computer science. Faculty who have witnessed the panic of such students will be the first to appreciate the importance of providing them with a firm grounding in basic mathematics. This is important for all students, but particularly for those who have been deprived educationally all their lives and for whom open admissions means nothing if not the opportunity to extend their options and alternatives.

Preparation for Everyday Life. Proponents of the preceding objectives are concerned with preparing students for subsequent coursework. Other professionals are interested in students' ordinary mathematical needs outside of college. The assumption is that as consumers and citizens, all students need to know some mathematics. They need to balance checkbooks, pay sales tax, cut recipes in half, and try to make sense of the graphs on television and in the newspapers. The mathematical skills required to cope with such tasks are basic and inescapable.

This objective is not immune to criticism. Millions of Americans have demonstrated that these demands of daily life can in fact be circumvented. They never attempt to balance their checkbooks without a pocket calculator (or even with it), they would not dream of cutting a recipe in half (a little extra never hurt), and they willingly pay accountants to prepare their income tax returns. More seriously, as we shall see, the content of courses with such objectives too often consists of little more than the traditional topics from arithmetic, many of which have been rendered all but obsolete by the growing popularity of pocket calculators. Nonetheless, the basic principle has provided the impetus for many remedial programs, and there is certainly merit in the idea that every student should attain at least a minimal level of mathematical literacy.

Preparation for Screening Procedures. Diverse as the above goals may be, they all reflect their proponents' conviction about the inherent value of mathematics. The next objective is more cynical: to help students survive the barrage of mathematical tests used for hiring, promotion, admission to graduate school, and the like. In many cases, such mathematics tests are used even though the relevance of the students' mathematical skills to the test's objectives are questionable. Thus, civil service tests for clerk-typists include arithmetic questions that would raise hackles on an expert; would-be cashiers are endlessly tested on arithmetic, despite the fact that their cash registers can easily handle all the necessary computations. Looking elsewhere, we find that mathematics comprises a significant part of the aptitude test required for law school (LSAT), although there is little evidence that the legal profession makes any substantial use of the content.

The authors make no effort to conceal their concern about this use of mathematics. Of course, where the content is germane to the job or academic program there is no issue. But to use questions in mathematics in place of outlawed intelligence tests or socioeconomic screenings, as a sifting device to narrow down the field of applicants, is an injustice both to the individuals involved and to mathematics itself. Nonetheless, for the present many students need to be prepared for such tests, and it may well be the obligation of remedial programs to meet this need.

Quantitative Sense. Finally, we come to an objective which, while related to content, goes well beyond it. This view is that the purpose of remediation is not to teach specific concepts or skills, but rather to instill what may be called *quantitative sense* — an insight into the general behavior of numbers. Quantitative sense, like most psychological constructs, is hard to define. Perhaps it is what faculty have in mind when they plead, "Never mind all the details; just give them a feeling for numbers"; perhaps it is what makes the difference between the student who can cope with later work in mathematics and the one who cannot. Yet this trait is rarely addressed directly; the expectation is that it will be acquired, if at all, as a by-product of conventional courses. Of course, the pedagogy of fostering traits is hardly on a firm footing, nor can we always identify the students who might benefit. Nonetheless, in many colleges the development of quantitative sense may be an important, if implicit, goal of mathematics remedial programs.

Process-Oriented Objectives

Transfer of Training. The claim has been made that while the content of mathematics courses is of interest only to a select few, the modes of thought involved—critical thinking, precision of expression, search for strategies of proof, generalization, and so on—are of importance to everyone. If students can acquire these abilities in a mathematics course and apply them to other areas, then we have a very powerful argument for teaching mathematics, remedial or otherwise.

Unfortunately, whether these patterns of thought can in fact be taught, much less applied, is a matter of controversy. Although the idea appears plausible, when it was tested at the turn of this century, results were negative; transfer of training simply did not take place. Recently, there has been another about-face. Several educators maintain that some mathematical principles and strategies, if properly taught, can in fact be transferred to other disciplines. If early experimenters missed the effect, they may merely have been using inadequate pedagogical and statistical techniques.

Today, the evidence is inconclusive, and further research has been urged. Questions have also arisen about the content of instruction; Whimbey, Boylan, and Burke (1979) have proposed that instead of being taught peripherally, rational thinking should become the focus of an entire course. In any event, to suggest rational thinking as a remedial objective raises some questions. If it can in fact be taught, then far from being remedial, it is of overriding importance; it should be one of the primary goals of most college-level "liberal arts" mathematics courses.

Moral Discipline. As if instruction in rational thinking were not enough, some parents and educators have advocated mathematics as a form of moral discipline. Jeremy Kilpatrick, in a recent talk presenting ideas developed by himself and James Fey (1979), remarked that "several case study observers noted in mathematics teaching something akin to the cultural rituals identified by sociologists and anthropologists. . . . When parents responded to the issue of hand calculators, for example, the emotion in their response suggested that the real issue was a sacred ritual of education, not practical utility. Teachers and parents also commented on the nonmathematical goals implicit in [mathematics] teaching. They believe students should be encouraged to work hard, keep busy, be polite, compete, aspire to improve, work independently, and prepare for things to come."

Here the harassed remediation instructors must beg off. They are grateful if they can teach their students the quadratic formula or the fine points of percent; they have neither the desire nor the qualifications to become moral leaders. Yet the view described above is pervasive, particularly among nonmathematicians, who are often the ones to approve remedial programs, examine the results, and control the budget.

Cultural Objectives

While proponents of the next two objectives acknowledge the value of mathematical content and processes, they also see other advantages. They approach mathematics as part of a broad cultural tradition spanning several thousand years and well worth continuing.

Traditionalism. The "traditionalist" argues that for years, entering college freshmen were required to complete the standard three-year sequence of academic high school mathematics, and such a time-honored tradition deserves to be respected. If, under relaxed admissions criteria, freshmen are admitted without this preparation, then they should enroll in courses that enable them to remove their deficiencies.

This point of view has been vigorously attacked and as vigorously defended. It has been criticized as outmoded and praised for "maintaining standards." Opponents claim that the traditionalist objective penalizes the very students who are supposed to benefit most from open admissions; supporters reply that anything less would prejudge those students as inherently unable to learn. The debate is particularly heated in that the recommended remedial sequence is often mandatory.

Humanism. The "humanists" share the traditionalist concern for historical values, but for different reasons. They see high school mathematics, in particular algebra and geometry, as an important influence on philosophy, science, and the arts, and hence as a major component of a liberal arts education. Even if students forget the details of their high school mathematics, they often retain a sense of its scope, methodology, and applications—in short, a feeling for its impact upon our culture. The college freshman who lacks this background should therefore have the opportunity to acquire it in mathematics remediation. Hayden and Mineka (1976, p. vi) suggest that such a program offers not merely "a sound background for further study of mathematics" but also an insight into "the role of active inquiry and discovery, not only in learning mathematics, but also in understanding its essential spirit."

Affective Objectives

The advocate of affective objectives is concerned less with the learning of mathematics than with the student's feelings in relation to the subject. The argument is that by the time remedial students enter college, they have had so many discouraging experiences with mathematics that they are ready to throw up their arms in despair. They dislike the subject, they dislike themselves in relation to the subject, and they see no chance for improvement. Affective objectives, designed to resolve the impasse, include enhancing self-image, overcoming "math anxiety," and improving attitudes toward mathematics.

The problem with affective goals is that one is never sure whether they are fostered for their own sake or merely to facilitate learning. In the first case, there can be no quarrel; who could with clear conscience object to the pursuit of happiness? However, the content of these courses suggests that affective goals are actually no more than stepping stones; the hope is that positive attitudes will translate into higher motivation and a correspondingly greater measure of learning. For this purpose, the importance of affective factors is far from established. Some authorities attach great importance to them; thus Kelley notes that "How one feels controls behavior, while what one knows does not " (1974, p. 86). On the other hand, a number of studies suggest that attitudes have little or no effect on mathematical learning (Aiken, 1976). As for questions of self-image or mathematics anxiety, programs are springing up by the dozens, particularly for women, but as yet the evidence is inconclusive.

Finally, we may note that colleges, as well as individuals, may be concerned about self-image. More than one school has initiated mathematics remediation less for the benefit of the remedial students than out of fear that its reputation will be tarnished by graduates who cannot add or subtract.

The preceding objectives have been sorted out for the purpose of discussion, but in practice many remedial programs have more than one objective. Thus, an algebra course may be taken by some students as a prerequisite for statistics, and by others to prepare for the LSAT or similar tests; or a remedial program may have the dual objectives of combating math anxiety and teaching arithmetic. Occasionally, additional objectives are grafted onto an existing program, as when a precalculus course is suddenly required to do double duty as preparation for a newly mandated proficiency test. So the influence of objectives is not quite as clear-cut as we might like it to be.

Nonetheless, it is our belief that objectives should be a key factor in the design of the entire remedial program. Moreover, they should be bona fide objectives, not rationalizations after the event. Too often, remedial faculty have no more than a diffuse feeling for the objectives of the program; even to raise the question takes them by surprise. It appears likely that time spent defining objectives at the beginning of a program will vastly improve its ultimate effectiveness.

Course Content

By and large, the content of remedial mathematics courses is chosen from the traditional precollege curriculum. Figure 1 suggests the range of this material. Roughly speaking, these topics are sequential from arithmetic through eleventh-year math, although Euclidean geometry is somewhat out of the main line of development.

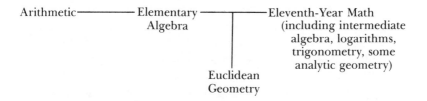

Figure 1. The Traditional Precollege Mathematics Curriculum

However, not all these subjects are covered in every remedial program. Some may not be offered at all, while others are taught in regular college-level courses.

Probably the major factor governing the selection of remedial content is the program's objectives. If the objective is traditionalist—to reconstruct the entire high school curriculum—then the content will include all the subjects just mentioned with the possible exception of arithmetic. If the goal is to prepare students for subsequent coursework, then the remedial content is likely to be arithmetic, algebra, or both.

Yet program objectives are themselves tempered by a more subtle factor: the college's expectations for entering freshmen. Few colleges are in a position to disregard the preparation, orientation, and ability of incoming students. To design a remedial program without realistically appraising what the average freshman knows or how long it will take him to learn it may be ill-advised and even counterproductive. Given that certain subjects are prerequisite to the college curriculum—say, algebra in a technical college— expectations may help define the boundary between remedial and nonremedial work. For example, colleges often weigh the psychological impact of classifying intermediate algebra as a remedial course if most of their freshmen are also deficient in arithmetic and elementary algebra. Requiring several terms of so-called remedial courses may create problems both in attracting students to the college and in motivating them once they have arrived.

When program objectives are less specific, the role of expectations may be even stronger. For example, if the goal is to help students keep their options open, how much math should students take? Is it realistic to encourage all students to study trigonometry or algebra? If students are being prepared for outside examinations, which students and which examinations? If the objective is to inculcate quantitative sense, how much and for whom?

Regardless of how the curriculum was determined, a remedial college course is likely to be less demanding than its high school counterpart. Often the college course will cover less material; for example, some elementary algebra courses omit simultaneous linear equations. One explanation for this difference is that traditional high school mathematics attracts the best students, while college remediation is intended for the weakest. Another is time: the content for which high schools allow five days a week over an entire year is compressed into a single one-semester three-hour college course. Moreover, college remedial courses are likely to emphasize skills and techniques, generally at the expense of concepts and proofs. Thus, a remedial geometry course may stress quantitative applications, reducing important theorems to mere rules-of-thumb. This filtering out of concepts is often as much a matter of policy as of feasibility; skills are easier not only to measure but also to justify in terms of subsequent needs.

Against this background, we can consider in detail the content of several specific remedial areas, starting with the most basic.

Arithmetic

Courses in arithmetic loom large in many remedial programs; a national survey of two- and four-year colleges found that arithmetic was offered at 84 percent of responding institutions (Baldwin and others, 1975). This is a natural emphasis; most remedial programs prefer to lay a secure foundation, starting with arithmetic and building up. The arithmetic course may have a number of objectives, among them preparation for the next course, for external tests, or for daily needs. When the goal is improvement of attitudes or self-image, arithmetic is often used to provide students with a taste of success.

Virtually all arithmetic courses cover operations with whole numbers, fractions, and decimals; other topics include ratio and proportion, percent, and word problems. Sometimes a course continues into operations with signed numbers, or it may branch off into a study of measurement. As a rule, the emphasis is on traditional pencil-and-paper manipulation; practice with algorithms occupies a good part of the period.

As yet, the impact of hand-held calculators on the arithmetic curriculum has been minimal. However, many educators feel that a change is inevitable; Vogeli (1975) asserts that certain topics in pencil-and-paper arithmetic will soon be as anachronistic as "sewing a fine seam." Already, courses in the use of pocket calculators are springing up, and wherever one turns there is talk of dropping entirely all proficiency requirements in conventional arithmetic.

Of course, such a radical change is not likely to gain wide acceptance overnight. While one issue—that of developing an unhealthy dependence on machines—may be suspect, the responsibility to prepare students for future admissions and employment exams cannot be ignored. This factor is serving to inhibit what many believe to be an appropriate adaptation of school curriculum to advancing technology.

Algebra

Elementary algebra is offered at even more colleges than is arithmetic—at nearly 90 percent of the colleges surveyed (Baldwin and others, 1975). Occasionally, the course parallels the traditional ninth year high school curriculum, particularly when articulation with intermediate algebra is important. However, many elementary algebra courses limit themselves to the more basic topics in the curriculum, especially if the course is designed for nonscience majors. These topics include: operations on polynomials and rational expressions, factoring, solutions of linear equations (by general consensus the most important topic in the course), and graphing linear functions; a few courses include simultaneous linear equations and quadratics.

Elementary algebra is a paramount example of a subject recommended in the interest of keeping the student's options open. It finds applications in virtually every technical area: in the physical sciences, the health sciences, and many of the social sciences. College faculty are more apt to mourn deficiencies in algebra than in any other subject, including arithmetic; indications are growing that of the two subjects, algebra is the more important.

Intermediate algebra courses, in contrast to elementary algebra, are widely considered too advanced to be designated as remedial. They are usually elective and are intended primarily for students with a specific interest in mathematics, science, or technology. Standard topics include polynomial functions, exponents and logarithms, and inequalities; stronger courses may also touch upon trigonometry and analytic geometry.

Geometry

According to Baldwin, geometry courses are offered by only about 35 percent of the colleges surveyed. When an entire course in geometry is offered, it is usually for traditionalist or humanistic reasons, or for transfer of training. In such cases, emphasis is on the methods of geometry and on the nature of mathematical proof. More often, however, topics from geometry are reduced to a unit in an arithmetic or algebra course. In this case, the treatment is informal. Few if any theorems are proved, and the emphasis is on more practical topics—polygons, circles, perimeter, area, and, as a token acknowledgment of the traditional curriculum, the Pythagorean Theorem.

Other Remedial Content

Although most remedial content is drawn from the traditional precollege curriculum, some quasi-remedial courses introduce new material as well. One type emphasizes applications, serving the special needs of students in a particular technical curriculum. Thus, a course for nurses may consider applications of arithmetic and algebra to unit conversions, medical dosages, and the like. Another type, the pre-science course, covers the mathematical topics needed in mandated science courses, including the metric system, scientific notation, and so forth.

A third type of quasi-remedial course, rather than emphasizing specialized applications, covers an amalgam of remedial and college-level content. This approach is usually called *sugar-coating*. Sugar-coating addresses several concerns: that remedial students arrive in college already bored and dispirited by customary approaches to remedial content, that their self-image is damaged by the need for this content, and that the intrinsic interest of the college-level component will provide motivation. The college-level material may be probability, statistics, computer science, or any other field combining numerical applications with a measure of popular appeal. In some colleges, the course in question may be used to satisfy the nonremedial graduation requirement in mathematics.

Sugar-coating was tried at several CUNY units in the early

years of open admissions, when there was particular concern about student acceptance of protracted remediation. Most of these programs, however, have since been dropped or significantly modified. One difficulty was that students found arithmetic and algebra too demanding to master peripherally while ostensibly learning something else. Furthermore, the sugar-coating is often no more palatable than the remedial content itself; students who are presumably enticed into learning arithmetic by the lure of statistics may end up turning their backs on both. Nonetheless, there are still those who contend that sugar-coating is a viable alternative, particularly for the marginally remedial student.

Two new trends appear to be taking shape in the content of remedial mathematics. One, already mentioned, is to place increasing emphasis on reasoning as an explicit part of the curriculum; Miles (1978) describes this as "the fourth R." Such topics as problem solving, recognizing cause and effect, using evidence, and classifying components are being taught as a separate body of knowledge in a number of courses around the country. While there is some question as to whether topics like these are part of mathematics, let alone remedial, the more significant issue is whether they can be learned and applied outside the classroom at all. While the evidence is not in, the prospects are exciting, and over the next few years such cognitive instruction may become "an important tool in the trade of developmental instruction" (Whimbey, Boylan, and Burke, 1979, p. 10).

The second trend involves the combining of topics from arithmetic, elementary algebra, and, to a lesser extent, geometry, to form a kind of remedial "general mathematics." An increasing number of colleges have organized courses around this content, serving all remedial students whatever their field of study. The approach here is extensive rather than intensive, intending to prepare the remedial student for a broad range of situations which require mathematical skills.

Diagnosis and Placement

Diagnosis and placement are among the most critical components of the remedial program. Where placement is unreliable, some students will waste time in courses they do not need, while others will enter classes for which they are altogether unprepared. If the procedure attempts not only to identify remedial students but also to diagnose their weaknesses, then it requires even more careful planning.

Placement procedures are usually based on an objective test, the high school record, a personal interview, or any combination of these. Ideally, the choice of procedure will reflect the content and goals of the remedial program.

Placement Tests

An objective placement test has several definite advantages. One practical consideration is that it can be graded by machine. In addition, the objective test measures all students by the same standard, it measures them as of the day of testing, and it can be administered with relative ease. By contrast, other criteria such as the high school record or a personal interview are apt to be outdated, unreliable, or cumbersome.

Once the decision is made to use a test for placement, the college must choose between developing its own in-house test and adopting a commercial instrument. Commercial tests offer several advantages. They have been extensively pretested to eliminate ambiguities and poor distractors. The test's norms enable the college to relate the performance of its students to that of comparable groups elsewhere in the nation. Grade levels, percentiles, and other data facilitate the interpretation of scores. When alternate forms of the test are available (an important consideration for retesting and for avoiding cheating), they have been carefully adjusted to ensure statistical equivalence. If the college's admissions procedure already requires the Scholastic Aptitude Test (SAT), American College Test (ACT), or similar instrument, a separate test may not be necessary. Finally, if the publisher is well established in the field of testing, then the prestige of the organization may foster acceptance of the test.

Commercial tests are listed and reviewed in Braswell (1974) and Buros (1975); the Educational Testing Service also compiles lists of tests from all sources. For reasons of security, specimen tests are not widely circulated, but they can sometimes be examined at university test libraries or bought from the publisher for a nominal fee.

Although commercial tests are widely employed, twice as many colleges have chosen to use tests they have prepared themselves (Baldwin and others, 1975). The chief advantage of in-house tests is that they are tailored to meet local requirements. There is no need to compromise content, emphasis, length, or style. Items can be devised to cover all major remedial topics at the appropriate level of difficulty. Moreover, for psychometric reasons, most standardized tests are apt to include items which are far too difficult for a potential remedial population.

Regardless of what type of test is chosen, the cutoff score (minimum passing score) is of manifest importance. Altering the cutoff by only a point or two may shift hundreds of students into remediation or out of it. Yet setting the cutoff is often treated more as an art than a science, resting primarily on the collective experience and judgment of the faculty. For a more empirical approach, local norms may be analyzed in order to gauge the minimum score needed to perform satisfactorily in the next math course. Still a third approach is more pragmatic; if remedial facilities are limited, the cutoff may be adjusted to reflect the number of available places. However the cutoff is determined, it may vary with curriculum; thus, a higher score may be required of science majors than of students in the arts.

The placement test may do more than separate those students who need remediation from those who do not. If the remedial program involves a sequence of courses or modules, test results may be used to place students within the sequence. If the program is offered in separate sections for stronger and weaker students, the test will determine the assignments to sections. Occasionally, an attempt is made to use the placement test as a more refined diagnostic instrument: to determine, for example, the specific topics in arithmetic with which the student needs help. However, this practice has been criticized on the grounds that the psychometric qualities of placement and diagnostic tests differ widely. Thus Thorndike and Hager (1969, p. 273) note, "To some extent, a 'group diagnostic test' is a contradiction in terms. Diagnosis is inherently individual and is appropriate for the individual who is having difficulty. A test that is pitched at a difficulty level suitable for identifying special difficulties of those in, perhaps, the bottom quarter of a grade group is not a good test for assessing achievement in the total group or even for separating the bottom one quarter from the top three quarters. Thus, classwide or systemwide use of a diagnostic test should generally be considered an inefficient procedure."

Mathematics faculty often have misgivings about the use of tests. As with any skill, test-taking has its techniques—making strategic guesses, using information from one question to answer another, and so on—and these techniques are better understood by traditional, academically oriented students than by a less sophisticated population. If the test is timed—and this is almost unavoidable given the usual constraints—it penalizes students who work slowly. If it has a large verbal component, it is unfair to those with a language handicap. And while some students fail unjustly, others pass by sheer luck.

From the student's point of view, the consequences of the test may be even more disturbing. On the one hand, students erroneously exempted from remediation may flounder in courses for which they are unprepared. On the other, those who are unnecessarily placed into remediation not only waste three to six class hours a week, but may be barred (until remediation is completed) from college-level work in mathematics, science, and even social science. Understandably, many students resent the fact that such important decisions are based on a single test. Appeals channels should be provided and publicized, but their availability does not always solve the difficulty; even capable students are often too shy or insecure to use them. For such reasons, some colleges bypass placement tests altogether, while others use them in conjunction with alternate procedures.

The High School Record

Use of the high school transcript for the purpose of placement is feasible when the courses and content coincide with the college's own remedial curriculum. A passing high school grade is usually accepted as proof of proficiency. Use of the high school record has certain advantages; it reflects performance over a sustained period rather than a single day, and it identifies students who may have latent knowledge and perhaps need only a brief review.

However, these advantages must be weighed against a number of drawbacks. High school grades are determined by teachers whose standards may vary from the college's and from one another's. Nor can one be sure that high school courses are uniform in content. Moreover, what a student once knew may be very different from what he has retained; this is especially true of adults who have been out of school for years. When the remedial content is arithmetic, the transcript may not provide applicable information. Finally, the records of some students, notably those with foreign or equivalency diplomas, cannot readily be translated into appropriate remedial placement.

Interviews and Other Procedures

At some colleges, an interview supplementing the test or high school record plays a large part in remedial placement. For example, at Bronx Community College, mathematics faculty interview all entering students as part of the registration procedure. If a borderline student seems capable of remedying his deficiencies without a formal course, he may be given the opportunity to do so. If placement test score and high school record point in different directions, the contradiction can be resolved. Students who plan to pursue a curriculum with little or no mathematics may be exempted from remediation altogether.

On some campuses, the school plays a minimal role in remedial placement; the decision is left to the student. In this view, remediation is a service, not an obligation; the college must offer appropriate courses, but it is the student who decides whether to avail himself of them. The student who knows no algebra, who knows that he knows no algebra, and who has been advised to take it, may be courting disaster by avoiding the subject; but the responsibility is his, not the college's. Apart from its effect on the students themselves, this policy poses one serious problem. Grossly unqualified students may bypass remediation and register in large numbers for entry-point college-level courses. In this case, instructors are placed in an untenable position; either they dilute the content of the course or they fail a large proportion of the class. In any event, the college's decision to make remediation optional does not eliminate the need for a placement procedure, since students who need help must still be identified and informed.

Instructional Systems

Once placement criteria are applied, the remedial population has been defined. Obviously, methods to teach this population must be designed around their backgrounds, abilities, and needs. Beyond their common deficiencies in mathematics, however, these students turn out to be very heterogeneous. Many of them, of course, fit Cross' description (1971, p. xiii) of "lowest third or low-A students, where the A stands for academic aptitude, ability or achievement." The difficulties of these students usually transcend their weakness in mathematics. Their study skills may be poor, and they often require remediation in reading and writing as well as in math. Their very orientation to college is apt to be shaky, and they may have little sense of what is expected of them.

A second group, however, consists of students who, while generally capable in other subjects, suffer from a specific, long-standing inability to cope with mathematics. They may see themselves as bright, functioning individuals who have a great deal to contribute, but who happen to be "dumb in math." Students in this group rarely challenge their placement into remediation. Instead, they often request outright exemption, on the grounds that their talents lie elsewhere and they will never learn the remedial content anyway. A few bring notes from their therapists.

For a third group of remedial students—often overlapping the previous two—all contact with mathematics throughout their high school years was kept to a minimum. A number were channeled into commercial or vocational tracks. Others bypassed academic math either on the advice of classmates or because they themselves thought it would be too taxing. Admittedly, such avoidance of mathematics, whether initiated by the school or the students themselves, often correlates with low ability or motivation.

Nonetheless, some of these students do surprisingly well; a few even go on to calculus and beyond.

Finally we have a group of students who may once have known the remedial content, but have since forgotten it. Often they believe themselves to be mathematically competent, and are genuinely surprised to find themselves assigned to remediation. Many such students need only a quick review. In a self-paced program, they often finish the work of the entire term within a month or two; in conventional classes, they use the time to catch up on homework from other courses.

It is a measure of the gap between mathematics and reading remediation that in reading, the counterparts of the last three groups hardly exist. Reading skills, once acquired, are reinforced every day, in and out of school; it is unthinkable that they would atrophy from disuse in a semester or two. Nor is it likely that high school students would be advised to avoid courses that call for reading; in fact, many states specify four full years of English as a high school graduation requirement. We may find occasional college freshmen with a specific disability in reading, but in all likelihood such students will be deeply concerned about their difficulty, and may already have taken steps to correct it.

In any event, the presence of these groups makes for a very diverse student population. They vary enormously in almost every respect: socioeconomic status, academic background, self-image, study skills, age, goals, and orientation to college. Even with respect to their mathematical deficiencies—the one trait they have in common—there may be a tremendous variation from one student to the next.

This diversity has an important impact on the conduct of remedial courses. In college-level classes, the instructor usually takes it for granted that students share a common mathematical background, on which he can base the new work of the semester. In remediation, where the entire content is drawn from the traditional precollege curriculum, everything is in a sense "background." Most students already know some of the material, no one knows all of it, and no two students know exactly the same topics to the same degree. This means that the distinction between background and new material loses its force; the terms have different meanings for each member of the class.

A second instructional concern is the required level of proficiency. In college-level courses the slower students (if they do not fail outright) squeak through with grades of C or D. In mathematics remediation, such grades are often unacceptable. Ideally, all the course content is essential; the student must learn every topic, and learn it at a fairly high level. In practice, the lowest passing grade on a remedial mathematics test may be 80 percent or even higher; sooner or later—although not necessarily on the first try—the student must attain this grade.

Given the normal variations among students, so high a standard would create problems in any class. But these problems are compounded by the third, and perhaps most far-reaching, factor in remedial instruction: the special responsibility that most colleges feel toward their remedial students. Typically, the need for remediation arises when a college pursues a policy of admitting students who, by traditional standards, lack the prerequisite academic preparation. In accepting such students, the college implicitly commits itself to providing whatever assistance is needed to help them catch up. As Ballard (1971, p. 39) noted, "Open Admissions wasn't going to work unless attention was paid to setting up an apparatus to literally surround the student in need of help from the time he entered college until the time he was ready to stand on his own two feet." A similar idea was expressed in a 1975 report by the Women's City Club of New York (p. 4): "The University has opened the doors of opportunity to all high school graduates, not in terms of come in and prove academic competence in six months or find the nearest exit. Instead, the invitation is to come, and extraordinary efforts will be made to help you to succeed." Admittedly, these are statements of ideals; the implementation often falls far short. Nonetheless, the commitment is clear: a "business as usual" attitude, with grades falling where they may, has no place in the remedial program. Rather, the goal is to develop instructional approaches so varied and effective that even the weakest students have a reasonable chance to learn.

Finally, the great problem with remedial instruction is that nothing can be taken for granted. This problem is particularly likely to arise in elementary algebra classes, where the instructor is often tempted to assume that everyone knows the small amount of arithmetic that is required. Granted, most students will know the prerequisite arithmetic, but provision must be made for the occasional exception.

If there is a single solution to these difficulties, it lies in the individualization of instruction. The advantages of individualization are too widely recognized to require enumeration here (Cross, 1976; McHale, Witzke, and Davis, 1969). In the context of remediation they are so important that despite innumerable administrative and financial constraints, the great majority of remedial mathematics programs provide at least some opportunities for individualized learning.

In this connection, one resource is all but indispensable: the mathematics laboratory, or math lab (also called learning center or resource center). Essentially, a math lab is a place where students can come for individual help in learning mathematics. The lab is usually open on a fixed schedule, which may include not only daytime hours but also evenings and weekends. Staffing almost invariably includes tutors; instructors, technicians, test proctors, or a coordinator may also be present. Other possible resources are primary learning materials such as texts and videotapes, and ancillary resources ranging from puzzles and worksheets to computer terminals for drill and practice. (The facilities available in a math lab are described more fully later under Learning Resources.)

A well-run lab can be all things to all students. Weak students use it to keep abreast of the work; better ones, to bypass their classes altogether. Students do not need to plan ahead; anyone with an unexpected half-hour of free time can drop in for a quick unscheduled study session. While well-planned math labs can be expensive, it is testimony to their worth that even with CUNY's repeated budget crises, virtually all of its seventeen colleges continued to operate their labs.

The way a math lab is used depends on the system of instruction. Three systems are widely used: self-pacing, classroom instruction (conventional or modified), and modularization.

Self-Paced Instruction

We have already noted that many remedial programs incorporate mastery learning; that is, students are required to master all topics at a relatively high level. Self-paced instruction allows students as much time as they need to achieve this goal. In principle, students move through the course at their own rate, taking each test as they feel ready for it. When the semester begins, each student receives an outline or set of lesson plans which serves as a guide to the course. Thereafter, he works individually from printed, audiovisual, or computerized materials, with help from tutors as needed. In some self-paced programs, an instructor provides occasional lectures, but attendance is optional. Tests cover specific points in the content, with passing grades of 80 percent or higher; students who fail a test restudy the material and repeat the test (in an alternate form) until they pass.

A popular form of self-paced instruction, developed in the 1960s by Fred Keller and others, is known as PSI (Personalized System of Instruction). In addition to self-pacing and mastery learning, PSI entails the use of peer tutors to help students through the course. (Another feature, the use of occasional lectures as a motivating device, has fallen into disuse.)

A number of studies have indicated that students who complete a self-paced course usually learn the material more thoroughly than their counterparts in conventional classes, and most would like to take other courses in the same mode (Kulik, Kulik, and Carmichael, 1974). However, the method presents its own difficulties. The most serious is procrastination. Without frequent prodding (and even with it), students may postpone their work, sometimes semester after semester. This may be particularly serious for remedial students, many of whom are neither self-disciplined nor highly motivated. Moreover, since most students have never taken a self-paced course, they often have trouble adjusting; the dropout rate in self-paced courses is apt to be much higher than in conventional ones (Akst, 1976). Self-paced instruction also poses problems for poor readers who are expected to work independently from printed materials. Other difficulties include administration, record-keeping, and the high cost of tutors, proctors, and special equipment.

To address some of these problems, a number of colleges are introducing modifications of self-paced instruction. For example, students may be required to maintain a minimum progress schedule. Alternatively, they may be allowed only a specified time period (usually one or two semesters) to complete the course, with the penalty of failing and starting all over again. Many programs allow only two or three attempts at each test, on the grounds that unlimited retesting encourages students to keep taking tests without actually studying for them. In some courses, an instructor concurrently covers the material in a series of lectures for students who prefer lectures to self-study.

In colleges with reservations about PSI, or with remedial programs too small to allow it, self-pacing may be achieved through independent study. Drawing upon math lab resources, the student works through the course content on his own. Visits to the lab may be scheduled in advance by the department, or they may be left entirely to the discretion of the student. As before, learning resources and tutors are available, and tests are administered when the student feels ready to take them. At some colleges, independent study is considered a regular course for which the student registers and may receive credit; at others, it is extracurricular. Time limits may or may not be imposed; participation may be mandatory or optional. The underlying approach remains the same: a facility is made available and the responsibility for using it rests with the individual student.

Classroom Instruction

Despite the value of self-paced programs in mathematics remediation, classroom instruction has several advantages. It dovetails with existing registration and scheduling procedures. Because it requires no special facilities or staffing, it can be quickly implemented. And it places students in a familiar situation which many of them find reassuring.

Often, instructors modify conventional classroom procedures, but even this is not always necessary; under some circumstances, conventional classroom instruction can work as well in a remedial program as anywhere else. For example, consider a geometry course for students with no background in the subject. The variations in ability and learning rate will be no greater than in the rest of the college. If the thrust of the course is conceptual and cultural, self-pacing may be inappropriate. In such a class, the presence of an enthusiastic instructor to lead discussions, foster interaction, and respond to students' questions and concerns may achieve more than an individualized program.

However, such a situation is admittedly the exception. More often, even when the traditional lecture-discussion paradigm is retained, modifications are necessary in the interest of individualization. The most common of these modifications is homogeneous grouping, which assigns students to different sections of the remedial course according to their performance on some specific criterion, usually a placement test. Since everyone in the class is presumably at the same level, the instructor can teach effectively to the entire group. Slower sections can proceed at a more leisurely pace by meeting for four or five hours a week instead of the conventional three, or they may extend over an extra semester. In any event, homogeneous grouping is only a partial solution to the problem of meeting individual needs. Although the classes are homogeneous in one respect, individual students differ in many respects. Furthermore, unless the student population is quite large, difficulties of programming and scheduling may arise.

More interesting are modifications devised by the department or individual instructor to meet the specific needs of the remedial class. Some of these modifications depend upon outside resources, but others cost nothing at all and can be implemented without difficulty. A few examples suggest the range of possibilities.

- The instructor devotes only part of each class to the usual lecture-demonstration; during the rest of the period, students work on their own or in small groups. The instructor remains available to resolve difficulties which the students cannot handle by themselves.
- During practice sessions, better students serve as tutors to help the rest of the class.
- The instructor selects a programmed text so that stronger students can skip superfluous explanations and exercises.
- The instructor begins each period with some problems covering the new work of the lesson. Students who complete the problems are allowed to leave. The instructor can then give a lecture at the level of the remaining students.

Suggestions like these can be implemented by the department or instructor without any outside support. If a math lab or tutoring staff is available, the range of possibilities is very much greater.

- One or more tutors may be brought into the classroom and used as needed. They may circulate around the room, helping the instructor check the work of individual students; or the class may be divided into several homogeneous groups, each with its own tutor.
- If supplementary learning resources are available, they may be assigned on an individual basis. Thus, one student may be required to complete an hour of computer-assisted drill on some particular topic; another may be directed to study a lesson from videotapes or other resources.
- Capable students may be allowed to work entirely from lab resources. Such students will in effect be replacing classroom instruction with self-paced independent study.
- The entire class may meet in the math lab once or twice a week, so that students can be helped on a one-to-one basis.
- Special sessions may be held in the lab during intersession so that students who have not quite finished the course can complete it before the start of the next semester.

Practical procedures like these are not usually prescribed or documented. They arise to meet immediate needs, and may be used one semester and dropped the next, according to the instructor's own sense of how the class can best be served. Perhaps faculty are best left to their own devices in this respect; with reasonable encouragement and administrative support, they will usually introduce a variety of ingenious and effective techniques to enrich classroom instruction.

Modularized Instruction

Modularized instruction attempts to combine the advantages of self-pacing with those of conventional instruction. The first step is to divide the content of the course into small, manageable modules, or mini-courses, each intended for, say, three weeks' work. The content of a basic remedial course, for example, could be divided as follows:

1. Operations with whole numbers and fractions.
2. Operations with decimals, percent.
3. Signed numbers, algebraic notation, positive exponents, operations on monomials and polynomials.
4. Linear equations in one or two variables; graphing, slope and intercept; systems of simultaneous linear equations with their graphic and algebraic solutions.
5. Types of factoring (common factoring, difference of two squares factoring, quadratic factoring); solution of quadratic equations by factoring and by the quadratic formula.

The separate modules are taught by different instructors in different classrooms, but all of them are taught simultaneously; in other words, we may have four or five instructors, in as many classrooms, all teaching at the same time and starting on the same day.

Before the beginning of the semester, each student takes a placement test covering the content of all the modules. On the basis of this test, he may be exempted from the entire course or from one or more of the beginning modules. He is placed in the appropriate module and proceeds consecutively through the rest of the program.

At the end of the first time period—three weeks, in our example—a departmental examination is administered in each module. Students who pass advance to the next module; otherwise, they repeat the module they just failed. Since all modules are offered at the same hour, and since each of them requires the same amount of time, there are no scheduling difficulties. In this way, students work their way through the course, taking a departmental test every three weeks. Depending on initial placement and number of modules repeated, a student may require only a single three-week period to complete the program, or as many as six, eight, or even more. Figure 2 shows the progress of three students.

Modularized instruction makes some accommodation to the needs of individual students while retaining the advantages of the

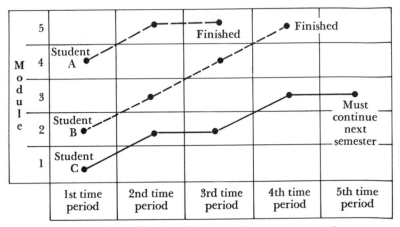

Time (Total = fifteen weeks or one semester)

Figure 2. Progress of Three Students in a Modular Program

classroom. Because grouping is relatively homogeneous, instructors can work at a level appropriate to most of the class. Moreover, as the semester progresses, better students complete the course, reducing overall class size so that weaker ones can receive more attention. The chief disadvantages are administrative. Not only does the method require a sizable remedial population, it also presupposes the availability of several instructors and classrooms at the same time. Because students may repeat modules or be excused from them, record-keeping can be difficult; in schools using this form of instruction, the mathematics department sometimes maintains its own computerized records. In any event, modularization cannot match the degree of individualization offered by self-pacing; the student who fails a test must repeat the entire module, even though he might need only a day or two of extra instruction.

In many respects modularization is as much an administrative innovation as a pedagogical one. What students actually experience—particularly those who never fail a module—is classroom instruction, with all its strengths and weaknesses. It is therefore not surprising that many colleges using this approach also offer tutoring, prerecorded lectures, and other supplementary resources.

Learning Resources

The term *learning resources* refers to the wide range of support services and personnel used in remedial instruction. When the teaching entails classroom instruction, learning resources are used for reinforcement. When the course is self-paced, they may be the primary vehicle of instruction.

While learning resources are particularly important in remediation, they have always had a place in instruction. The instructor's office hours, the free tutoring provided by math clubs, the mimeographed supplementary exercises that faculty prepare—all these qualify as learning resources. What is unique in remediation is the degree to which they are needed and used. Today's remedial students may have very limited time to give to their studies and limited skill in making use of that time, yet they have a particular need for effective review, practice, and drill. To help these students, instructors may need to rely upon resources far more elaborate and varied than the traditional ones.

Tutors

To the remedial mathematics instructor, no resource is more valuable than a competent tutor. If funds are available, such tutors can be recruited from a variety of sources. Students with an interest in teaching are often quite effective. So are former students of the remedial program itself, although some schools prefer to wait until the student has completed at least one more mathematics course. Two-year colleges, which have no upperclassmen to draw on, may recruit tutors from the community or from nearby universities.

A program can have tutors even if there are no funds to pay them. Tutoring is a suitable project for a math club or honor society. It may be incorporated into independent study programs in mathematics, education, or psychology; it may even be mandated as part of a program for prospective teachers. Volunteer tutors may be recruited from the community; retired teachers, accountants, and business personnel often make excellent tutors.

At the very least, tutors must be competent in the content of the remedial course. If allowed to grade papers, they may need guidelines, if only to maintain uniform standards. When the philosophy and techniques of the program have a special effect on its implementation, tutors will benefit from an orientation session before the start of the semester as well as an occasional meeting during the term. Beyond this, however, tutors should be encouraged to develop their own methods and tutoring styles. There is no single effective approach; tutors who are allowed to follow their own bent often do better than those who are expected to conform to some rigid criterion.

Tutors can perform a variety of tasks, including:

• Going over assignments and practice problems
• Making the rounds while students work individually from texts and other resources
• Working with the weaker students
• Grading papers
• Assisting in record-keeping
• Proctoring tests
• Staffing a math lab or tutoring room
• Staffing a telephone "hot line" when other facilities are closed
• Tutoring and monitoring students in certain types of self-paced instruction
• Helping students who are working independently
• Sharing the instructor's responsibilities during office hours

Printed Resources

Remedial mathematics programs use texts and ancillary printed resources of every sort. They serve several functions: to explain or review content, to provide practice and drill, and to supply students with material for informal self-testing. Ancillary resources have a number of virtues. First of all, they are cheap: cheap enough to distribute freely without concern or fuss. They are portable; students can carry them around, take them home, use them at odd moments during the day. They are readily individualized to meet the needs of specific students, curriculums, or schools. Finally, they have been known to be reasonably entertaining.

Ancillary materials are marketed commercially, but they are so easily prepared that even apart from considerations of cost, it may be more convenient to produce one's own. Suggestions can be found in *The Mathematics Teacher* and other professional journals, as well as in sourcebooks like Sobel and Maletsky's *Teaching Mathematics* (1975). Texts and other widely-used printed resources are described below.

Texts. A remedial text, like any other, should be attractive, readable, and rich in worked out examples. However, the remedial text must also meet several other criteria. The chief of these is that the format of the text be appropriate to the teaching method in use. Of course traditional texts will continue to be used in conventional classroom instruction. Appropriate texts are also available in nontraditional systems. For self-paced instruction, there are several choices. Programmed texts allow the student to complete the entire course independently, working at his own pace. Typically, the text consists of short explanatory passages, each followed by a question testing the student's understanding. Students who miss the question are directed to additional passages that amplify the same content; those who are correct move to the next topic. Such texts are an inexpensive and convenient solution to the requirements of self-pacing, but students often find them tedious. As one alternative, we have the newer texts written primarily for PSI instruction. In these books, content is divided into small, manageable lessons—often one for each day's work. At the beginning of each lesson is a short pretest, designed to measure whether the student already knows the material and should therefore move on to the next lesson. Each lesson ends with a posttest similar to the pretest. In this way students proceed through the course, devoting time only to those topics that give them trouble. Some of these texts are accompanied by supplementary audiovisual resources. Such packages are the backbone of many self-paced remedial programs.

Finally, for modularized courses, there are remedial texts bound into separate pamphlets, each covering a single topic or module. Students are directed specifically to those modules that meet their needs and buy only the corresponding materials. Thus, the nursing student and the business administration student may both begin with arithmetic but then branch out into modules on medical dosages and basic accounting, respectively. In this way, the modular format provides flexibility at modest cost.

Remedial texts differ from conventional ones in other respects. Many use simple vocabulary and syntax—sometimes at an eighth- or ninth-grade level—not only because the students may be poor readers but because even good readers have trouble making sense of mathematical materials. Explanations often take the form of common-sense or intuitive arguments rather than formal proofs. Instructor's manuals usually include tests, often in several equivalent forms; in this case, the student's text may provide sample tests of the same type.

In the last few years, excellent texts have appeared in all remedial areas. Reviews can be found in such professional journals as *The Mathematics Teacher, The Two-Year College Mathematics Journal,* and the *MATYC Journal,* as well as in *Science Books and Films,* published by the American Association for the Advancement of Science.

Worksheets. Typically, worksheets are handouts providing extra drill and practice. A worksheet can cover a single topic, or even a single aspect of a topic. For example, worksheets on addition of fractions can develop in succession addition of fractions with the same denominator, addition in which one denominator is a multiple of the other, addition with unrelated denominators, addition of mixed numbers, and so on. Other worksheets can treat the same material at different levels of computational difficulty. A short review or worked-out example at the top of each sheet makes it even more useful. Students usually correct their own worksheets, but help should be available to explain mistakes. If students are encouraged to save their corrected worksheets, they will have a valuable individualized learning resource.

Short Lessons on Specific Topics. Teachers may distribute lessons on topics which are omitted from the text, which are of interest only to selected students, or which are included primarily for enrichment. Typical lessons treat the use of pocket calculators, properties of prime numbers, accuracy and precision of measurement, and statistical mean, median, and mode. Materials may be prepared by faculty, obtained commercially, or even clipped from journals and other sources.

Recreations. Recreations include puzzles, magic squares, riddles, brain teasers, games—all sorts of diversions based on mathematical themes. While their purpose, of course, is to teach, students are apt to see them in the opposite light: not as a continuation of the learning process but as a welcome interruption. Particularly popular are crossword puzzles that use numbers instead of words. Recreational materials should be well within the ability of the students attempting them. Puzzles that might frustrate or discourage the student have no place in the remedial program.

Task Cards. Task cards are sets of index cards, each with a single task or problem on a specific topic at a specific level of difficulty; the answer is explained on the back of the card. Such cards are useful in meeting individual needs within a classroom setting; for ten or fifteen minutes of each period, students can select appropriate cards from the file and work independently. Task cards provide students with evaluation as well as practice; they can gauge their progress from the range and difficulty of the task completed. Attractively color-coded task cards are available commercially, or instructors may prepare their own.

Sample Tests. Because testing often plays a major role in remedial programs, many instructors provide students with samples of the course tests. Students are always delighted, because the tests indicate so clearly what is expected of them. For the instructor, however, sample tests are a mixed blessing. They are likely to result in some students' "studying to the test" (although this is not a drawback if the test is well-designed and covers all the important points). Instructors may face difficulties in the design of alternate forms, since some students become indignant when a new form deviates in any respect from the sample. Finally, sample tests introduce a practice effect which may to some extent invalidate the result of the actual test. Nonetheless, sample tests are a popular and useful resource in many remedial courses.

Audiovisual Resources

Audiovisual resources include audiotapes (with or without accompanying slides or filmstrips), videotapes, films, and the like. They may be incorporated into remedial programs in a variety of ways. Instructors may assign audiovisual resources to the entire class for outside study on a regular basis or may use them during class for enrichment, motivation, or simply as a change of pace. In PSI courses, an audiovisual series is often the primary vehicle of instruction; the entire course is available on film or tape, and the student learns the material directly from the resources. The instructor is then free to provide individual assistance or to work with small groups.

Audiovisual materials have some compelling advantages over the printed page. They are ideal for poor readers and students with different learning styles. They help solve the problem of absence; if a student misses a class or two, he can easily make up the work. They make learning a private affair between student and resource; students can repeat a tape, take notes, pause for problem solving or review, even take a break and come back—all without fear of faculty disapproval. Finally, audiovisual resources have the advantage of novelty; even the most disgruntled student may be cheered by a bright, attractive videotape.

But there are also major disadvantages. The first is cost: not only the cost of the resources themselves but the ultimately greater cost of viewing equipment, electricity and wiring, maintenance, replacement, and repair. As a rule, audiovisuals are not portable; the student is locked into the machine. Finally, audiovisual materials tend to promote rigidity. They represent a considerable investment; an elaborate audiovisual resource, once adopted, is apt to dominate course pedagogy long after questions have arisen about its continuing effectiveness.

If the decision is made to use audiovisual materials, the faculty must decide whether to buy commercial resources or produce their own. A number of books are available on the preparation of resources; we will note here only that it is not a job to be undertaken lightly. Commercial resources are often reviewed in *The Mathematics Teacher* and in *Science Books and Films*. Inquiries may also be addressed to the Educational Media Committee of the Mathematical Association of America; this committee has published an annotated list of available audiovisual series and attempts to monitor new developments in the field.

Calculators and Computers

Few developments have had as many repercussions in the field of mathematics education as the development of inexpensive hand-held calculators. Their impact on curriculum is discussed elsewhere; here we will consider them only as a support service. When used in this way, the calculator does not so much replace old skills as reinforce them.

One plan for using calculators requires students to learn all the usual pencil-and-paper algorithms, but allows them to check their results by machine. The advantage of this plan is that students can check their work immediately; and if wrong, they can direct their energies to finding their own mistakes. One might think that the ease of doing problems by calculator would cause the class to rebel against learning pencil-and-paper techniques at all. However, this does not seem to be the case; on the contrary, experience suggests that such use of calculators, limited as it may be, is both enjoyable and motivating.

A second advantage of the calculator is that it permits the introduction of complex scientific or practical computations. Thus, students may compute compound rather than simple interest, or apply statistical techniques to actual, real-life data. The approach is particularly valuable when the instructor's goal is to emphasize the structure of a problem rather than its computational details.

Of course, the use of calculators is hardly limited to arithmetic classes. For example, algebra or trigonometry students, working with calculators that have preprogrammed exponential, logarithmic, or trigonometric functions, can determine specific values of these functions at the touch of a key. Here the student is liberated not only from the burden of computation but even from the use of a table. As a result, many more problems can be considered in a class period, and broader principles demonstrated.

With all the practical uses of calculators, we should not overlook their recreational value. Innumerable games, puzzles, and tricks have been devised to help the student play as well as work with numbers. There are by now a substantial number of popular books on calculators, and most of them have chapters devoted to such applications.

A variation on the calculator has been developed which serves a different purpose; instead of answering arithmetic questions, it asks them. To start, the display might flash a multiplication problem. The student is given a fixed amount of time to solve the problem (mentally or on paper) and key in the answer. The right answer leads to another, more demanding problem; if the answer is wrong, the problem is repeated. The student receives his score at the end of the session.

At one time the cost of calculators was a deterrent to their widespread use. Today, with beginning prices well below those of typical textbooks, most students are quite willing to buy one. In any case, math labs usually keep a few on hand for the convenience of the student; at some colleges, calculators may be borrowed or rented for the semester.

Computers, too, have found a place in the remedial mathematics program. Their uses to date fall into four categories: drill-and-practice, instruction, testing, and record-keeping.

In drill-and-practice, the student works at a terminal and begins by identifying himself to the system, which has a record of his background and previous performance. On the basis of this information the computer displays a question appropriate to the student's needs in content and level of difficulty. If his answer is incorrect, he may receive hints, diagnostic comments, a worked-out example, an explanation—indeed, anything considered appropriate by the author of the computer program. When the student's answer is correct, he will be asked a somewhat more demanding question. Slow students may be called upon to solve many simple problems; those who are more capable may reach the end of the lesson in relatively few steps.

To many remedial students, the computer represents the complexity of twentieth century technology; just to be able to communicate with it is often enormously gratifying. Computers have been described as impersonal, but even this may be a refuge to the remedial student; no matter how many times he fails, the computer will keep his secret. Responsive, tireless, accurate, the computer may well become the ultimate instrument for individualizing drill-and-practice.

When the computer is used in its instructional or "tutorial" mode, the student's lesson—expository passages interspersed with occasional exercises—is itself displayed at a terminal. If the student's answer to an exercise is incorrect, he may be presented with a more elementary development of the content; if correct, he advances to the next topic. At present, the merits of this kind of individualized instruction have not been established, and only a handful of colleges are using the computer in this way.

The above uses of computers require complex interactive programs. Applications to testing may be much simpler. Typically, a bank of test items is stored in the computer, which is programmed to generate alternate equivalent forms of each test. This is particularly useful in mastery learning, where students may take several versions of a test before they pass. In some cases, students are actually tested at the terminal; they work out the problems with pencil-and-paper and enter their answers into the system. However, not only is this expensive but it leads to mayhem if the computer "goes down" in the middle of a test. More often, tests are printed out and the student takes them as usual in class or in a testing room. The computer, linked to an optical scanner, may also be used in grading. Dozens of papers can be marked in a few minutes, and the results automatically analyzed and stored.

The last major role of the computer is for record-keeping. The computer can use test scores or other information to determine placement, which is then printed out either in a list or directly on the registration form. This greatly expedites the assignment of students to the appropriate courses. Computerized record-keeping may also be valuable within the program. When instruction is self-paced, the computer can monitor students' progress, including number of test tries, test scores, attendance, time spent in drill and practice, and so on. In modularized programs, as we have seen, computers are often used at the end of each module to update students' records and make note of their progress.

Weighed against these benefits is the question of cost. Although recent technological advances have reduced prices by several orders of magnitude, and although proponents insist that computers are ultimately more economical than tutors, a computer and labful of terminals are still far beyond the budget of many colleges. A second problem relates to the difficulty of finding suitable programming. While excellent materials are available commercially (Splittgerber, 1979), their content may not coincide with the curriculum of the remedial course. In this case, computer programs must be written locally, usually at great expenditure of time and money.

Several journals report extensively on calculators and computers in education. Current developments are described in *Computers in Education, Educational Technology,* and *Programmed Learning and Educational Technology.*

Pedagogical Issues and Suggestions

In this section we will consider some pedagogical questions which we feel are particularly important in the remedial mathematics classroom. We have tried to limit ourselves to issues that may be of concern to the individual instructor; questions of policy are reserved until the next section. While we hope that the following suggestions will be useful, they are intended only as guidelines. Within the classroom, final jurisdiction on pedagogy should usually rest with the instructor; certainly no one knows the students better than he. The reader should have no qualms about taking exception to this or that recommendation, at least as it applies to his class; we would probably be the first to agree.

Instructor-Student Interaction

In an upper-division mathematics course, faculty may perhaps allow themselves the luxury of ignoring the students' progress. They may assign homework without determining whether students even attempt it. They give only one or two tests a semester. They may pause for questions without always providing full answers; if the question relates to previous work, they may dismiss it with the pointed observation, "We covered that last week." When students are bright, motivated, and self-propelled, the method may do no harm—or not much, anyway.

However, in the remedial mathematics class students may not be bright, motivated, or self-propelled. Instructors must keep informed not only about the students' progress but also about possible deterrents to their progress.

Perhaps the instructor's first task is simply to cheer up the students. Many, despite the evidence of their placement scores, may insist that they do not belong in the course; such students should be directed to the appropriate appeals channels. Others may admit their deficiencies, but despair of ever learning the material. They may be helped by being told how widespread the problem is, and how many students have succeeded.

On the first day of class the instructor should orient students to the course, familiarizing them with the text (including index, notation, and answers) and course requirements. The role of homework may be discussed, with emphasis on the critical importance of practice in developing technique. This may also be the time to indicate that reading mathematical material is not like reading the evening paper; in math, a four-page reading assignment may take an hour or more. Even such specific suggestions as studying rote material in several short sessions rather than a single long one, or "sleeping on" an intractable problem and making a fresh start the next morning, prove valuable to many students.

Instructors should also discuss the importance of asking questions. In mathematics, it too often happens that only the best students are in a position to ask coherent questions; knowing most of the material, they can identify the small gaps. Unfortunately, remedial students in need of help are more likely to be in a state of confusion, possibly about entire blocks of material. Even if they have the courage to reveal their difficulties, they may have trouble finding the words. Yet communication at such times is essential. One instructor has solved the problem by advising students simply to announce, "I'm sorry, but I don't know what's going on." At first students hesitate to identify themselves in this way, but they soon discover (as does the instructor) that their problems are shared by great numbers of their more timid classmates.

During the first few class meetings, the instructor should work at getting to know the students—individually if at all possible. It may help to think of every student as a "special case." If a student is chronically late, is he chatting in the corridor, or is he the victim of an unreliable babysitter? If another is repeatedly unprepared, is it laziness or might his text have been stolen? Obviously, not all students need or want this degree of concern. Many simply go about their business, learning the work of the semester. However, those with particular problems should be aware that while poor work will not be condoned, the instructor will consider the circumstances and help improve them if possible.

During the semester, the instructor must continue to monitor the students' progress. In particular, it is essential to determine whether students are keeping up with their assignments and to identify the types of errors encountered. In the rare cases where assignments are done on a computer, this task poses no problems. Otherwise, the instructor may personally collect and check homework; where this is not feasible, spot-checking and calling on students in class are practical alternatives. Some instructors allow a limited number of "unprepareds," so that anyone with a valid excuse is not penalized. Others make a point of announcing that all test questions will be selected from the problems assigned for homework.

Many remedial students put off doing their homework, either through inertia or lack of time. Some instructors have the class start the assignment during the last ten minutes of the period (working independently or in small groups); this allows students to ask about difficult problems in class, rather than having to struggle alone at home. Or the instructor may make himself available in the math lab (or elsewhere) on a fixed schedule, so that students who come in to do their homework at that time can receive immediate help. Occasionally, the class schedule includes one period a week of individual "catching up" in the lab, but this excellent practice is usually beyond the jurisdiction of the individual instructor.

Instructors can also judge the students' progress by giving frequent quizzes—perhaps as many as a dozen or more during the semester. Quizzes highlight the important ideas, keep students studying, and alert the instructor to problems requiring prompt corrective action. Short quizzes, two or three questions requiring about fifteen minutes, will suffice. Test questions should be clear and manageable; complex questions, or those requiring special tricks or insights, should be avoided. The purpose of a remedial test is not to discover unsuspected brilliance but simply to determine who is learning the material and who is not.

Formal, Intuitive, and Rote Learning

It is generally agreed that the remedial classroom is not the place for formal development of mathematical topics. However, this does not mean that learning must be reduced to rote. Often, faculty find a middle ground by presenting demonstrations that, without actually proving the mathematical results, render them intuitively acceptable.

Thus, certain theorems about inequalities—for example, if $a < b$, then $a+c < b+c$—can be convincingly demonstrated simply by moving one's hands along a number line. The approach also works with the related theorem, if $a < b$ and $d > 0$, then $ad < bd$. Such demonstrations are in no sense proofs, but they enable students to sense the validity of the results. Similarly, in teaching that the decimal equivalent of a rational number either terminates or repeats, the class may be convinced merely by carrying out the conversion for several common fractions. Not only will students observe the pattern, but they will probably agree that it is inevitable when any fraction is converted to a decimal. Again, students will accept the fact that the sum of the angles of a triangle is 180 degrees if every student simply cuts out a triangle, snips off the vertices, and lines them up.

The approach has some limitations. First, intuitively satisfying demonstrations cannot always be devised; thus, in teaching the quadratic formula, the authors have found no middle ground between developing it from scratch and asking students to take it on faith. More seriously, a demonstration must not do violence to underlying mathematical principles. For example, the procedure with triangles just described may cause students to conclude that mathematical generalizations can be established inductively—an idea so misguided as perhaps to outweigh the benefits of the demonstration. Finally, the approach may fail if the topic is comparatively complex. Thus, demonstrating inequalities on a number line works well in the examples given. However, it is less serviceable in persuading students that if $a < b$ and $d < 0$, the direction of the inequality is reversed: $ad > bd$.

In such cases the instructor may be well advised simply to present the result as a fact to be accepted, learned, and used. There is no need to apologize for rote learning in a remedial course, particularly if the course is designed to emphasize skills. It may help to indicate that a proof exists but is beyond the scope of the class. Most students are relieved to be spared the proof; the handful who are interested can meet with the instructor after class.

Mastery Learning

The concept of mastery learning refers to the viewpoint of Bloom (1976), Block (1971), and others that every student must learn each topic at a specified, fairly high level—usually about 80 percent—before continuing to the next one. In practice this means that if a student fails a test, he must return to the material, study further, and try again until he attains the required score. Some programs allow unlimited retesting; others limit students to three or four attempts, on the grounds that this encourages more intensive study between tries.

A strong case can be made for mastery learning in remedial mathematics. If the objective is to teach specific techniques and skills required later, whether in or out of college, then students should be able to handle the material with assurance and ease. Even within the remedial course, the content is usually cumulative, so students need a strong grasp of each topic before going on. Moreover, Kulik and Kulik who, with Carmichael, reported that PSI is more effective than conventional instruction (1974), later concluded that the most important factor in explaining this success is mastery learning (1975).

Nonetheless, mastery learning has its critics. Some claim that the full significance of a mathematical topic cannot be perceived on first encounter, but only after seeing how it interacts with subsequent material. This, in effect, is the traditional educational theory of spiral learning: a topic is introduced, set aside, and then re-examined with new insight and sophistication. A second argument is that once the student attains a minimum proficiency level—usually well below that required in mastery learning—he can improve on his own while concurrently continuing with the coursework. Another objection is that unless mastery of a topic is reinforced throughout the semester, students' skills deteriorate once the test is over. Finally, if program objectives are cultural or affective, mastery learning may be inappropriate.

In any event, it can be very difficult for an individual instructor to attempt mastery learning within the confines of a single classroom. Not only must students be provided with an opportunity for retesting, but quantities of tests must be prepared and kept on hand. The problem is ameliorated if a math lab is available. Otherwise, the instructor might do better to pool forces with several like-minded colleagues, or raise the subject at the departmental level.

Selecting Techniques and Algorithms

When introducing a new topic, the nonremedial instructor has the prerogative of choosing the technique which he feels works best. In remediation, where so much of the content is review, the instructor must decide whether to avail himself of the same prerogative or to build on less effective approaches which the students may already have encountered. Whatever the ultimate advantages of the new method, its first effect may be to terrify the students; fragmentary as their prior knowledge may be, it at least provides a toehold.

In making the choice, the instructor should consider the circumstances. Certainly, if a student knows a method—any method—and uses it correctly, he should be allowed to continue using it. This is particularly important for foreign students, whose algorithms may differ somewhat from ours. But students whose algorithms are shaky should be urged at least to give the new approach a chance. For example, in the traditional treatment of percent, problems are divided into three types: rate, base, and percentage. However poorly understood, this distinction may loom large in the student's mind, obscuring the advantages of developing the topic from scratch as an application of ratio and proportion. In each case, then, the instructor must weigh the merits of the new method against the importance to the student of using the old one as a security blanket.

The remedial instructor must also think carefully about introducing short cuts. To people at home in mathematics, it can be infuriating to watch a student solve a problem by some plodding, mechanical procedure when a simple short cut allows the job to be done in far less time. Nonetheless, the view has been expressed that in remediation, short cuts—particularly short cuts of limited applicability—should be avoided. Insight is often required to recognize when the short cut may or may not be used, and such insight is precisely what the remedial student lacks. Weak students, governed by the very reasonable principle that it's better to be safe than sorry, usually prefer a single method that works in every case.

Challenging the Remedial Student

Every course should provide some degree of challenge, but in remediation a little goes a long way. Many remedial mathematics students have been challenged beyond their endurance for years; the remedial instructor might better foster an atmosphere of reassurance and calm. The goal is a "no-fail" situation; while the development of each topic should include successively more demanding concepts and applications, the steps should be very small indeed. Students who claim that they are bored by the lack of challenge need not always be taken at their word; sometimes the alleged boredom is a mask for secret panic. (In the case where the claim is true, the student may not belong in the class at all.) If one must choose between too much challenge and too little, the latter is probably preferable.

Talking Down to the Student

Years ago, beginning mathematics teachers were told that the secret of success lay in one word: KISS. KISS, it turns out, is an acronym for Keep It Simple, Stupid—an expression which makes up in accuracy what it lacks in elegance. The advice is as good today as it was then. An instructor's colleagues may criticize him for "talking down to the students"; students themselves rarely see it in that light. On the contrary, their reaction is likely to be, "You really understand us. You make everything so clear." This is true even of students who do excellent work outside of mathematics. The instructor who successfully communicates the often demanding content of remedial mathematics is not talking down to the students; he is simply talking to them.

Recommended Academic and Administrative Policies

In earlier sections, we have described alternate approaches to mathematics remediation, usually without indicating our own preferences. Now we will identify some policies that we think work best. While we cannot claim to exhaust the issues, we have chosen those areas that we feel are of greatest importance. Our recommendations are based on personal experience as remediation teachers and coordinators, on discussions with faculty and students at CUNY and other institutions, and on an examination of the intrinsic constraints of the field. This having been said, we hasten to add that we certainly do not have answers to all the problems in remedial mathematics. Here and there the reader will detect a note of hesitancy where the authors themselves fail to agree. Furthermore, it is unlikely that there is any campus where all the following recommendations represent the best possible choices. Each of them is a compromise, a weighing of pros and cons; other remedial faculty are bound to weigh the factors differently. However, we hope that at the very least we are providing a basis for discussion among those interested in mathematics remediation.

Jurisdiction over Mathematics Remediation

The primary administrative decision about a remedial mathematics program is whether it should be under the jurisdiction of the mathematics department or of a separate department of remedial or developmental skills. On balance, we believe that mathematics remediation should be offered in the mathematics department. This position can be defended with reference both to its own advantages and to the disadvantages of the alternative.

Only by housing mathematics remediation in the math department can continuity be maintained between remedial and nonremedial courses. Remedial content and emphasis will be determined by qualified faculty, who know the entire curriculum and recognize what skills students require.

Students are thus assured that the remedial program and subsequent courses form an integrated sequence. Moreover, both the mathematics faculty and the students benefit from these early encounters. Today's remedial students are tomorrow's population in entry-point college courses; faculty will have only themselves to blame if, later on, their college-level students fall short of expectations. From a practical point of view, having the same faculty teach remedial and nonremedial courses provides greater flexibility in scheduling as the proportion of remedial to nonremedial enrollments fluctuates from term to term. Finally, the mathematical competence of remedial faculty and their courses can be safeguarded by having appropriate departmental criteria apply.

The alternative design—a single department embracing remedial courses in all fields—presents the immediate problem of internal governance. It is extremely unlikely that a chairperson can be found who is equally committed to remediation in mathematics and in language skills. Polarization may occur, not only between remedial faculty in the two areas but also between mathematics faculty in remediation and those in the mathematics department. Moreover, the sheer size of a remedial department may make it too unwieldly to administer.

The claim has been made that a separate remedial department provides a "community of learning specialists who can collectively know and relate to each individual student as a person" (Roueche and Kirk, 1973). However, mathematics remediation—typically the largest of the remedial programs—usually enrolls many competent students who have trouble only in this one area, who do not need the services of a "community of learning specialists," and who prefer to dissociate themselves from an explicitly remedial department.

Remedial Objectives

Objectives should be formulated at the outset of the remedial program and should govern every detail of implementation. They must be the foundation of the program, not an afterthought. If the faculty encounter difficulty in defining the objectives of a remedial program, they should refine and clarify their thinking until they can state exactly what goals the program is to achieve.

However, not all objectives have equal merit. Of the objectives described earlier in this chapter, the authors have a strong preference for those immediately related to course content: providing skills needed in subsequent courses, keeping the students' options open, preparing them for daily life, and the like. Cultural objectives seem difficult to justify, particularly for career-oriented students. The role of mathematics in promoting logical thinking has not been demonstrated, and there is a great danger of confusing cause and effect in this area. As for affective objectives, they appear to be poorly understood, even by their proponents; if our ultimate goal is to promote learning, then we cannot ignore the formidable body of evidence (Aiken, 1976; Scheirer and Kraut, 1979) that affective factors play no part.

At present the objective of preparing students for external tests is an unavoidable, if unsavory, remedial goal. Therefore, the mathematical community should examine the extent to which mathematics is being used as an artificial screening device and should exert pressure to eliminate such use.

Remedial Content

While we recognize the continuing importance of arithmetic, we feel that the remedial curriculum must reflect the increasing importance of the hand-held calculator. We do not at this time advocate the abandonment of pencil-and-paper computation; it is required of students in far too many situations. However, we propose that the student should concurrently develop competency in the use of calculators. Above and beyond this, mathematics educators should urge businesses, graduate schools, and other institutions to permit calculators on the job, in coursework, and even on employment and standardized tests. As calculators assume greater importance outside the classroom, it will become increasingly practicable to de-emphasize the traditional arithmetic skills.

By and large, the most important subject in remedial mathematics is elementary algebra. Prerequisite to virtually every mathematics-related course, it is also important as an example of mathematical generalization and technique. Algebra is particularly valuable when the objective of the remedial program is to keep options open.

We see little justification, however, for including Euclidean geometry in the remedial curriculum. The content is outside the mainstream of college mathematics and of limited intrinsic interest to the nonspecialist. The subject is usually introduced as a vehicle for demonstrating the axiomatic method, but this application may not be appropriate to the remedial classroom; in any event, other, more central mathematical topics (such as elementary group theory) can be used for the same purpose. It is worth noting that Euclidean geometry is rarely offered in European secondary schools, and even in the United States it has been omitted from some of our most innovative high school programs.

Implementing the Remedial Program

The remedial program must include a means of individualizing instruction. The varied backgrounds and needs of remedial students have already been discussed. We believe that these differences cannot be addressed within the framework of the conventional classroom. Techniques for individualizing instruction have already been suggested. The reader should review them carefully; if none seems applicable, he should devise his own. In remedial mathematics any degree of individualization is better than none at all.

We recommend that remedial programs adopt the strategy of mastery learning. Arguments for and against mastery learning were presented earlier. We feel that, on balance, mastery learning is easily justified. The remedial curriculum, if properly constructed, will be relatively free of peripheral topics; students must therefore be encouraged to master all of the course content, not merely part of it. Mastery learning provides exactly the impetus which is needed.

In light of the value of individualization and mastery learning, we urge all programs to consider self-paced instruction, which fulfills both these needs. Self-pacing is particularly useful in arithmetic and elementary algebra classes, where some students may be only marginally remedial while others know next to nothing. Although self-pacing presents difficulties of its own (notably administration, preparation of resources, and student procrastination), these difficulties tend to diminish with time, while the advantages of the method continue semester after semester.

Regardless of the method of instruction, the importance of a math lab cannot be overemphasized. Even the simplest math lab, staffed by tutors and open for only a few hours a day, can make an enormous difference to the remedial program. Not all resources are expensive: worksheets, sample tests, and even supplementary texts cost very little and can be of great value. The lab is particularly important if the program uses conventional classroom instruction.

While classroom pedagogy may be left to the individual instructor, the content and standards of remedial courses are the concern of the entire department, if not of the college itself. Therefore, the department should take responsibility for preparing the final examination, which should be uniform throughout all sections of a remedial course. A departmental exam encourages instructors to cover all the content at the required proficiency level. Extending the same policy to class quizzes poses administrative problems but is worth trying when feasible. One fringe benefit for instructors is that they are spared the chore of preparing their own tests.

Remedial courses should be staffed by faculty who are sympathetic to the students and the material. Ideally, of course, this describes the entire department. In practice, however, certain faculty, particularly in the four-year colleges, may feel very far removed from the problems of underprepared students. The remedial program is probably best served by excusing such faculty from participation.

For all but the smallest remedial mathematics programs, one or more members of the faculty should be given time to serve as remedial coordinator. Most remedial programs entail a host of administrative tasks: overseeing the preparation of materials, directing lab staff, addressing the grievances of individual students, working with various offices of the college, and so on. It is appropriate that whoever assumes responsibility for this work receive tangible compensation.

Placement and Appeals

All placement tests should be administered by a central agency; moreover, this agency should develop a system for "flagging" remedial students so that they can be directed to the appropriate courses. The first part of this recommendation is followed on most campuses. Less widespread, however, even on campuses where placement is presumably mandatory, is the practice of ensuring that such students take their remedial courses at the appropriate time. When a college has thousands of remedial students, many of whom have multiple remedial obligations, and when for whatever reason remediation is postponed beyond the first semester, vast numbers of students will deliberately or accidentally "slip through the net." An interdisciplinary computerized system is essential to correct this situation. At registration, a printout may be available indicating each student's remedial status, or the information may be printed onto the student's registration form. In addition, the class roster of college-level mathematics courses should indicate those students whose remedial mathematics obligation has not been met.

Whatever the placement procedures—tests, high school record, interviews—none is infallible. The student who disagrees with his remedial designation must have the opportunity to appeal his placement and even to be retested. Moreover, if this appeals procedure is to be available to all students, and not only the more outspoken of them, it must be widely publicized. Outright exemption from mandated remediation is a thornier issue, but we believe that in special circumstances even this is warranted. Few of us would want to deny Shakespeare a degree from our institutions on the grounds that he could not factor the difference of two squares.

We are not prepared to make an across-the-board recommendation concerning the value of mandatory remedial placement. However, where the student may choose to bypass remedial courses, it is imperative that faculty maintain the standards of entry-point college-level courses. Instructors should be assured that the department will condone a high failure rate if it results from the deliberate enrollment of unprepared students.

Granting Credit

Arithmetic remediation should not receive college credit. Remediation in other areas of mathematics may or may not receive credit, depending on the college, the student body, and possibly on financial-aid considerations. Few issues are more controversial than this one. Recommendations have been made that remedial courses receive full credit, partial credit, no credit, "in-house" credit (computed into the grade-point average, but not applicable toward graduation), and even negative credit. Opponents of credit argue that granting credit for work traditionally covered in high school or even earlier cheapens the degree. Advocates of credit claim that in an open admissions college, the concept of traditional high school courses is no longer meaningful; in any case, college credit is given to other courses which overlap the high school curriculum, such as beginning language classes. Moreover, no-credit remediation works a hardship when financial aid is tied to a minimum credit load. Hecht (1975) has proposed that in granting remedial credit, the college apply the same criteria used in evaluating transfer courses. A student who has received credit once for the content— who, for example, passed elementary algebra in the ninth grade and applied it toward high school graduation—should not receive credit a second time; but if the so-called remedial course is effectively new material for the student, credit should be given. This proposal has not been widely adopted, but even by this criterion, arithmetic would receive no credit. For other courses, the granting of credit should probably reflect circumstances on the particular campus.

Grades

We advocate the use of letter grades in preference to Pass-Fail (or the equivalent), even when the remedial program carries no credit. High grades are a mark of achievement; students take pride in a grade of A or B, regardless of its effect on grade point average. Low passing grades serve a different purpose; the student who receives a C or D may find it worthwhile to review the material as preparation for the next course. Finally, the grade of F should be available for students who consciously neglect their studies.

However, grades in remedial courses should be motivating rather than punitive. Thus, a neutral grade such as *Repeat* is appropriate for the student who attends regularly, uses supplementary resources, and makes some progress, but who still does not meet all course requirements by the end of the term.

Funding and Evaluation

The remedial program must be allocated sufficient resources to carry out its mandate. Class size must be held down. Tutors must be funded. Perhaps most important, the capacity of the program must match the number of students who are mandated to enroll. On some campuses the backlog of students waiting to get into remediation numbers in the thousands; not only does this discourage the students, but it can seriously impede the operation of college-level courses. The administration must show its commitment to remedial programs by allocating funds and hiring needed faculty.

One excellent way to maximize cost effectiveness is to have neighboring colleges share the cost of resources. Tests, exercises, audiovisual materials, and computer programs all lend themselves to sharing; it may even be possible for several colleges jointly to operate a computer center or math lab. Administrators should join forces in exploring channels like these.

Finally, we suggest that all remedial programs be formally evaluated at regular intervals. Appropriateness of content, reliability of placement procedures, and effectiveness of instruction all benefit from outside review. Ideally, a blue-ribbon panel or external evaluator should be called in periodically to assess the program and suggest improvements. Evaluation of remedial programs is discussed in Chapter Five.

5

Program Evaluation

Geoffrey Akst
Miriam Hecht

❉ ❉ ❉ ❉ ❉ ❉ ❉ ❉ ❉ ❉ ❉ ❉ ❉ ❉ ❉ ❉ ❉ ❉

The literature on evaluating college remedial programs leaves the reader with two strong impressions: the first is that current evaluation procedures are enormously diverse; the second is that there has been little effort to systematize that diversity. Moreover, in most studies it is not clear whether procedures were chosen on the basis of intrinsic merit, expediency, or ignorance of the alternatives. The last possibility cannot be dismissed, if only because there is no single source which describes and compares the alternative methodologies. General texts on evaluation, even educational evaluation, are useful but unfocused. Published evaluative studies of individual remedial programs are not uncommon, but they usually employ specific approaches rather than exploring the range of possibilities. Moreover, most studies on remedial evaluation deal with a particular discipline, so that a study of methodological weaknesses in the evaluation of reading programs, for example, may escape the attention of the researcher in remedial writing or mathematics.

The discussion which follows presents an overview of the interests, constraints, pitfalls, and opportunities confronting the evaluator of any college remedial program. After considering the role and importance of remedial evaluation, we survey a variety of evaluative designs and conclude with suggestions for implementing an evaluative study.

The Role of Remedial Evaluation

In an age of shrinking budgets and growing demands for accountability, the evaluation of academic programs hardly requires justification. However, the need for evaluation is particularly acute in college remedial programs. Such programs are apt to be large and expensive; it has been estimated that the City University of New York (CUNY) spends some $35 million a year on remediation. Programs that obtain funds from government or foundation grants may be required to submit evaluations. Often, the programs employ innovative teaching strategies which invite comparison with more traditional instruction. And perhaps most important, the viability of the entire curriculum may be determined by the effectiveness of the remedial program; only if the student body is properly prepared in basic skills can standards be maintained in later courses.

Despite these factors, relatively few remedial programs have been carefully evaluated. In mathematics, a national survey showed that three quarters of the responding colleges had never formally evaluated their remedial programs (Baldwin and others, 1975), and this may well be the case in reading and writing as well. Such studies as have been attempted vary widely in quality; while some appear to be thorough and objective, others are oversimplified or consist of little more than unfounded reassurances.

Why have so many colleges skirted the evaluation of their remedial programs? There are several explanations. For one thing, remedial staffs, often overworked and pressed for resources, may feel that time and effort spent on evaluation could be put to better use. For another, the idea of deliberately withholding remediation from a group of weak students to permit comparison with the remediated population has been widely opposed (Cross, 1976). And to assess any college program by systematic empirical research appears alien to the thinking of many academics; many faculty feel that learning is a slow and subtle process, more readily revealed through sympathetic interaction with students than by the application of yardsticks. Nonetheless, there is little doubt that on some campuses, faculty avoid evaluation for a less laudable reason: they themselves have misgivings about the outcome. Roueche (1973, p. 26) reports charges that "community college leaders deliberately did not evaluate remedial programs because they knew beforehand how disastrous the results of such an evaluation might be." And in fact, the results of some remedial evaluative studies have been so negative that programs have been curtailed or in some cases entirely abolished (Cross, 1976; Sharon, 1970).

Before considering this type of comprehensive or "summative" evaluation, let us say a few words about "formative" evaluation, which is typically more modest in its goals (Scriven, 1967). The purpose of formative evaluation is to identify those elements of the instructional program which contribute to its effectiveness and those which need improvement. Formative studies are particularly valuable near the beginning of a program, while it is still taking shape. By contrast, summative evaluation sums up the worth of an ongoing program, not with reference to the separate components but to the value of the program as a whole; it often serves as a basis for deciding whether to continue or drop the program. In practice, the difference between formative and summative evaluation is sometimes blurred, but the activities appropriate to the two types differ sufficiently to justify the distinction.

Some evaluators believe that in terms of practical consequences, formative evaluation far outweighs summative (Gordon, 1970). Thus, Worthen and Sanders (1973, p. 47) observe that "the greatest service evaluation can perform is to identify aspects of the course where revision is possible." Several examples of formative evaluation show the wide range of possibilities. Middleton (1977) examined the relation between section size and success in remedial English and math classes; he found that large sections were at least as effective as smaller ones. A study of reading classes by Kingsborough Community College (1973) showed that classes in which tutors worked along with instructors were more successful than those in which instructors worked alone. Lachica and Brookes (1976) found that in an English as a Second Language (ESL) program, students taking ESL for the first time had a higher passing rate than those repeating the course. Akst (1976) examined a self-paced remedial mathematics program to determine whether reading ability was a factor in mathematical achievement; he found that the two were unrelated.

Studies like these are quick, simple, and informative. They may be designed to examine any aspect of a remedial program, from texts to methods of instruction, from testing procedures to exit criteria, from which of the students are learning the content to what content is being learned. Such studies may not lend themselves to generalization nor be intended for publication. However, if judiciously planned and executed, they are invaluable in putting the remedial program on the right track.

Summative evaluation—our major concern—is usually more elaborate. Properly done, it calls for careful planning and implementation, possibly over a period of years, and may best be carried out by an external evaluator. Summative evaluation may cover a number of areas, such as:

1. Appropriateness of objectives: One may take the position that program objectives are not open to question, since they are presumably the premises on which the rest of the program is based. Occasionally, however, an evaluator may take exception to objectives that appear to be misguided or unrealistic (for example, the objective in a writing program of having foreign students attain the same proficiency level as native speakers).

2. Appropriateness of content to program objectives: At the inception of a remedial program, faculty determine the appropriate content and proficiency level, using their experience to guide them. Thus, reading faculty decide that students entering social science courses should be able to read texts at a certain indicated level of comprehension; mathematics instructors teach compound interest in the belief that it will help students in later

life. In some cases—by no means all—such curricular decisions can subsequently be evaluated on empirical grounds. For example, if we can identify two groups of students, differing only in the extent to which they have mastered reading skills, we can compare their performance in subsequent social science courses. However, it may be virtually impossible to follow the math students beyond graduation to determine whether an understanding of compound interest has in fact been useful.

3. Appropriateness of placement procedure: Whatever the basis of the placement procedure—high school record, interviews, a battery of tests, or self-selection—the procedure itself should be subject to careful scrutiny (Zwick, 1965). Issues meriting investigation include content and cutoff score of a test, and reliability of interview ratings, essay scores, and high school grades. Both judgment and empirical research play a role in addressing these concerns.

4. Effectiveness of instruction: The question here is whether students are in fact learning the remedial content and if so, whether their learning is the result of remedial instruction or extraneous factors.

5. Efficiency of instruction: Can the same learning be provided at a smaller investment of time or money? Alternatively, can more learning be obtained for the same investment? (Carman, 1971; Cosby, 1975).

Few evaluative studies consider all the above areas of inquiry. Colleges may not seek out an evaluator's views on the appropriateness of objectives—a question which is in any event a matter of judgment rather than empirical research. The investigation of content or placement is often precluded by the difficulty of long-term follow-up studies. And questions of efficiency or cost-effectiveness may well be considered the province of a financial specialist rather than the academic evaluator. In practice, therefore, most remedial evaluations have focused on the effectiveness of instruction: whether students are learning the remedial content, and whether their performance in subsequent coursework is improved as a result. Even within these bounds, however, the summative evaluation of remedial programs is far more complex than one might expect.

Collecting Data

No matter how great the expertise of the program evaluator, an objective evaluation must be based, in part at least, on empirical data. Particularly important are the *preprogram* and *postprogram measures*—indexes of what remedial students know before and after participation in the program.

The preprogram measure is used in several ways: as a base line for later comparisons, a device for sorting out groups to be compared, and a gauge of whether groups were equivalent before the start of remedial instruction. Often, it serves more than one of these functions in the same study.

In most remedial evaluations, a test score is used as the preprogram measure. One reason for this choice is obvious. Often, an appropriate test is already being administered for purposes of remedial placement; by using the same score as a preprogram measure, the test is made to do double duty. But a single test score provides a convenient preprogram measure even when placement is based on other factors (for example, the high school record). Alternatively, the student's college grade-point average (GPA) may serve as the preprogram measure, but this is feasible only if placement occurs after the first semester (Entwistle, 1960).

When we turn to postprogram measures, used to gauge knowledge after remedial instruction, we find a far greater variety of indicators. These may be classified as short- or long-range. *Short-range measures* describe the students' behavior while they are still in the course; examples are grade on final examination and average quiz grade. *Long-range measures* are concerned with students' performance after they leave the remedial program; they include grade in the next course, GPA after a specified number of semesters, verbal GPA (for reading, writing, and ESL remediation), quantitative GPA (for mathematics remediation), credits earned, and persistence in college. Tests administered after the student leaves the remedial program, or measures involving follow-up studies after college, are seldom practical and are not considered here.

The choice of postprogram measure is a matter of lively

debate. Proponents of long-range measures argue that if the goal of the remedial program is to prepare students for college-level coursework, then the program has met this goal only to the extent that students subsequently perform better than they would have otherwise. Robinson (1950, p. 83) has characterized short-range measures as "specious, ill-considered or clearly superficial." The opposing camp, defending short-range measures, point out that the remedial instructor can do no more than improve students' skills while they are in the program; whether students retain these skills over succeeding semesters is not the instructor's responsibility. Moreover, in nonremedial courses it is common practice to measure learning no later than the end of the semester; holding remedial staff to more stringent standards would therefore be unfair. The choice of measure is particularly important because results based on short-range measures are usually positive whereas those based on long-range measures are more likely to be equivocal (Piesco, 1978; Santeusanio, 1974).

Of course, the same evaluative study can use several post-program measures, some short-range and some long-range. Indeed, some studies have used as many as a half-dozen. Roueche and Snow (1977, p. 107) conclude that "the most successful developmental education programs are generally those that . . . use a number of indices on which to evaluate their efforts."

After choosing the preprogram and postprogram measures, the evaluator must extract from data collected about individual students a single quantity—a number—that provides information about the entire group. This number, which we refer to as the *grouping statistic,* can be obtained in either of two ways. In the first, the evaluator is concerned only with the proportion of students who succeed—where success is defined as, say, passing the course (however poorly) or scoring above a specified cutoff on a posttest. For each student the question is only, "Did he succeed?"; no attempt is made to quantify the result by asking, "How well did he succeed?" In the second, the evaluator is concerned with averages (average test score or average GPA), which actually measure the extent of the student's knowledge instead of merely separating the wheat from the chaff. The choice of grouping statistic—

proportion or average—can have a significant effect on the outcome of an evaluation (Akst, 1976) and warrants careful consideration.

Although preprogram and postprogram measures comprise the most essential data in remedial evaluation, other types of information may also be needed. In particular, it is important to document in detail the actual implementation of the program; this information can be obtained from faculty and student interviews, syllabi, texts, departmental memoranda, and, of course, from direct observation. Other data of possible interest include peripheral effects of the program, costs, and attitudes of students, faculty, or other concerned groups.

Finally, the evaluator must decide which students should participate in the evaluative study. In sufficiently small remedial programs, the entire remedial population can serve. However, when the population is large, this is not only unwieldy but unnecessary; in such cases a randomly selected subset, representative of the larger group, may serve quite as well. Another strategy for controlling the volume of data is the statistical technique known as *multiple matrix sampling*. This newly developed procedure permits the evaluator to administer only a few test items to each participant in the study and then, by extrapolation, estimate how the entire population would perform on the complete test. For details of this technique, the interested reader should consult Wolf (1979) or Shoemaker (1973).

Measuring Learning

Clearly a critical component of program evaluation is measuring how well the content has been learned. Novices usually see this as a fairly straightforward matter. "There's nothing to it," they will say. "Just give all the students a test at the beginning, another at the end, and see how much they've improved." This procedure is in fact the first of the eight evaluative designs which we will consider.

The Single-Group Pretest-Posttest Comparison

Of all the designs to be discussed here, the single-group pretest-posttest design is undoubtedly the simplest. It is concerned only with the remedial population—hence the term *single-group*—and uses as preprogram and postprogram measures two equivalent forms of the same test. Often this test is the one originally used for remedial placement, so that by definition everyone in the study will initially have fallen below the cutoff. If the grouping statistic is an average, then the pretest and posttest scores are averaged separately, and the difference between the two results is taken to be the measure of learning. If, on the other hand, the grouping statistic is a proportion, then the effectiveness of the program is gauged by the proportion of students who score above the cutoff on the posttest.

The single-group pretest-posttest comparison can be represented by the diagram shown below:

$$(\text{Remedial})$$
$$M_1\text{- - -Remediation- - -}M_2$$

Here M_1 stands for the preprogram measure (pretest) and M_2 for the postprogram measure (posttest). The broken time line and the word *Remediation* signify that remedial instruction has taken place between administration of the two tests, and the word *Remedial* in parentheses indicates that all the students in the evaluative study belong to the population originally placed into remediation.

The single-group pretest-posttest comparison is probably the design most commonly used in the evaluation of remedial programs. The main reason for this popularity is that the design is so easy to implement. In contrast to other evaluative designs, it avoids such difficulties as withholding remediation from students who need it, rounding up exempted students for posttesting, and waiting a semester or more to investigate GPA or grade in the next course.

Unfortunately, while it is the design most convenient to implement, it is also the one of least value. Even if postprogram scores are significantly higher than preprogram scores—and as we will

see, they usually are—the evaluator cannot automatically attribute
the gain to the effectiveness of the remedial program. This problem is so serious that Wolf (1979, p. 143) notes, "Specialists in research design generally dismiss the single-group pretest-posttest
design as useless. The evaluation worker may not be able to because
the alternative—no study at all—is unacceptable."

Here the novice is apt to become defensive. Eager for quick,
positive results, he challenges such objections with questions like,
"Why shouldn't test gains be attributed to the effectiveness of the
program? How else can they possibly be explained?"

One reason that the gains cannot be attributed solely to the
remedial course is that the favorable results may have been obtained by chance. Fortunately, there are reliable, statistical techniques (t-test, chi-square test, and others) for indicating when a
result is merely accidental and when it is statistically significant.
These techniques are discussed in any standard text on inferential
statistics and the evaluator should certainly be familiar with them.

Far more serious is the fact that the single-group pretest-
posttest comparison is particularly vulnerable to a host of extraneous factors, known as *biases,* which distort results and cloud interpretations. In fact, Wolf (1979, p. 143), having already warned
against the design, later makes the point, "If used—no matter how
reluctantly—the only course open to the evaluation worker is to
systematically eliminate each competing alternative explanation so
that the presumptive conclusion of a treatment effect is tenable." It
is to these "competing alternative explanations," or biases, that we
now turn.

Evaluative Biases

The biases described below are of two types. Some relate to
learning that does in fact occur but is not attributable to the remedial program. Others relate to spurious gains resulting not
from any learning at all but from peculiarities of tests and testing
procedures.

Test Administration Bias. If, in an educational study, the administration of the pretest differs in a significant way from that of
the posttest, gains may result merely from this difference and not

from any actual learning. Test administration bias is of particular concern in remedial evaluation; often the pretest is part of a large battery of tests, given in a poorly-lit auditorium over a period of hours, while posttests are given separately in the relative comfort of the remedial classroom. Here the pretest scores may be artificially lowered by the students' discomfort or fatigue. To compound the difficulty, posttests are often administered by the remedial teachers themselves; for reasons altruistic and otherwise, these teachers may answer leading questions, allow extra time, and otherwise contribute to exaggerated gains.

Student Attitude Bias. Scores on tests may be affected by the student's attitude. Students frequently underestimate the importance of the pretests and do less than their best work, thereby contributing to an illusory gain later on. However, students who are overly anxious on the posttest (which may also serve as the final examination) sometimes perform poorly, so that program effectiveness is underestimated.

Teaching to the Test. Often the remedial instructor is familiar with the content of the posttest. As a result, he may perhaps unconsciously stress topics he knows are included, at the expense of other equally important material. Thus, an instructor may emphasize one type of algebra problem over another because he knows the former appears on the test. The outcome, of course, is an artificial increase in scores.

The Practice Effect. The mere experience of taking the pretest may prepare students to do better later on. They will be informed about the format of the test, the use of the answer sheet, the allocation of their time, and so on. If the same form is used twice, they may simply remember answers. In any event, the outcome is again an artificially high posttest score.

Instrument Bias. If the pretest and posttest are to reflect relevant learning, they must be both valid (that is, the content and minimum proficiency level must be appropriate) and reliable (the results must be consistent). Otherwise, any indicated changes, whether gains or losses, may be either irrelevant or simply a matter of chance.

The Hawthorne Effect. It has often been noted that students' performance is apt to improve merely because they realize that they are receiving special attention. This phenomenon, known as the Hawthorne effect (after a classic study conducted in Hawthorne, Illinois), results in gains which, while genuine for the experimental population, may not be sustained for subsequent groups.

Dropout (Mortality) Bias. It is all but inevitable that more students will start an educational program than finish it. This is particularly serious in evaluating remedial courses, not only because dropout rates are commonly high but because it is apt to be the weaker students who drop out; in effect, the bottom of the class is sifted out rather than taught. Posttest scores for these dropouts are seldom included in the statistical analysis; hence a comparison of pretest and posttest averages may suggest an exaggerated gain.

Regression Toward the Mean. Regression toward the mean is a surprising but well-documented statistical phenomenon: if a group of students is given a test and then retested, those who initially scored at the extremes (whether very high or very low) will, when retested, tend to move toward the middle of the distribution. This shift will probably take place regardless of any learning or forgetting, and in fact tends to occur even if the second test is given immediately after the first.

Many people find the regression phenomenon difficult to accept; perhaps the following analogy will help. Suppose that each member of a group rolls a die twice. Those who initially rolled a one, the lowest possible score, will very likely go up toward the group mean on their second roll, while those who initially rolled a six will go probably down. Similarly, all chance events (and every test score incorporates an element of chance) exhibit regression toward the mean, so that extreme scores tend to be moderated on a second try.

This bias is particularly relevant to the evaluation of remedial programs, since frequently remedial students are those who have scored low on a pretest (placement test). Their scores tend to rise on retesting because of regression, whether learning has taken place or not. It should be noted, however, that when the remedial population includes the vast majority of entering freshmen—and instances have been reported as high as 98 percent (Anderson and Grady, 1977)—the effect of regression is minimal.

External Learning Bias. Students often improve their basic skills for reasons having little or nothing to do with remedial instruction. Thus, their arithmetic may improve through self-study; their reading may become more proficient as a result of assignments in nonremedial courses. The sheer excitement of being in college provides some students with the impetus to sharpen their skills. For example, Robinson (1950) found that college students improved their reading skills even when given no remedial instruction at all.

History Bias. This bias concerns the possible impact of accidental, often unpredictable, external events on the program under evaluation. Thus, a one-year grant may result in small classes and exceptional performance; a crippling snowstorm or strike may have the effect of reducing achievement. The longer the duration of the evaluative study, the greater the risk of such atypical events.

Maturation Bias. A posttest-over-pretest gain may simply reflect the student's normal maturation or mental growth. However, among students of college age this is probably a minor factor.

Controlling Biases

When the remedial evaluator uses a pretest-posttest comparison, this formidable array of biases may seriously distort results. The problem is compounded by the fact that of the eleven biases described, eight tend to operate toward making the remedial program appear more effective than it actually is. The remaining three—attitude, instrument, and history—may either exaggerate or underestimate the apparent effectiveness of the program, depending on circumstances (see Table 1). This may explain why Piesco (1978, p. 20), in her review of research on CUNY remedial programs, found that "one-group pretest-posttest designs demonstrated, without exception, that students who completed remedial courses showed some improvement in basic skills." By the same token, Cross (1976, p. 33), reviewing remedial evaluations of the 1940s and 1950s, notes, "It is significant that generally speaking, the better designed studies showed less glowingly positive results than the simpler but less adequate research studies." In short, the cumulative effect of these biases may be to represent as very successful a program which is in fact of questionable value.

Table 1. Single-Group Pretest-Posttest Comparison:
Probable Direction of Biases.

Bias	Probable Direction of Bias
Test administration bias	up
Student attitude bias	?
Teaching to the test	up
Practice effect	up
Instrument bias	?
Hawthorne effect	up
Dropout bias	up
Regression toward the mean	up
External learning bias	up
History bias	?
Maturation bias	up

If an evaluative study is to produce justifiable conclusions, the effect of the above biases must be minimized. In some cases, the very recognition of the bias suggests appropriate remedies; in others, remedies may be relatively technical or obscure. Examples of steps that may reduce the influence of biases, if not eliminate it altogether, include the following:

- Test administration bias: Avoid having classroom instructors administer posttests.
- Student attitude bias: Persuade students of the importance of doing well on the placement examination.
- Teaching to the test: Use a "secure" posttest, unfamiliar to the instructional staff.
- Practice effect: Use alternate rather than identical forms for pretest and posttest.
- Instrument bias: Use tests of established validity.
- Hawthorne effect: Conceal from the remedial population (if not from the instructors themselves) the fact that the program is being formally evaluated.
- Dropout bias: Average pretest scores for only those students who also take the posttest; analyze separately the pretest scores of students who do not complete the course.

- Regression toward the mean: Use instruments of established reliability. A more complex technique is to use a separate pretest
for the purpose of program evaluation, distinct from the placement examination originally given (Sparks and Davis, 1977).
Although students placed into remediation perforce score near
the low end of the *placement test* distribution, this may not be true
of the separate pretest. Thus, regression is not operative.

Three biases are absent from the above list: external learning, history, and maturation. These three may be described as *biases of false
attribution;* that is, they are associated with learning gains which,
while real, are not attributable to remedial instruction. To compensate for these and other biases, a number of remedial studies have
abandoned the basic single-group pretest-posttest design in favor
of alternatives using a control group.

The Control Group

A control group, in this context, is a population of students
who, while initially comparable to those entering the remedial program, are nevertheless excluded from the program. The term may
refer either to a group of students receiving no remedial instruction or to one receiving an alternate form of remedial instruction.

In the single-group design just described, the success of the
remedial *population* does not necessarily imply the success of the
remedial *program.* As we have seen, improvement may be entirely
illusory; even if real, it may be due to one or more of the three
false-attribution biases mentioned above. When the remedial
group is compared to a control group, however, we can assume that
the biases affect both groups equally and can therefore be disre-
garded. Having thus neutralized the effect of the biases, we are
free to attribute any difference between post-program measures
for the two groups to the effectiveness of the program itself. Thus,
the use of a control group is a strategy for "turning back the clock"
and determining how remediated students would have fared had
they received alternate remedial assistance or none at all.

We will begin our discussion of control-group designs with two in which the controls receive no remediation at all: the remediated-unremediated comparison and the marginally-remedial, marginally-exempted comparison.

The Remediated-Unremediated Comparison

The remediated-unremediated comparison requires the division of the remedial population into two comparable groups, one of which receives remedial instruction while the other does not. Assignment to the two groups should be random in order to increase the likelihood that the groups are initially equivalent. As indicated here, the unremediated group (Remedial$_2$) serves as a control group for the remediated group (Remedial$_1$).

$$(\text{Remedial}_1)$$
$$M_1 - - - \text{Remediation} - - - M_2$$
$$M_1 - - - \text{No Remediation} - - - M_2$$
$$(\text{Remedial}_2)$$

The average preprogram measures (M_1) for the two groups are compared to check initial equivalence. The extent to which the post-program measures (M_2) differ is the gauge of program effectiveness.

The major disadvantage of the remediated-unremediated comparison is that the deliberate withholding of remediation is ethically questionable. Arguments on this score often become very heated, replete with allusions to open doors becoming revolving doors, essential medications being withheld from the sick and dying, and sheep being led to slaughter. However, none of these metaphors addresses the very cogent argument that until the effectiveness of the remedial program is clearly demonstrated, any ethical questions are somewhat premature; the program may in fact be an outright waste of time. Thus, Piesco (1978, p. 4) writes, "Although no evidence exists regarding effectiveness . . . colleges offering remedial programs have been generally reluctant to randomly exempt from remedial work a proportion of those students identified as being in need of remediation. This reluctance has prevented the conduct of the experimental research which might enable educators to determine which remedial techniques are effective, for whom, and under what conditions."

While a number of evaluative studies have employed unremediated control groups (for example, Losak, 1968; Sharon, 1970), they are certainly in the minority. Frequently, various strategies are introduced to circumvent the ethical issues. One such strategy, used when remedial placement is voluntary, is to consider as a control group those students who test into remediation but elect not to participate. Another practice, employed when placement is purportedly mandatory, is to identify and use as controls those students who nonetheless manage to evade it (Berger, 1972). A third approach is to use as a control group students who, having been among the last to register, are closed out of the requisite remedial classes. Unfortunately, in each of these cases, the two groups are apt to differ with respect to such traits as motivation, self-image, attitude toward mathematics, and so on, thus biasing the results. Perhaps preferable is the strategy of randomly choosing a control group and then postponing, rather than eliminating, their remedial obligation. This approach may moderate, if not completely resolve, the ethical issues.

The Marginally-Remedial, Marginally-Exempted Comparison

The marginally-remedial, marginally-exempted design involves a comparison between a remediated population and an exempted control group. However, the participants in the study are chosen in a special way. The marginally remedial students are those who narrowly fail the pretest and therefore receive remediation; the marginally exempted students are those who narrowly pass. The premise is that since the two groups are separated by only a few points, they start off so similar as to be considered equivalent. As before, the difference in postprogram measures serves as an indication of program effectiveness.

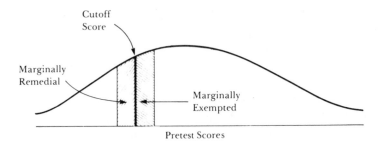

Figure 1. Comparing Marginal Students

(Marginally Remedial)
M_1- - - - - - - -Remediation- - - - - - - -M_2
M_1- - - - - - -No Remediation - - - - - - -M_2
(Marginally Exempted)

While this design avoids the moral dilemma posed by the remediated-unremediated comparison, it poses its own problems. One is that it measures the program's effectiveness only for the best of the remedial students; but the performance of these students is not necessarily representative of the entire remedial population. Another problem is that since the two groups are only approximately comparable at the outset, the postprogram measures may be difficult to interpret. If the remedial group surpasses the exempted one, there is some evidence of the remedial program's success. However, if the exempted group surpasses the remedial one, we are hard-pressed to decide whether the program has some value (although perhaps not enough), or whether it is altogether useless. This design might thus be called *inequitable;* results can be interpreted if they go in one direction, but not if they go in the other. The problem of inequitable designs will be considered again later in the discussion.

Biases in Cross-Group Designs

Apart from the eleven biases presented earlier, the two control-group designs just considered introduce biases of their own. These new cross-group biases are *differential biases* and *initial differences.*

Differential Biases. In introducing a control group, we proceeded on the assumption that even if the original biases continued to operate, they would operate equally on the two groups and could therefore be discounted. If this is not the case—that is, if the biases affect the two groups to different degrees—our assumption is unwarranted, and the results are again distorted. For example, in a remediated-unremediated comparison, the dropout bias may favor one group over the other; in a marginally-remedial, marginally-exempted study, regression toward the mean will usually favor the remedial group. In such cases, postprogram measures may be difficult to interpret. A good strategy for controlling any differential bias is to follow the earlier recommendation for the corresponding single-group bias.

Initial Differences. In comparing groups on postprogram measures, we would like to associate the superior performance of one group with a superior instructional experience. Such a conclusion is invalid if the higher-scoring group was superior even prior to instruction. This problem arose in considering the marginally-remedial, marginally-exempted comparison. It also arises in connection with the remediated-unremediated comparison if, one way or another, students place themselves into the two groups instead of being randomly assigned. Reed (1956) and Santeusanio (1974) have found that overlooking the initial difference bias produced by such self-selection has weakened a large number of studies.

While the best way to control the initial difference bias is by random assignment, this is not always feasible. In such cases, other approaches must be found. A number of early studies tried to equate remedial and control groups by matching students across groups on variables believed to be educationally significant; for example, age, sex, IQ, and the like (Entwistle, 1960; Gordon, 1970). This procedure had the obvious disadvantage of restricting the evaluative study to students who might in no way have been representative of the populations from which they were drawn, and has been generally abandoned. Recent remedial evaluations have employed complex statistical techniques, notably analysis of covariance (ANCOVA), to compensate for initial differences. Ary, Jacobs, and Razavieh (1972, p. 275) characterize analysis of covariance as "a superior method of control . . . which permits a compensation to be made in the analysis of the data for the lack of equivalence in the groups initially." However, other researchers have called the technique into question. Thus, Wolf (1979, p. 133) admonishes, "No amount of statistical manipulation and adjustment can be done to compensate for the fact that the groups come from inherently different populations."

An alternate statistical approach for overcoming the initial dissimilarity of two comparison groups is a rather subtle technique known as regression-discontinuity analysis. This technique is central to our next evaluative design.

The Regression-Discontinuity Design

Of all the designs which we will consider, the regression-discontinuity design (not to be confused with the regression bias) is the most complex, both conceptually and in terms of the requisite statistical analysis. Because it involves some quite technical considerations (such as the *line of best fit*), we will outline only the principle; readers may consult Sparks and Davis (1977), Tallmadge and Horst (1976), or Thistlethwaite and Campbell (1960) for a more detailed presentation.

The regression-discontinuity design involves two groups: the remedial population, which receives remediation, and the exempted group, which does not.

(Remedial)

M_1- - - - - - - -Remediation- - - - - - - -M_2

M_1- - - - - - -No Remediation - - - - - - -M_2

(Exempt)

However, because the two populations are not initially equivalent, we cannot talk of a "control group." Rather, we must find a way to compare postprogram measures from these two disparate groups so that we can draw conclusions about the effectiveness of remedial instruction.

For the sake of discussion, let us assume that the preprogram and postprogram measures are both tests. The first step in
the regression-discontinuity analysis is to graph each student's test
scores, with one axis representing pretest and the other, posttest.
The result is a scatter diagram like that shown in Figure 2.

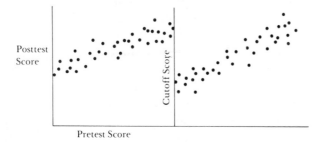

Figure 2. A Scatter Diagram of Pretest and Posttest Scores

Each point to the left of the cutoff line represents a student whose
pretest score placed him into the remedial program; the points to
the right represent students who were exempted. Next we draw the
two *lines of best fit;* that is—to oversimplify considerably—lines
which most nearly pass through each of the two sets of points.
This is shown in Figure 3, where line R is the line of best fit for the
remediated students, and line E the line of best fit for the exempted students. Had there been no remediation at all, one would

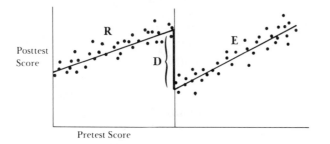

**Figure 3. Lines of Best Fit for Remediated and
Exempted Students, Case 1**

expect a single continuous line across the entire graph. Therefore the size of the gap—that is, the length of the line segment D—provides a measure of program effectiveness.

The regression-discontinuity design has several serious drawbacks, chiefly related to the statistical analysis. One is that the two lines of best fit are something of a compromise; if in fact they do not "fit" their points well, there is little to be learned from further analysis. Another is that focusing on the length of line segment D has the effect of undervaluing programs which are particularly successful with the weakest students. This is suggested in Figure 4; although the posttest scores of such students have been raised substantially, so that line R is nearly horizontal, the length of segment D remains unchanged. (Horst, Tallmadge, and Wood, 1975, describe a variation of the regression-discontinuity design which meets this objection, although it introduces difficulties of its own.)

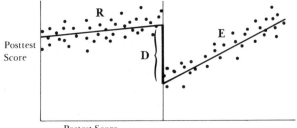

**Figure 4. Lines of Best Fit for Remediated and
Exempted Students, Case 2**

Finally, there is at present no standard for determining whether the length of the line segment D is statistically significant (Wolf, 1979); this leaves open the possibility that program gains were due to chance.

Evaluating Learning

To evaluate is to ascribe value, which in turn implies the availability of a standard. From this point of view, the four designs considered up to now have not so much evaluated remedial effectiveness as measured it; nowhere was there a serious attempt to translate this measurement into a value judgment. Yet such judgment is essential. If a study, regardless of design, reports an average gain of ten points, we still cannot characterize the program as a success or failure, because the magnitude of the gain exists in a vacuum.

To remedy this situation, four evaluative standards have been proposed, each leading to a new design. In the first, the *remediated-exempted comparison,* the performance of the exempted population is used as the standard for assessing the achievement of remediated students. In the second, the *norm-group comparison,* our standard is the performance of a national population. The *cross-group comparison* compares the effectiveness of two different remedial programs, usually at separate institutions. Finally, the *historical comparison* contrasts the effectiveness of a current program with that of one previously offered at the same school. In each case, the design has a genuine evaluative component, insofar as an appropriate criterion is available for comparison with the remedial postprogram measure.

The Remediated-Exempted Comparison

Like the regression-discontinuity design described earlier, the next design involves exempted as well as remedial students. However, the statistical analysis is more straightforward.

$$\text{(Remedial)}$$
$$M_1 - - - - - - - \text{Remediation} - - - - - - - M_2$$
$$M_1 - - - - - - \text{No Remediation} - - - - - - M_2$$
$$\text{(Exempted)}$$

The remediated-exempted comparison usually employs a long-term postprogram measure, such as GPA or performance in some college-level course. The preprogram measure is usually the original placement score so that those who fell below the cutoff received remediation while the rest of the student population did not. Since preprogram and postprogram measures are not comparable, it is clearly impossible to compute gains. Instead, the evaluator compares postprogram measures for the two groups.

The great drawback of the remediated-exempted comparison is that it is *inequitable,* in the specialized sense used earlier. If the remedial group surpasses, or even matches, the exempted one, we have strong evidence that the program is successful. If, on the other hand, the remedial group continues to lag behind, no conclusion can be drawn with certainty. Possibly the program is worthless; possibly it is good, but not good enough to compensate for the initial handicap of this group.

Moreover, to compare remedial and exempted students sets a very stringent standard for the remedial program. Of course, any remedial population will include individual students who ultimately perform as well as those who were exempted, or even better. However, to expect that the two group *averages* be equal—much less favor the remedial group—is asking a great deal. To see this more clearly, imagine an ESL program serving nonnative students. Even if everyone in the program were raised to the level of the cutoff score, the population as a whole would probably remain substantially weaker than the initially exempted native speakers. In such a case, the very real effectiveness of the remedial program is obscured by the evaluative design. This problem often arises in a remediated-exempted comparison; Piesco (1978), studying CUNY's program evaluations, found that only rarely did remediated students attain the performance level of their exempted counterparts. This is true despite the fact that several biases (notably the dropout bias and the maturation bias), operating differentially, tend to inflate the postprogram measure of the remediated group.

The Norm-Group Comparison

In the norm-group comparison, preprogram and postprogram measures consist of scores on standardized tests—usually two forms of the same test. The design is frequently used in reading programs, especially if a standardized test is already being used as a

placement or exit mechanism. The improvement of the local remedial population is compared with that of the corresponding national population on which the test was normed. While test manuals
provide tables to facilitate the comparison, the procedure itself is
technical; the interested reader is referred to Tallmadge and Horst
(1976) or Horst, Tallmadge, and Wood (1975).

$$(Remedial)$$
$$M_1 - - - - - - - \text{-Remediation-} - - - - - - - M_2$$
$$M_1 - - - - - - - - - - - ????? - - - - - - - - - - - M_2$$
$$(National\ Norm)$$

One virtue of the norm-group design is its relative simplic-
ity; the comparison is based on information which is already available. Moreover, the design is *equitable;* that is, we may draw conclusions about the value of the program regardless of whether local
gains are higher or lower than those of the norm group.

However, these advantages are outweighed by the drawbacks of the design. The most serious of these is the likelihood that
the norm group and the local population are not initially comparable. Even if the two groups achieve the same average pretest score,
they may differ on any of a dozen educationally significant variables—age, sex, ethnicity, socioeconomic status, and so on. If the
norm group is receiving instruction, we know nothing about the
amount or type. We may not even know how long ago the test
norms were established. And of course all such differences will
tend to invalidate any comparisons based on these norms. For
example, even when the content of a standardized test is suitable, if
its norms are based on a junior high school population, these
norms are entirely unacceptable for purposes of evaluating college
programs. Test-makers are becoming aware of this problem and
are beginning to offer college-level remedial placement tests with
appropriate norms, but the match may still be far from perfect.

A second drawback of the norm-group design is the difficulty of finding a standardized test that corresponds, in content
and level of difficulty, to the requirements of the individual program.
Often the selection of a test entails a succession of compromises,

each of which further invalidates the use of the norms. For these and similar reasons, Wolf (1979, p. 135) concludes that "the use of the norm group for a standardized test for contrast purposes is a somewhat unappetizing compromise which should probably be made only as a last resort."

The Cross-Program Comparison

The cross-program comparison employs as a standard of success the achievement of a comparable remedial population, typically at another college. The design may be diagrammed as follows:

$$(\text{Remedial}_1)$$
$$M_1\text{- - - - - - -Remediation}_1\text{- - - - - - -}M_2$$
$$M_1\text{- - - - - - -Remediation}_2\text{- - - - - - -}M_2$$
$$(\text{Remedial}_2)$$

Note that Remedial_1 and Remedial_2 stand for remedial populations at different colleges, while Remediation_1 and Remediation_2 indicate the corresponding remedial programs. It is assumed that the two remedial populations are initially equivalent, that the two programs have comparable objectives, content, and placement procedures, and that the colleges have agreed on common preprogram and postprogram measures. The preprogram measure is used as evidence of initial comparability; the difference in postprogram measures becomes the basis for evaluating the two programs.

A major advantage of this design is that the results have formative as well as summative value. They indicate not only the effectiveness of one remedial program relative to the other but also the direction in which the weaker program should be modified.

Like other two-group designs, the cross-program comparison is subject to the initial difference and differential biases discussed earlier. The problem may be even greater here because random selection across programs, the usual technique for controlling individual differences, is generally impossible. Therefore initial comparability of populations must be established by careful analysis of pretest scores, socioeconomic status, age, and so on.

There may also be problems of implementation if the staffs of the two colleges, feeling themselves in competition, are reluctant to cooperate.

The cross-program comparison is seldom used because it is difficult to locate programs with matching populations, objectives, content, and placement procedures. However, the current trend toward uniform proficiency testing within entire college systems (for example, at CUNY, the public colleges of Georgia, and those of New Jersey) may tend to standardize these variables, in which case the design may become more feasible.

The Historical Comparison

The historical comparison is a variation on the cross-program comparison. Here, however, the study is conducted at a single college, and the groups being compared consist of students receiving remediation in different semesters.

(Present Remedial)
$$M_1--------Remediation_1--------M_2$$
$$M_1--------Remediation_2--------M_2$$
(Previous Remedial)

Preprogram measures establish the initial comparability of the two groups, while the achievement of the earlier group becomes the standard for that of the later one.

The historical comparison is easily implemented—often, one simply lists passing rates for several consecutive terms—and is therefore frequently used. However, it is particularly vulnerable to differential historical bias. For example, when tuition was first imposed at CUNY in 1976, a number of colleges reported higher success rates; apparently, students were willing to work harder to avoid repeating a remedial course for which they had to pay tuition. There is also a strong likelihood of subtle initial differences, even when the populations appear to be comparable.

The historical comparison is particularly valuable when there have been deliberate changes either in the remedial program or in the college environment. However, it is also useful for detecting unsuspected changes which may have arisen.

If a program has undergone no significant internal or external modifications, the use of the historical comparison serves simply to replicate the evaluation, a procedure not without its own value. In this event, differences in achievement should be minor and attributable to random fluctuations.

Implementing the Remedial Evaluation

To the extent that evaluation may be considered a science, it is far from an exact one. Whatever conclusions are drawn, they may be plausible or even probable; but as Fadale (1977) points out, no study, however strong its design and careful its implementation, can demonstrate an indisputable cause-and-effect relationship. Therefore no amount of psychometric expertise or statistical analysis should obscure the pivotal role played by judgment in an evaluative study. In choosing a design, in weighing strategies to minimize the effect of biases, in interpreting results—here and in many other areas, the evaluator's insight is critical.

Thus, the choice of evaluator could have a considerable impact on the resulting evaluation. While a number of programs have been evaluated by their own coordinators, it may be difficult for someone so intimately connected with the program to be sufficiently objective. Perhaps it is preferable to have the evaluation conducted by a department or college committee, by the college's office of institutional research, or by an outside evaluator. In any event, the choice also depends on a number of other factors, including available funding, the qualifications of local staff, and the purpose of the evaluation.

It is essential that an evaluator be selected and decisions shaping the evaluative study be made early in the proceedings. Following this, the evaluator should lay out a schedule of what must be done, when, and by whom. Tests must be chosen and administered and questionnaires completed before the start of classes; once instruction has begun, essential preprogram measures may be irretrievably lost.

As we have seen, the evaluator is responsible for several

important choices: preprogram measure, postprogram measure, evaluative design, and grouping statistic. In making these choices, one important consideration is that each of them reflect the objectives of the remedial program. If the purpose of a remedial writing course is to prepare students for Freshman Composition, then grade in this course is a natural postprogram measure. If the program's objective is to raise as many students as possible to criterion level (rather than merely improving the skills of each participant), then the grouping statistic should be the percentage of students who pass, *not* an average. If objectives are not already this explicit, then the evaluator should insist that they be clarified; this may serve not only to strengthen the evaluation but to improve the program itself.

A second factor in making choices is feasibility. The evaluator must consider such constraints as time and funding as well as local policy with respect to testing, withholding needed remediation, and related concerns.

Lastly, the evaluator must assess the intrinsic strengths and weakness of each alternative, while recognizing that certain methodological choices exclude others.

We will consider these factors in the discussion which follows. While it is impossible to spell out the ramifications of each alternative, we will indicate a few guidelines for making the necessary decisions. Some information which has a bearing on such decisions is summarized in Table 2.

The Preprogram Measure

As we see from Table 2, test scores are the most common preprogram measure, whatever the evaluative design. If the norm-group comparison is being considered as the evaluative design, then a pretest with suitable content and norms must be available. We may also note that if the evaluator plans to compensate for the regression bias by using separate pretests for placement and evaluation, then both tests must be scheduled before the start of the program.

In rare cases, college GPA or high school average may be used as the preprogram measure. Both have the advantage that

Table 2. Considerations in the Choice of Evaluative Designs.

Design	Preprogram Measure	Postprogram Measure	Feasibility Problems
Single-Group Pretest-Posttest Comparison	Test (GPA)	Must be comparable to preprogram measure	
Remediated-Unremediated Comparison	Test	GPA, grade in next related course, retention or graduation rate (test)	Ethical question of withholding remediation (assembling unremediated students for posttest)
Marginally-Remedial, Marginally Exempted Comparison	Test (or other placement criteria)	GPA, grade in next related course, retention or graduation rate (test)	Assembling exempted students for posttest
Regression-Discontinuity Design	Test	Test, (GPA)	Assembling exempted students for posttest.
Remediated-Exempted Comparison	Test (or other placement criteria)	GPA, grade in next related course, retention or graduation rate (test)	Assembling exempted students for posttest
Cross-Program Comparison			
(a) Separate colleges	Test	Test	Finding comparable cooperating colleges
(b) Same college	Test (or other placement criteria)	GPA, grade in next related course, retention or graduation rate, course grade, test	Avoiding cross-influences among experimental groups
Norm-Group	Standardized test	Must be comparable to preprogram measure	Finding test with appropriate content and norms
Historical Comparison	Test	Test	Requires continuing use of same test

Note: Entries in parentheses are less feasible and are seldom employed.

Possible Biases	Compre-hensive?	Equi-table?	Provides an Educational Standard?
Test administration, student attitude, teaching to the test, practice effect, instrument, Hawthorne effect, dropout, regression toward the mean, external learning, history, maturation	yes	yes	no
Initial differences, test administration, teaching to the test, student attitude, Hawthorne effect, differential operation of other biases	yes	yes	no
Initial differences, test administration, teaching to the test, student attitude, Hawthorne effect, differential operation of other biases	no	no(?)	no
Initial differences, test administration, teaching to the test, student attitude, Hawthorne effect, differential operation of other biases	yes	yes	no
Test administration, teaching to the test, student attitude, Hawthorne effect, differential operation of other biases	yes	no	yes (too stringent in some cases)
Initial differences, history, differential operation of other biases	yes	yes	yes
Initial differences, history, differential operation of other biases	yes	yes	yes
Initial differences, history, differential operation of other biases	yes	yes	yes

they are part of the student's record and, in the absence of more appropriate data, can be retrieved at any point in the evaluative study. However, neither is sufficiently reliable to serve as an acceptable preprogram measure; in addition, the GPA is not feasible unless the student attended college for at least a semester prior to the start of remediation.

Related to the collection of preprogram measures is the recording of demographic data—age, sex, high school courses, native language, and so on. Such data may be essential for establishing the comparability of student populations, determining the types of student for whom the remedial program is most effective, and so on. Information of this kind should be obtained before the start of the program; attempts to reconstruct it after the event are notoriously expensive, frustrating, and ineffective.

The Postprogram Measure

The choice of postprogram measure reflects a complex play of forces. As we have seen, the most important question in connection with the postprogram measure is whether it should be short- or long-range. In theory, at least, this choice should depend upon the objectives of the program. If the remedial content is offered for its own sake, then a short-range measure is reasonable. However, if remediation is intended primarily to prepare students for college-level courses, a long-range measure is more appropriate.

Beyond this, the choice of postprogram measure is also dictated by evaluative design. The reader will note from Table 2 that four of the eight evaluative designs virtually mandate the use of a posttest as the postprogram measure. In the single-group and norm-group comparisons, the statistical analysis demands a posttest similar to the pretest. In the cross-program and historical comparisons, there are already so many unavoidable differences between groups that the evaluator should attempt to standardize where he can.

There is also a final complication. In any study comparing students who receive remediation with those who, for whatever reason, do not, administering a uniform posttest may pose a problem. It is difficult to contact the unremediated students, and even more difficult to assemble them for a test from which they have nothing to gain. The use of a posttest may also be discouraged by faculty concerned about overtesting the students.

If we have dwelt on these points, it is not to dishearten the prospective evaluator, but rather to demonstrate once more the role of judgment in an area of conflicting pressures. The choice of a postprogram measure is all the more critical in that, as has been noted earlier, short-range measures usually yield positive results, while long-range measures tend to be more equivocal. Hence there is a danger that the choice of postprogram measure will become a mechanism for manipulating the outcome of the evaluation.

The Evaluative Design

The selection of an evaluative design should be closely related to the objectives of the remedial program, and it is usually among the first decisions made.

The intrinsic merit of a design may be gauged by the answers to the following questions: (1) Is the design relatively free from the effect of biases? (2) Is it equitable; that is, does it provide evidence equally well of success or of failure? (3) Is is comprehensive; that is, does the sample reflect the entire remedial population? (4) Does it provide a reasonable educational standard?

Offsetting these considerations is the question of feasibility. Of course, the feasibility of a design cannot be determined categorically; it depends on conditions at the particular college. Nonetheless, it is probably safe to say that the strongest designs are apt to be the least feasible. There is more than sheer perversity at work here; if a single design were both feasible and strong, it would obviously preempt the field. Thus, we have the powerful remediated-unremediated comparison, which is often ruled out because the ethical problems it raises render it impracticable. At the other end of the spectrum is the single-group pretest-posttest design, extremely easy to implement but so prone to bias as to be of minimal value. Fortunately, the use of one design does not preclude the use of any other; combining designs can only give a more rounded picture of program effectiveness.

Grouping Statistic

Whereas the preprogram measure, postprogram measure, and design may impinge on one another, the grouping statistic is independent of all three. It is important that the grouping statistic be chosen at the start of the evaluative study and that it be related to program objectives. Otherwise there may be a great temptation to compute the results in various ways, reporting only the most favorable. The danger (as with the postprogram measure) is that the choice will be made to whitewash the remedial program rather than to evaluate it.

Recommendations

Certainly no single chapter can answer all the questions raised in as complex a field as program evaluation—complex in terms of the skills required, the issues demanding attention, and the many factors that must be taken into account. We have attempted in these pages to introduce some order into the relatively uncharted territory of remedial program evaluation. Although we might wish to conclude with a definitive statement of the best plans and procedures, we are in fact unable to commit ourselves to a single "best" strategy. This is not only because circumstances vary from campus to campus but also because there are unresolved issues in which it would be premature to say that one position is correct and another in error. Instead, we have chosen to conclude with a list of brief caveats. Perhaps they are oversimplified, but we feel that they will help readers maintain their perspective amid the many details and alternatives which have been brought to their attention.

1. Be objective. The objectivity of an evaluative study may be gauged by the extent to which it is based on concrete, appropriate data. The judgments of blue-ribbon panels and the diffuse impressions of faculty or students may play a role, but they should not be allowed to dominate the study. Specific criteria for success or failure must be agreed upon in advance. Moreover, the appearance of being partisan can discredit an evaluator as much as the fact of partisanship; thus, evaluation by the program coordinator or other interested party is suspect from the start.

2. Be informed. Familiarity with the range of design options is critical in planning the evaluative study. Although we have stressed such options throughout this discussion, the topic has been far from exhausted. The reader may wish to consult other sources, such as the two excellent books published by the U.S. Office of Education (Horst, Tallmadge, and Wood, 1975; Tallmadge and Horst, 1976) or any of the fine texts on general evaluation.

3. Be comprehensive. We have emphasized the need to assess the overall effectiveness of remedial instruction, but the reader should not overlook other legitimate areas of evaluation—cost effectiveness, reliability of placement procedures, and so on. In particular, the utility of formative evaluations should be borne in mind, especially in the early stages of the program.

4. Be pragmatic. Plan to do only what is feasible, taking into account the local limitations of resources, equipment, staffing, and time. The most ambitious study, if left unfinished, is worth less than a modest one brought to fruition.

5. Be politic. In planning and implementing the study, be alert to the policy of the college and the misgivings of the staff. Keep all parties informed of your procedures, and avoid strategies that may discourage cooperation.

6. Be selective. Although the study should include all significant areas, the types of data to be collected should be chosen with the greatest care. Great masses of raw data, collected without clear purpose or direction, defy analysis. Identify precisely the necessary data; then, in advance of the study, draw up a collection schedule so that data are not irretrievably lost. In the final report, highlight the major results, lest they be drowned in a sea of peripheral information.

7. Be prepared to compromise. Every evaluation represents a compromise between the attainable and the ideal. If randomization is impossible or small quantities of data are lost, settle for the best of what is possible—at the same time gauging the extent to which such shortcomings may result in misleading conclusions.

References

＊ ＊ ＊ ＊ ＊ ＊ ＊ ＊ ＊ ＊ ＊ ＊ ＊ ＊ ＊ ＊ ＊

Ablon, L. "A Modular Approach to Preparatory Mathematics." *American Mathematical Monthly*, 1972, *79*, 1126–1131.

Adams, W. R. *How to Read the Sciences*. Glenview, Ill.: Scott, Foresman, 1970.

Adler, M. J., and Van Doren, C. *How to Read a Book*. New York: Simon & Schuster, 1972.

Aiken, L. R., Jr. "Update on Attitudes and Other Affective Variables in Learning Mathematics." *Review of Educational Research*, 1976, *46* (2), 293–311.

Akst, G. R. "A Study of the Effect on Learning of Pacing and Testing Procedures in a Two-Year College Remedial Mathematics Course." Unpublished doctoral dissertation, Teachers College, 1976. *Dissertation Abstracts International*, 1976, *37*, 2035A.

Algeo, J., and Pyles, T. *Problems in the Origins and Development of the English Language*. New York: Harcourt Brace Jovanovich, 1966.

Allen, R. L. *English Grammars and English Grammar*. New York: Scribner's, 1974.

297

Allen, R. L., Pompian, R., and Allen, D. *Working Sentences.* New York: Crowell, 1975.

Anderson, H., and Grady, M. *Harvest: A Study of 1,775 Students Who Entered El Paso Community College in the Fall of 1973.* Educational Resources Information Center, ED 137 323. Colorado Springs, Colo.: El Paso Community College, 1977.

Anderson, S. B., and Ball, S. *The Profession and Practice of Program Evaluation.* San Francisco: Jossey-Bass, 1978.

Ary, D., Jacobs, L. C., and Razavieh, A. *Introduction to Research in Education.* New York: Holt, Rinehart and Winston, 1972.

Baldwin, J., and others. *Survey of Developmental Mathematics Courses at Colleges in the United States.* Educational Resources Information Center, ED 125 688. Garden City, N.Y.: American Mathematical Association of Two-Year Colleges, 1975.

Ballard, A. B. "The Academic Program in Senior Colleges." In *Open Admissions at the City University of New York,* testimony before the Joint Legislative Committee on Higher Education by the City University of New York. New York: City University of New York, 1971.

Baskoff, F. *American English: Guided Composition.* New York: American Language Institute, New York University, 1971.

Bender, L. *Visual-Motor Gestalt Test.* New York: American Orthopsychiatric Association, 1946.

Berger, D. *Effectiveness of College Skills and Basic Writing Courses in Preparing Students for Regular College Courses.* New York: Office of Research and Testing, City College of New York, 1972.

Bernstein, L. "Using Materials from Other Disciplines." In *Proceedings of the CUNY Association of Writing Supervisors Conference, May 1979.* New York: City University of New York, forthcoming.

Block, J. H. *Mastery Learning: Theory and Practice.* New York: Holt, Rinehart and Winston, 1971.

Bloom, B. *Human Characteristics and School Learning.* New York: McGraw-Hill, 1976.

Bowles, D., and others. "Comprehensive Reading Program Competency Examination of College-Level Reading and Study Skills." Unpublished manuscript, Brooklyn College, 1976.

Braswell, J. S. *Mathematics Tests Available in the United States.* (3rd ed.) Washington, D.C.: National Council of Teachers of Mathematics, 1974.

Brookes, G., and Withrow, J. *10 Steps: Controlled Composition for Beginning and Intermediate ESL Students.* New York: Language Innovations, 1974.

Brown, C. M., and Adams, W. R. *How to Read the Social Sciences.* Glenview, Ill.: Scott, Foresman, 1968.

Brown, J. I. *Programmed Vocabulary.* (2nd ed.) Englewood Cliffs, N.J.: Prentice-Hall, 1971.

Bruffee, K. *A Short Course in Writing.* Cambridge, Mass.: Winthrop, 1972.

Bryant, N. D. "Diagnostic Test of Basic Reading Decoding Skills." Unpublished manuscript, 1975.

Buros, O. K. (Ed.). *Mathematics Tests and Reviews.* Highland Park, N.J.: Gryphon Press, 1975.

Burt, M. K. "Error Analysis in the Adult EFL Classroom." *TESOL Quarterly,* 1975, *9* (1), 53–63.

Campbell, D. T., and Stanley, J. C. *Experimental and Quasi-Experimental Design for Research.* Chicago: Rand McNally, 1966.

Carman, R. *A Cost-Effectiveness Analysis of Various Methods of Instruction in Developmental Mathematics.* Educational Resources Information Center, ED 057 793. Santa Barbara, Calif.: Santa Barbara City College, 1971.

Christiansen, F. *Notes Toward a New Rhetoric: Six Essays for Teachers.* New York: Harper & Row, 1967.

Collier, J. *Visual Anthropology: Photography as a Research Method.* New York: Holt, Rinehart and Winston, 1967.

Communications Research Machines. *Psychology Today: An Introduction.* Del Mar, Calif.: Communications Research Machines, 1970.

Conference on College Composition and Communication. "Conference on College Composition and Communication Resolution on Testing." Adopted April 1, 1978. Reprinted in *College Composition and Communication,* 1979, *30,* 391–392.

Cooper, C. R. "Holistic Evaluation of Writing." In C. R. Cooper and L. Odell (Eds.), *Evaluating Writing.* Urbana, Ill.: National Council of Teachers of English, 1977.

Cooper, C. R., and Odell, L. (Eds.). *Evaluating Writing.* Urbana, Ill.: National Council of Teachers of English, 1977.

Cosby, J. P. *Remedial Education—Is It Worth It?* Educational Resources Information Center, ED 099 067. Fort Lauderdale, Fla.: Nova University, 1975.

Coursen, H. *As Up They Grew.* Glenview, Ill.: Scott, Foresman, 1970.

Courtney, L. "Methods and Materials for Teaching Word Perception in Grades Ten Through Fourteen." In H. M. Robinson (Ed.), *Sequential Development of Reading Abilities. Conference on Reading,* Supplemental Educational Monographs No. 90. Chicago: University of Chicago Press, 1960, pp. 42–46.

Cross, K. P. *Beyond the Open Door: New Students to Higher Education.* San Francisco: Jossey-Bass, 1971.

Cross, K. P. *Accent on Learning: Improving Instruction and Reshaping the Curriculum.* San Francisco: Jossey-Bass, 1976.

Crowell, T. L., Jr. *Index to Modern English.* New York: McGraw-Hill, 1964.

Curran, C. A. *Counseling-Learning: A Whole-Person Model for Education.* New York: Grune & Stratton, 1972.

Czarnecki, K. E., and Ramos, J. A. "Counseling-Learning: A Wholistic View of the Learner." *TESOL Newsletter,* 1975, *9* (6), 1, 4.

Daiker, D., Kerek, A., and Morenberg, M. *The Writer's Options.* New York: Harper & Row, 1979.

D'Angelo, F. J. *Process and Thought in Composition.* Cambridge, Mass.: Winthrop, 1977.

Decker, A., Jody, R., and Brings, F. *A Handbook on Open Admissions: Success, Failure, Potential.* Boulder, Colo.: Westview Press, 1976.

D'Eloia, S. "The Uses—and Limits—of Grammar." *Journal of Basic Writing,* 1977, *1* (3), 1–48.

D'Eloia, S., and others. *The English Modules and Workbook.* Albany: State University of New York, 1976.

Dickerson, L. J. "The Learner's Interlanguage as a System of Variable Rules." *TESOL Quarterly,* 1975, *9* (4), 401–407.

Diederich, P. B. *Measuring Growth in English.* Urbana, Ill.: National Council of Teachers of English, 1974.

Duke, C. R. *Basic Writing Skills Assessment Project: An Interpretive Report.* Educational Resources Information Center, ED 153 245. Plymouth, N.H.: Plymouth State College, 1978.

Elbow, P. *Writing Without Teachers.* New York: Oxford University Press, 1973.

Entwistle, D. "Evaluations of Study Skills Courses: A Review." *Journal of Educational Research,* 1960, *53,* 117–125.

Epes, M., Kirkpatrick, C., and Southwell, M. "The COMP-LAB Project: An Experimental Basic Writing Course." *Journal of Basic Writing*, 1979, *2* (2), 19–37.

Epes, M., Kirkpatrick, C., and Southwell, M. *COMP-LAB Exercises.* Englewood Cliffs, N.J.: Prentice-Hall, 1980.

Fadale, L. M. *Developmental Studies for Occupational Students: Post-secondary Programs.* Ithaca, N.Y.: Cornell Institute for Research and Development in Occupational and Continuing Education, 1977.

Farrell, T. "Slaying the Dragon Error: A Response to Patricia Laurence." October 1977, *39*, 233–237.

Fawcett, S., and Sandberg, A. *Grassroots: The Writer's Workbook.* Boston: Houghton Mifflin, 1976.

Fey, J. T. "Mathematics Teaching Today: Perspectives from Three National Surveys." Paper presented at the annual meeting of the Mathematical Association of America, Biloxi, Miss., January 1979.

Field, J. P., and Weiss, R. H. *Cases for Composition.* Boston: Little, Brown, 1979.

Finn, P. J. "Computer-Aided Description of Mature Word Choices in Writing." In C. R. Cooper and L. Odell (Eds.), *Evaluating Writing.* Urbana, Ill.: National Council of Teachers of English, 1977.

Flower, L., and Hayes, J. "Problem-Solving Strategies and the Writing Process." *College English*, 1977, *39* (4), 449–461.

Fries, C. C. *Linguistics and Reading.* New York: Holt, Rinehart and Winston, 1963.

Fry, E. "Fry's Readability Graph: Clarifications, Validity and Extension to Level 17." *Journal of Reading*, 1977, *21*, 242–252.

Gallingane, G., and Byrd, D. *Write Away.* New York: Collier Macmillan, 1977.

Gans, H. J. *The Urban Villagers: Group and Class in the Life of Italian-Americans.* New York: Free Press, 1962.

Gattegno, C. *Teaching Foreign Languages in the Schools: The Silent Way.* (2nd ed.) New York: Educational Solutions, 1972.

Gattegno, C. "Some Remarks and Additions on the Silent Way." *IDIOM*, Winter 1974, *4* (2), 3.

Gehle, Q. L., and Rollo, D. J. *The Writing Process.* New York: St. Martin's, 1977.

Giordano, G. "Semantic Anticipation in Adolescent and Adult Reading Instruction." *Reading World,* 1977, *17,* 146–150.

Goldman, R., Fristoe, M., and Woodcock, R. W. *Goldman-Fristoe-Woodcock Test of Auditory Discrimination.* Circle Pines, Minn.: American Guidance Services, 1970.

Gordon, E. W. "Compensatory Education: Evaluation in Perspective." *IRCD Bulletin.* New York: Columbia University Press, 1970.

Gould, G. L. *Groundwork.* New York: Harcourt Brace Jovanovich, 1977.

Grant, M. K., and Hoeber, D. R. *Basic Skills Programs: Are They Working?* AAHE-ERIC Higher Education Research Report No. 1. Washington, D.C.: American Association for Higher Education, 1978.

Gray, B. Q., and Trillin, A. "Animating Grammar: Principles for the Development of Video-Tape Materials." *Journal of Basic Writing,* 1977, *3,* 77–91.

Hake, R. "With No Apology: Teaching to the Test." *Journal of Basic Writing,* 1978, *1* (4), 39–62.

Harris, A. J., and Sipay, E. P. *How to Increase Reading Ability: A Guide to Developmental and Remedial Methods.* (5th ed.) New York: McKay, 1970.

Harris, A. J., and Sipay, E. P. *How to Increase Reading Ability: A Guide to Developmental and Remedial Methods.* (6th ed.) New York: McKay, 1975.

Harris, A. J., and Sipay, E. P. *How to Teach Reading: A Competency-Based Program.* London: Longmans, 1979.

Haskell, J. F. "An Eclectic Method?" *TESOL Newsletter,* 1978, *12* (2), 19–24.

Hayden, S., and Mineka, J. *Algebra and Geometry: An Introduction with Applications.* Baltimore, Md.: Williams & Wilkins, 1976.

Hechinger, F. "For the 'Writing Crisis,' Help Is on the Way." *New York Times,* Sept. 18, 1979, p. C5.

Hecht, M. "Should High School Subjects Receive College Credit?" *Journal of the CUNY Mathematics Discussion Group,* 1975, *3,* 43–45.

Hecht, M., and Hecht, C. *ModuMath Arithmetic.* Boston: Houghton Mifflin, 1978.

Hodgins, R. C. "Text Is the Adversary." *Teachers College Record,* 1970, *72,* 7–22.

Holmes, J. A., and Singer, H. *Speed and Power of Reading in High*

School. Cooperative Education Research Monograph 14. Washington, D.C.: U.S. Department of Heaith, Education, and Welfare, 1966.

Horst, D., Tallmadge, G., and Wood, C. *A Practical Guide to Measuring Project Impact on Student Achievement.* Washington, D.C.: U.S. Government Printing Office, 1975.

Hunt, K. "Syntactic Maturity in School Children and Adults." *Monographs of the Society for Research in Child Development,* 1970, *35* (1, Serial No. 134).

Jelfo, D. *An Evaluation of the Developmental Education Program at Cuyahoga Community College, Eastern Campus.* Educational Resources Information Center, ED 099 036. Fort Lauderdale, Fla.: Nova University, 1974.

Johnson, D. D., and Pearson, P. D. *Teaching Reading Comprehension.* New York: Holt, Rinehart and Winston, 1978.

Kaplan, R. B. "Cultural Thought Patterns in Intercultural Education." *Language Learning,* 1966, *16,* 1–20.

Kelley, E. C. "The Importance of Affective Learning Outcomes." In P. Paynes (Ed.), *Curriculum Evaluation.* Lexington, Mass.: Heath, 1974.

Kendrick, S. A., and Thomas, C. L. "Transition from School to College." *Review of Educational Research,* 1970, *40* (1), 151–179.

Keystone Visual Survey Tests. Meadville, Pa.: Keystone View, 1956.

Kingsborough Community College. "The Freshman English Program Revisited (1972–1973)." Unpublished report, Office of Institutional Research, Kingsborough Community College, 1973.

Kirk, S. A., Kleibhan, J. M., and Lerner, J. W. *Teaching Reading to Slow and Disabled Learners.* Boston: Houghton Mifflin, 1978.

Kogen, M., and Seltzer, S. New York: Harper & Row, forthcoming.

Kulik, J. A., and Kulik, C. "Effectiveness of the Personalized System of Instruction." *Engineering Education,* 1975, *66* (3), 228–231.

Kulik, J. A., Kulik, C., and Carmichael, K. "The Keller Plan in Science Teaching." *Science,* 1974, *83,* 379–383.

Kunz, L. A. *26 Steps: Controlled Composition for Intermediate and Advanced ESL Students.* New York: Language Innovations, 1972.

Kunz, L. A. *X-Word Grammar: An Editing Book.* (Experimental ed.) New York: Language Innovations, 1976.

Kunz, L. A. "X-Word Grammar: Offspring of Sector Analysis." *Journal of Basic Writing,* 1977, *1* (3), 63–76.

Kunz, L. A. *Twenty-Six Steps.* (Rev. ed.) New York: Language Innovations, 1979.

Kunz, L. A., and Viscount, R. R. *Write Me a Ream: Exercises in Controlled Composition.* New York: Teachers College Press, 1973.

Kytle, R. *Clear Thinking for Composition.* (2nd ed.) New York: Random House, 1973.

Lachica, G. M. "Studies in Remediation, 1976–1977." Unpublished report, Office of Instructional Testing and Research, Borough of Manhattan Community College, 1977.

Lachica, G. M., and Brookes, G. "A Study of Factors Related to Success in the ESL Program, Fall 1975." Unpublished report, Office of Instructional Testing and Research, Borough of Manhattan Community College, 1976.

Lavin, D. E., Alba, R. D., and Silberstein, R. A. "Open Admissions and Equal Access: A Study of Ethnic Groups in the City University of New York." *Harvard Educational Review,* 1979, *49* (1), 53–92.

Laurence, P. "To Thomas J. Farrell." *College English,* 1977, *39* (2), 230–233.

Lay, N. D. S. "Chinese Language Interference in Written English." *Journal of Basic Writing,* 1975, *1* (1), 50–61.

Levy, W. J. *More Powerful Reading.* New York: Amsco, 1969.

Lloyd-Jones, R. "Primary Trait Scoring." In C. R. Cooper and L. Odell (Eds.), *Evaluating Writing.* Urbana, Ill.: National Council of Teachers of English, 1977.

Loewe, R. E. *The Writing Clinic.* Englewood Cliffs, N.J.: Prentice-Hall, 1973.

Losak, J. G. *An Evaluation of Selected Aspects of a Junior College Remedial Reading-Writing Program.* Educational Resources Information Center, ED 027 021. Miami: Miami-Dade Junior College, 1968.

Lyons, R. *Autobiography: A Reader for Writers.* New York: Oxford University Press, 1977.

McHale, T. J., Witzke, P. T., and Davis, G. W., Jr. *Mathematics for the Majority.* Milwaukee: Milwaukee Area Technical College, 1969.

Macrorie, K. *Writing to be Read.* New York: Hayden, 1968.

Macrorie, K. *Telling Writing.* New York: Hayden, 1970a.

Macrorie, K. *Uptaught.* New York: Hayden, 1970b.

Matthews, R. S. "The Evolution of One College's Attempt to Evaluate Student Writing." *Journal of Basic Writing,* 1978, *1* (4),

63–70.

Maxwell, M. *Improving Student Learning Skills: A Comprehensive Guide to Successful Practices and Programs for Increasing the Performance of Underprepared Students.* San Francisco: Jossey-Bass, 1979.

Mellon, J. C. *Transformational Sentence-Combining: A Method for Enhancing the Development of Syntactic Fluency in English Composition.* Urbana, Ill.: National Council of Teachers of English, 1969.

Mellon, J. C. *National Assessment and the Teaching of English.* Urbana, Ill.: National Council of Teachers of English, 1975.

Memering, D. "Forward to the Basics." *College English,* 1978, *39* (5), 553–561.

Metzger, E. "A Scheme for Measuring Growth in College Writing." *Journal of Basic Writing,* 1978, *1* (4), 71–81.

Middleton, J. R. "Successful Outcomes and Class Size in Remedial Programs: Intensive Writing and Reading Skills, Spring 1974 to Fall 1975." Unpublished Report, Office of Instructional Testing and Research, Borough of Manhattan Community College, 1977.

Miles, C. "Reasoning: The Fourth 'R.'" *Journal of Developmental and Remedial Education,* 1978, *2* (1), 22–24.

MLA Handbook. New York: Modern Language Association of America, 1977.

Mouley, G. S. "A Study of the Effects of a Remedial Reading Program on Academic Grades at the College Level." *Journal of Educational Psychology,* 1952, *43,* 459–466.

Muscatine, C., and Griffith, M. *First Person Singular.* New York: Knopf, 1973.

National Assessment of Educational Progress. *Writing Mechanics, 1969–1974: A Capsule Description of Changes in Writing Mechanics.* Report number 05-W-01. Washington, D.C.: U.S. Government Printing Office, 1975, 1.

New York City Board of Higher Education. Minutes, July 9, 1969.

O'Connor, J. *English Vocabulary Builder.* Vol. 1. Boston: Human Engineering Laboratory, 1948.

O'Hare, F. *Sentence-Combining: Improving Student Writing Without Formal Grammar Instruction.* Urbana, Ill.: National Council of Teachers of English, 1973.

O'Hare, F. *Sentencecraft: An Elective Course in Writing.* Lexington, Mass.: Ginn, 1975.

O'Rourke, J. P. *Toward a Science of Vocabulary Development.* The Hague: Mouton, 1974.

Palumbo, E. "Teaching ESL from the Aesthetic Realism Point of View." Paper presented at the New York State Teachers of English to Speakers of Other Languages and Bilingual Educators Association Annual Conference, Syracuse, N.Y., 1974.

Parsegian, V. L., and others. *The Life Sciences.* New York: Academic Press, 1970.

Pearson, P. D., and Johnson, D. D. *Teaching Reading Vocabulary.* New York: Holt, Rinehart and Winston, 1978.

Percy, W. *The Message in the Bottle.* New York: Farrar, Straus & Giroux, 1975.

Petrie, A. (Ed.). *Basic Writing Anthology I.* New York: The City College, City University of New York, 1972.

Piesco, J. "Research on Remedial Programs at the City University of New York: A Review of Evaluative Studies." Unpublished report, Office of Institutional Research and Analysis, City University of New York, 1978.

Piesco, J., Shrier, I., and Podell, L. "Review of the Evaluative Literature on Open Admissions at CUNY." Unpublished report, Office of Program and Policy Research, City University of New York, 1974.

Ponsot, M. "Total Immersion." *Journal of Basic Writing,* 1976, *1* (2), 31–43.

Praninskas, J. *A Rapid Review of English Grammar.* (2nd ed.) New York: Prentice-Hall, 1975.

Raimes, A. *Focus on Composition.* New York: Oxford University Press, 1978.

Rardin, J. "A Counseling-Learning Model for Second Language Learning." *TESOL Newsletter,* 1976, *10* (2), 21–22.

Reed, J. C. "Some Effects of Short-Term Training in Reading Under Conditions of Controlled Motivation." *Journal of Educational Psychology,* 1956, *47* (5), 257–261.

Rizzo, B. "Peer Teaching in English I." *College Composition and Communication,* 1975, *26,* 394–396.

Rizzo, B. *The Writer's Studio.* New York: Harper & Row, 1978.

Rizzo, B., and Villafane, S. "Spanish Language Influence on Written English." *Journal of Basic Writing,* 1975, *1* (1), 61–71.

Robinson, H. A. "A Note on the Evaluation of College Remedial Reading Courses." *Journal of Educational Psychology,* 1950, *41,* 83–96.

Robinson, H. A. *Teaching Reading and Study Strategies: The Content Areas.* Boston: Allyn & Bacon, 1975.

Robinson, L. *Guided Writing and Free Writing.* New York: Harper & Row, 1975.

Roueche, J. E. *Salvage, Redirection or Custody — Remedial Education in the Community Junior College.* Educational Resources Information Center, ED 019 077. Washington, D.C.: American Association of Junior Colleges, 1968.

Roueche, J. E. "Accommodating Individual Differences." *Community College Review,* 1973, *1,* 24–29.

Roueche, J. E., and Kirk, R. W. *Catching Up: Remedial Education.* San Francisco: Jossey-Bass, 1973.

Roueche, J. E., and Snow, J. J. *Overcoming Learning Problems: A Guide to Developmental Education in College.* San Francisco: Jossey-Bass, 1977.

Roueche, J. E., and Wheeler, C. L. "Instructional Procedures for the Disadvantaged." *Improving College and University Teaching,* 1973, *21,* 222–225.

Samuels, M. S. "A Mini-Course in the Research Paper." *College English,* 1976, *38* (2), 189–193.

Santeusanio, R. P. "Do College Reading Programs Serve Their Purpose?" *Reading World,* 1974, *14* (4), 259–271.

Scheirer, M. A., and Kraut, R. E. "Increasing Educational Achievement via Self-Concept Change." *Review of Educational Research,* 1979, *49* (1), 131–150.

Scriven, M. "The Methodology of Evaluation." In R. E. Stahe (Ed.), *Curriculum Evaluation.* AERA Monograph Series on Evaluation, No. 1. Chicago: Rand McNally, 1967.

Seeley, H. W., and Van Demark, P. J. *Microbes in Action.* (2nd ed.) San Francisco: W. H. Freeman, 1972.

Sharon, A. T. *Effectiveness of Remediation in Junior College.* College Entrance Examination Board Research and Development Report RDR-70-71, No. 2. Princeton, N.J.: Educational Testing Service, 1970.

Shaughnessy, M. "Open Admissions and the Disadvantaged

Teacher." *College Composition and Communication,* 1973, *24,* 401–404.

Shaughnessy, M. "Introduction." *Journal of Basic Writing,* 1975a, *1,* 1–3.

Shaughnessy, M. (Ed.). "Reading Comprehension and the High School Graduate." In National Institute of Education, *Summaries of Panel Reports 1 Through 10 of the Conference on Studies in Reading.* Washington, D.C.: National Institute of Education, 1975b, pp. 85–94.

Shaughnessy, M. "Basic Writing." In G. Tate (Ed.), *Teaching Composition: Ten Bibliographical Essays.* Fort Worth: Texas Christian University Press, 1976a.

Shaughnessy, M. "Diving In: An Introduction to Basic Writing." *College Composition and Communication,* 1976b, *21,* 234–239.

Shaughnessy, M. "The Miserable Truth: An Address to the CUNY Association of Writing Supervisors." In *Congressional Record,* September 9, 1976c, E4955–E4956.

Shaughnessy, M. "Speaking and Doublespeaking of Standards." In J. R. Banister (Ed.), *Proceedings of the California State University and Colleges Conference on the Improvement of Student Writing Skills, Spring 1976.* Long Beach: Trustees of the California State University and Colleges, 1976d.

Shaughnessy, M. "Patterns: Observations on the Efforts of Inexperienced Writers." Unpublished speech delivered at the Modern Literature Conference, Michigan State University, East Lansing, Mich., October 1977a.

Shaughnessy, M. *Errors and Expectations: A Guide for the Teacher of Basic Writing.* New York: Oxford University Press, 1977b.

Shaughnessy, M. "Some Needed Research on Writing." *College Composition and Communication,* 1977c, *28,* 317–320.

Shaughnessy, M. "Introduction" to special issue on testing. *Resource* (a publication of the Instructional Resource Center, City University of New York), March 1978, 1–3.

Shoemaker, D. M. *Principles and Procedures of Multiple Matrix Sampling.* Cambridge, Mass.: Ballinger, 1973.

Shor, S., and Fishman, J. *The Random House Guide to Basic Writing.* New York: Random House, 1978.

Singer, H., and Ruddell, R. (Eds.). *Theoretical Models and Processes of Reading.* Newark, Del.: International Reading Association, 1970.

Skurnick, B. Composition Text. New York: Random House, forthcoming.

Smith, F. *Understanding Reading: A Psycholinguistic Analysis of Reading and Learning to Read.* New York: Holt, Rinehart and Winston, 1971.

Sobel, M. A., and Maletsky, E. M. *Teaching Mathematics: A Sourcebook of Aids, Activities, and Strategies.* Englewood Cliffs, N.J.: Prentice-Hall, 1975.

Sparks, J., and Davis, O. "A Systems Analysis and Evaluation of a Junior College Developmental Studies Program." Paper presented at the annual meeting of the American Educational Research Association, New York City, April 1977.

Splittgerber, F. "Computer-Based Instruction: A Revolution in the Making?" *Educational Technology,* 1979, *19* (1), 20–26.

Stevick, E. W. "Review of Gattegno 1972." *TESOL Quarterly,* 1974, *8* (3), 305–314.

Stotsky, S. L. "Towards More Systematic Development of Children's Reading Vocabulary in Developmental Reading Programs for the Middle to Upper Elementary Grades." Unpublished doctoral dissertation, Harvard University, 1976.

Stotsky, S. L. "Teaching the Vocabulary of Academic Discourse." *Journal of Basic Writing,* 1980, *2* (3), 15–39.

Strong, W. *Sentence Combining: A Composing Book.* New York: Random House, 1973.

Suchman, E. A. *Evaluative Research.* New York: Russell Sage Foundation, 1967.

Tallmadge, G., and Horst, P. *Procedural Guide for Validating Achievement Gains in Educational Projects.* Washington, D.C.: U.S. Government Printing Office, 1976.

Thistlethwaite, D. L., and Campbell, D. T. "Regression Discontinuity Analysis: An Alternative to the Ex Post Facto Experiment." *Journal of Educational Psychology,* 1960, *51,* 309–317.

Thomas, L. *Relevance of Patterns.* Palo Alto, Calif.: Westinghouse Learning Press, 1973.

Thorndike, R. L., and Hagen, E. *Measurement and Evaluation in Psychology and Education.* (3rd ed.) New York: Wiley, 1969.

Troyka, L., and Nudelman, J. *Taking Action: Writing, Reading, Speaking, and Listening Through Simulation Games.* Englewood Cliffs, N.J.: Prentice-Hall, 1975.

Turabian, K. L. *A Manual for Writers of Term Papers, Theses, and Dissertations.* Chicago: University of Chicago Press, 1967.

Vogeli, B. "Pocket Calculators: Their Impact on Mathematics Instruction." Paper presented at the 5th annual CUNY Conferences on Open Admission, Mathematics Section, New York City, December 1975.

Wallen, C. J. *Competency in Teaching Reading.* Chicago: Science Research Associates, 1972.

Walpole, R. E. *Introduction to Statistics.* New York: Macmillan, 1969.

Weinstein, G., and Fantini, M. *Towards a Humanistic Education: A Curriculum of Affect.* New York: Praeger, 1970.

Wepman, J. M. *Auditory Discrimination Test.* Chicago: Language Research Association, 1973.

Whimbey, A. *Problem-Solving and Comprehension: A Short Course in Analytic Reasoning.* Philadelphia: Franklin Institute, 1979.

Whimbey, A., Boylan, H., and Burke, R. "Cognitive Skills-Oriented PSI for Students." *Journal of Developmental and Remedial Education,* 1979, *2* (2), 7–10.

White, E. *Comparison and Contrast: The California State University and Colleges English Equivalency Examination.* Long Beach: Chancellor of the California State University and Colleges, 1973–1979 (yearly).

Williams, J. "Reevaluating Evaluating." *Journal of Basic Writing,* 1978, *1* (4), 7–17.

Wolf, R. M. *Evaluation in Education.* New York: Praeger, 1979.

Women's City Club of New York. *The Privileged Many: A Study of the City University Open Admissions Policy, 1970–1975.* New York: Women's City Club of New York, 1975.

Wood, N. V. *College Reading and Study Skills.* New York: Holt, Rinehart and Winston, 1978.

Worthen, B., and Sanders, J. *Educational Evaluation: Theory and Practice.* Worthington, Ohio: C. A. Jones, 1973.

Yorkey, R. *Study Skills for Students of English as a Second Language.* New York: McGraw-Hill, 1970.

Zwick, E. J. "An Evaluation of the Effectiveness of the Remedial Mathematics Program at the Ohio State University." Unpublished doctoral dissertation, Ohio State University, 1964. *Dissertation Abstracts,* 1965, *25,* 6323.

Index

❋ ❋ ❋ ❋ ❋ ❋ ❋ ❋ ❋ ❋ ❋ ❋ ❋ ❋ ❋ ❋ ❋ ❋